Developmental Transitions across the Lifespan

Leo B. Hendry is one of the foremost developmental psychologists of his generation. His diverse range of interests have included studies on young people's involvement in competitive sports, investigations into teacher and pupil relations in school, adolescents' leisure pursuits and their family relations, parenting styles, youth workers and mentoring, youth unemployment, adolescent health behaviours, and transition to early adulthood. His research interests now include work on ageing and retirement.

Developmental Transitions across the Lifespan is the first collection of Hendry's works, and essentially joins the dots to provide an overarching perspective on lifespan development through a dynamic systems theory approach. Underpinned by empirical research, this collection of journal articles and book chapters is linked by a contemporary commentary which not only contextualizes each piece within today's research climate, but builds to provide an unorthodox, comprehensive but above all compelling perspective on human development from childhood to old age.

Leo B. Hendry's research output has been significant and influential. This is an important book that will provide students and researchers in developmental psychology not only with an opportunity to view his contribution holistically, but in connecting his range of research interests, provides a new contribution to our understanding of lifespan development in its own right.

Leo B. Hendry is former Professor of Psychology at the Norwegian University of Science and Technology, Trondheim, and at the University of South Wales, Glamorgan, and of Education at the University of Aberdeen, and also taught at the University Institutes of London and Leeds. He is now Emeritus Professor, University of Aberdeen. He has been Visiting Professor to many universities in Europe, Canada and the Americas, and worked as a psychological advisor to the Family Support Division, American Forces (Europe) till 1989. He has carried out research projects for both national and international funding bodies and published over 150 research articles, 30 book chapters, and 22 books, which have been translated into 9 foreign languages.

Developmental Transitions across the Lifespan
Selected works of Leo B. Hendry

Leo B. Hendry

First published 2015
by Psychology Press
27 Church Road, Hove, East Sussex BN3 2FA

and by Psychology Press
711 Third Avenue, New York, NY 10017

Psychology Press is an imprint of the Taylor & Francis Group, an informa business

© 2015 Leo B. Hendry

The right of Leo B. Hendry to be identified as the author of this work has been asserted by him in accordance with sections 77 and 78 of the Copyright, Designs and Patents Act 1988.

All rights reserved. No part of this book may be reprinted or reproduced or utilised in any form or by any electronic, mechanical, or other means, now known or hereafter invented, including photocopying and recording, or in any information storage or retrieval system, without permission in writing from the publishers.

Trademark notice: Product or corporate names may be trademarks or registered trademarks, and are used only for identification and explanation without intent to infringe.

British Library Cataloguing in Publication Data
A catalogue record for this book is available from the British Library

Library of Congress Cataloging in Publication Data
Hendry, Leo B.
[Works. Selections]
Developmental transitions across the lifespan : selected works of
Leo B. Hendry / Leo B Hendry. — 1st Edition.
    pages cm. — (World library of psychologists)
1. Adolescent psychology. 2. Developmental psychology. I. Title.
BF724.H464 2015
155—dc23
                                                                    2014040448

ISBN: 978-1-84872-279-8 (hbk)
ISBN: 978-1-31572-639-7 (ebk)

Typeset in Times New Roman
by RefineCatch Limited, Bungay, Suffolk

Printed and bound in Great Britain by
CPI Group (UK) Ltd, Croydon, CR0 4YY

This book is dedicated to the four people who best represent, for me, my past, my present and my future:

- My late grandfather, LEO BROUGH, who inspired me and gave me the belief that I could achieve whatsoever I wanted to achieve in this life.
- My loving partner and co-researcher, PROFESSOR MARION KLOEP, for together we are lucky in being able to share so many academic ideas and discoveries, wonderful journeys, joyous experiences and good fortune.
- My grandchildren, CHLOE and CONNOR, for whom I wish success in achieving whatever they wish for themselves as they make their individual, developmental transitions across the lifespan.

Professor Leo B. Hendry
Chiclana de la Frontera
España
October 2014

Contents

Acknowledgements		ix
Introduction		1
1	Aspects of the 'hidden curriculum'	12
2	Constructed case studies in a school context	21
3	Educational pathways and interactive factors	33
4	Differing perceptions	50
5	Young people's views on people and places	68
6	Young people talking	89
7	Adolescents speaking out about health	110
8	Challenges, risks and coping in adolescence	122
9	Young people's unemployment lifestyles	137
10	Young people in modern society	150
11	Challenging the orthodoxy: what is 'emerging adulthood'?	159
12	Parental views of emerging adults	171
13	Pathways to retirement	192

14	Reflecting on theories	201
15	The lifespan challenge model re-visited	218
	Concluding remarks	236
	Index	239

Acknowledgements

In line with the ideas behind Dynamic Systems Theory, this book came about by the interactions of several elements in the system of my life. So, I would like to thank a variety of people for making it possible.

First, I am grateful to all my British academic mentors, from Brian Foss, through John Whiting and Lou Cohen to John Nisbet and to all the brilliant researchers and theorists I have met internationally, for helping to develop my thoughts as expressed in my writings.

Next, to all the students I have worked with worldwide, and perhaps especially all the Master's and Doctoral students at the University of Aberdeen, from whom I have learned so much. I thank them for sharing and commenting on my ideas as they developed.

Then, my thanks to all my co-authors, who have allowed me to present various journal articles and book extracts from our shared publications in the past.

Bernard Cornwell also deserves a mention for introducing me to Uhtred of Bebbanburg and for personally informing me of what the future holds in store for my Viking hero.

I would also like to express my thanks to Russell George and Michael Fenton at Taylor & Francis for giving me the opportunity to publish some of my earlier works in a thematic form.

Finally, my grateful thanks go to Libby Volke, who has acted as my 'Mamacita' for this book – guiding and nurturing it carefully and tenderly to completion – and to Suzy McGill and the whole Production Team at Psychology Press, Taylor & Francis Group for such a fine tome.

Additionally, I am grateful to the following individuals and organisations for their kind permission to reproduce material in this book:

1. International Review of Sports Sociology

Hendry, L B and Welsh, J (1981) Aspects of the hidden curriculum: Teachers' and pupils' perceptions in physical education. International Review of Sports Sociology, 16, 4, 27–40.

x   *Acknowledgements*

2. Bloomsbury
Hendry, L B (1978) School, Sport and Leisure: Three Dimensions of Adolescence. A & C Black. London, pp. 73–85. Originally Lepus. 0-86019-037-4.

3. Bloomsbury
Hendry, L B (1978) School, Sport and Leisure: Three Dimensions of Adolescence. A & C Black. London, pp. 155–157.

4. Taylor & Francis
Hendry, L B and Love, J (1994) Youth workers and youth participants: Two perspectives of youth work? Youth and Policy, 46, 43–44 & 51–55 (Discussion).

5. Taylor & Francis
Hendry, L B, Kloep, M and Wood, S (2002) Young people talking about adolescent rural crowds and social settings. Journal of Youth Studies, 5, 4, 357–374.

6. Peter Lang
Hendry, L B and Kloep, M (2005) 'Talkin', doin' and bein' with friends': Leisure and communication in adolescence, pp. 163–184. In Williams, A and Thurlow, C (Eds), Talking Adolescence: Perspectives on Communication in the Teenage Years. London, Peter Lang.

7. Taylor & Francis
Shucksmith, J S and Hendry, L B (1998) Health Issues and Adolescents: Growing Up, Speaking Out. London & New York: Routledge, pp. 128–142. 0-415-16849-X.

8. Taylor & Francis
Kloep, M and Hendry, L B (1999) Challenges, risks and coping in adolescence, pp. 400–415. In Messer, D and Millar, S (Eds) Exploring Developmental Psychology. London Arnold–Hodder. 0-340-67682-5.

9. Taylor & Francis
Hendry, L B, Raymond, M and Stewart, C (1984) Unemployment, school and leisure: An adolescent study. Leisure Studies, 3, 175–187. 0261-4367/84; Spon Ltd.

10. British Psychological Society
Kloep, M. and Hendry, L B (2007) 'Over-protection, Over-protection, Over-protection!' Young people in modern Britain. Open dialogue, The Psychology of Education Review, 31, 2, 4–7 and 18–20. 0262-4087.

11. John Wiley and Sons
Hendry, L B and Kloep, M (2007) Conceptualizing emerging adulthood: Inspecting the Emperor's new clothes? Child Development Perspectives, 1, 2, 74–79.

12. John Wiley and Sons, British Psychological Society
Kloep, M and Hendry, L B (2010) Letting go or holding On? Parents' perceptions of relationships with their children during emerging adulthood. British Journal of Developmental Psychology, 28, (4), 817–834.

13. British Psychological Society
Kloep, M and Hendry, L B (2007) Retirement: A new beginning? The Psychologist, 20, 12, 742–745.

14. Taylor & Francis
Hendry, L B, Kloep, M, Espnes, G A, Ingebrigtsen, J E, Glendinning, A and Wood, S (2002) Leisure transitions – a rural perspective. Leisure Studies, 21, 1, 1–14.

15. Oxford University Press
Kloep, M, and Hendry L B (2011) A Systemic approach to the transitions to adulthood, pp. 53–60 and 63–75. In Arnett, J, Kloep, M, Hendry, L B and Tanner, J (eds) Debating Emerging Adulthood: Stage or Process? New York, Oxford University Press. 978-0-19-975717-6.

Every effort has been made to contact copyright holders for their permission to reprint all third-party material in this book. The publishers would be grateful to hear from any copyright holder who is not here acknowledged.

Introduction

Personal introduction

As I sit here to write my commentary to the selected extracts of my published writings over the years, I feel somewhat like Bernard Cornwell's semi-fictitious Viking hero, Uhtred of Bebbanburg, who, in old age, finally decided to set down his life story. However, unlike Uhtred, I am enjoying retirement in sunnier climes and do not intend recalling battles or kings or women I have known and loved, but rather academic themes, theoretical frameworks, research methods and modelling!

Nevertheless, like Uhtred's need to demonstrate his authority and experience in reporting the progress of battles or the strategies of monarchs by his involvement in these events, I too feel I have to very briefly outline my academic qualifications and experience – and mention the names of some better known academic theorists I have encountered – in order to offer support for what I will write in the remainder of the text.

As I grew up I was crazy about sports of all kinds and attained a reasonable level of ability as an amateur boxer, a sprinter of County standard, a springboard diver of national level giving diving displays at galas across Scotland, a gymnast of sufficient ability to take part in public gymnastic displays in stadia, exhibition halls and at county fairs whilst doing military service in the Royal Army Education Corps and I played as an amateur soccer player with professional clubs in both Scotland and England (Dumbarton F.C. and Weymouth F.C.) – only taking up golf in late middle-age and acting as a part-time Sports Psychologist to a number of young golf tour professionals and club golfers in Scotland.

Thus, in my late teens, it seemed inevitable that I should train as a physical education teacher at Strathclyde University (Jordanhill Campus) rather than be the classroom teacher I would have become if, instead, I had taken a degree in English and History at Glasgow University. At Jordanhill, I gained a Diploma of the Scottish School of Physical Education after three years of study, and a Post-Graduate Diploma in Education one year later.

Hence, my entry into the world of academic writing and publishing was both late – having had a career as a schoolteacher for some years before being appointed to a university post at one of London University Institute's colleges – and unusually different, given that I had previously been a professional sportsperson and sports-coach in soccer, gymnastics, athletics and swimming, and not an academic. Nevertheless, over time I did gain a number of academic credentials, namely:

M.Ed. (with Distinction, University of Leicester, 1970), M.Sc. in Psychology and Sociology (Bradford University, 1971), Ph.D. (Aberdeen University, 1975), D.Litt. (Aberdeen University, 1994), Fellow British Psychological Society (1984) and a Chartered Psychologist. I am currently Emeritus Professor, University of Aberdeen, Scotland, and I have been presented with a Lifetime Achievement Award of the European Association for Research on Adolescence for my published contributions to European research.

To date, I have written a number of academic papers and books:

- over 150 research journal articles;
- 30 book chapters; and
- 22 books (published in several languages, including Spanish, Italian, Japanese, Korean, Norwegian and Danish).

In my career I have worked full-time in several British universities – London, Leeds, Aberdeen, Glamorgan – and in Trondheim, Norway (as a Psychology Professor, Health Psychology Professor and in the Norwegian Centre for Childhood Research), and have been a Visiting Professor to several universities in both Europe and North America, including Giessen, Ankara, the Free Universities of Amsterdam and Brussels, Mid-Sweden University, Boston, Penn State and Cornell; acted as Psychological Advisor to the Child and Family Services Department, American Forces (Europe) with the honorary rank of Lieutenant-Colonel until the mid-1980s; and have been a fairly regular, invited keynote speaker to social science conferences worldwide.

These global invitations have enabled me to get to know, and be helped by, a number of international, academic 'celebrities' including Professor Sir Michael Rutter, Professor Richard Lerner, Professor Glen Elder, Professor Mihalyi Csikszentmihalyi and the late Professor Uri Bronfenbrenner.

Significantly, my meetings, and collaborations, with a number of well-known British academics and theorists gave me inspiration to research and write on various topics as my career progressed. For instance, Professor Brian Foss, Department of Psychology, University of London, encouraged me to take the data I had collected while acting as a Psychological Advisor at an Easter training course run by the English Amateur Swimming Association for elite young swimmers and their coaches and publish my first research papers internationally. Later, he supported my application to Leicester University to study for a Master's degree when I was appointed to a Head of Department position within one of Leeds University Institute's Colleges and could not complete my Master's course in London.

When in Leeds I developed a close working relationship with Professor H. T. A. ('John') Whiting, and a more orthodox one, with Professor George Meredith, Department of Psychology, which nevertheless led me to learn about laboratory-based research. My research partnership with John Whiting was extremely fruitful and produced a variety of articles and books on topics within the allied areas of sport, physical education and human movement. However, because my publications in these areas were somewhat contextually focused, they do not figure strongly in this text. Nevertheless, what we wrote seems to me as relevant now for athletes, coaches, teachers and other professionals who work with young people as mentors and trainers (see e.g. Whiting *et al.*, 1974; and Whitehead and Hendry, 1976).

At Bradford University I encountered a number of inspirational academics as I followed a part-time taught Master's course. Professors Frank Musgrove, Louis Cohen and Dennis Child introduced me to sociological, as well as psychological perspectives on behaviour, and perhaps especially the applications of role theory, which I utilised for my Master's dissertation where I studied teacher and pupil relations. Thereafter, when I accepted appointment to a Lectureship in the Department of Education, University of Aberdeen, Lou Cohen said to me (prophetically as it turned out!): 'Leo, John Nisbet is the King-maker. You'll be a professor in a few years!'

Within my post at Aberdeen, the late Professor John Nisbet (then Head of Department) gave me 'free' time, and the Department's Research Officer, the late Dr Jennifer Welsh, as my field assistant, to collect data from over 3,000 adolescents and their teachers, for my doctoral project. Several conference papers, articles, books and chapters emerged from that research, and I was grateful to enlist the help of Professor David Kerridge, Head of the Statistical Department, as my Statistical Assistant in that study.

A few years later I also contributed to a book, commissioned by the Scottish Office, as a way of evaluating developments in community education and based on an in-depth study of different participations in various community settings (see Nisbet *et al.*, 1980).

After subsequent promotions through Senior Lecturer to a Personal Chair, John Nisbet suggested that I put forward a selection of my published works from a range of externally funded projects on adolescence, together with a linking commentary, for the degree of Doctor of Letters, which I was awarded by Aberdeen University in 1996.

The mention of the University of Aberdeen brings to mind a significant event in my professional life and here I digress to tell a story that both inspired me in my work, but also unsettled me a little by its intensity and, frankly, by its spiritual quality: The Dalai Lama was in Aberdeen University to receive an honorary degree. At the luncheon after the ceremony he dined at the High Table and I sat some distance from that table among several hundred people. When the Dalai Lama was on his way out of the Hall and everyone was applauding him, he suddenly stopped on the platform when he came opposite me and pointed. When I realised it was 'me' he wanted to address, we made eye contact, and as he continued to look and point to me he said: 'You and I, we are both interested in young people: Keep up the good work!' Then he walked out. I am still amazed and powerfully moved by that encounter.

I was appointed to the Established Chair and became Head of Department when the late John Nisbet retired and Janet Shucksmith (now a Professor at Tyne-Tees

4 *Introduction*

University), who had previously worked on a project with John, became my Research Officer on a funded, seven year longitudinal study of 10,000 young Scots. From that project Janet and I wrote a number of articles and books together with other members of my research-team (see, e.g., Hendry *et al.*, 1993).

Another significant partnership has been that of my co-writings with Professor John Coleman, University of Oxford (previously, Director of the Trust for the Study of Adolescence). The benefits of this collaboration have been two-fold: First, the opportunity to co-write two further editions of a book whose first edition had been commercially successful and translated into several languages; and second, to be able to present my ideas within these editions to practitioners and policymakers as well as academics. However, as a textbook on adolescence, offered within a general theoretical framework of normal and constrained development, it does not figure significantly in this anthology.

The most recent, most endearing and lasting partnership that has influenced my work, has been my co-teaching, co-researching and co-writing with Professor Marion Kloep, firstly, in Scandinavia, and, ultimately, in Wales. Without doubt, our joint ventures and informal discussions have enriched my work and extended my thinking about lifespan transitions (see several extracts from our joint publications below).

Perhaps at the outset it is important to say something about the selection of extracts that form the major part of this book. Why have I chosen these particular extracts? My answer is to say that the book is an attempt to offer some perspectives and insights into developmental contexts from adolescence to old age and to provide illustrative examples of the ways in which I sought explanatory frameworks to better understand human change and how this influenced my research methodologies.

I did not simply choose what I consider to be the best-written texts and somehow link them together into a coherent series of readings. My rationale was to present particular themes within human development as they emerged from my published works and my comments on them may allow readers insights into my ideas, research approaches and how theoretical frameworks emerge and develop. In addition, I hope that they might offer ideas about developmental interactions, contexts and transitions.

Equally illuminating for the reader, may be for me to explain why I have discarded – beyond the limitations of space – particular examples of my research and theoretical ideas. It was not ego, it was not random extraction, it was not simply to allow a presentation of my best pieces of writing. Rather, some themes were omitted because they were basically under-developed or focused too narrowly on a particular aspect of human behaviour.

As examples of interesting research I have discarded from my selections in this book I cite the following:

1. The traditional literature on adolescents' mentors essentially describes the mentoring figure as a caring adult. Yet it seemed to me that young people were more strategic in finding relationships that helped them to resolve a current

life-issue irrespective of age differences between themselves and a mentor. In a study we carried out to explore this topic (e.g. Hendry and Philip, 1996), results illustrated the different needs that directed adolescents towards seeking guidance and help from a range of chosen individuals – adults and peers – and that some young people did not possess the social skills to enable them to 'find' a mentor in times of trouble. Further, we noted that choice of mentor was usually based on specific contextual issues, which often enabled the adolescent to act as the instigator of the relationship. A companion piece offered mentors' views of these relationships (Philip and Hendry, 2000)

2. Then, I was privileged to win a grant to conduct a longitudinal project involving 10,000 young Scots (see e.g. Hendry *et al.*, 1994), which enabled a rich array of methods to come into play.

However, since the findings from these researches were mainly descriptive of relationships and longitudinal developmental transitions, they do not figure in my selected extracts. Thus, I have omitted several potentially useful texts to include what I consider to be more illuminating extracts that illustrate and display the key forces and factors and contextual influences in lifespan development.

So, what the reader *will* find within these covers are articles, some of them published in more 'obscure' journals, some book extracts from earlier decades and examples of more up-to-date writings. Taken together, and including an academic debate, these may offer some challenge to mainstream ideas and interpretations of development.

Broadly, the book will take the reader from an outline of a derived ecological lifespan model and two earlier studies, that attempted to look at both general trends and sub-group and/or individual variations; through an examination of aspects of teenage life, to early adulthood; then an examination of family relations during a developmental 'turning-point', and an examination of trajectories into retirement and old age. Finally, these illustrative extracts lead on to re-assessment of the lifespan model, together with a brief discussion of future directions for developmental psychology. In doing so, I hope readers will find insights, ideas and inspiration to take into their own endeavours in exploring and uncovering the inter-linked mechanisms and processes that bring about developmental change.

A brief outline of themes

When I reflect, like Uhtred, looking back on my academic publications, what strikes me most forcibly is the pattern of themes that run through my writing, despite the shift of research topics, and how the conceptual and theoretical interpretations of my empirical investigations became building-blocks for my current thinking about the forces and factors influencing development. Further, I will present an introductory comment to each selected extract, in addition to the overall commentary. Additionally I believe my writings will appeal to practitioners as well as academics, because I have always attempted to offer certain general recommendations that could be of value to professionals.

So, reflecting on the basic principles and topics that have emerged in my writings over the years, the following seem most salient:

a) *Disaggregation:* I was never a believer in *one-variable answers* to questions about human behaviour or how effectively means and standard deviations truly demonstrate findings in the real world, and where averages may not truly reflect the range of behaviours or responses in research populations. In a book titled *The Numbers Game: The Commonsense Guide to Understanding Numbers in the News, in Politics and in Life* Michael Blastland and Andrew Dilnot wrote that if one were to present the average of the colours of a rainbow it would be grey! Hence, I have always sought to provide for *disaggregation and variability* to take account of the range of differences in any sample.

b) *Discipline Orthodoxy:* Because my academic qualifications were gained alongside a lecturing career, my writings reflect perhaps a greater *multidisciplinarity* than some of my academic peers. This has enabled me to note that most aspects of behaviour are influenced by a variety of forces and factors, some psychological, some social, some material and some biological. Additionally, because different disciplines have different approaches to developmental (and other) questions in human change, I have always been alert to the limitations contained in many studies. While I always had respect for academics presenting such results and propounding certain theories, it has never stopped me questioning them. As a rebel, I have always opposed orthodoxy!

c) *Individual–Environment Compatibility: Person-environment interaction* is inherent in my writings because of the influences of ecological theorists such as Bronfenbrenner (with whom, on one visit to the University of Cornell, I team-taught research methods), Elder, Lerner, Rutter and, more recently, Valsiner. All these writers in their various ways have posited the importance of the individual's encounters with differing contexts as vital to change, how contexts can 'suit' the individual's endeavours or constrain them, and how the individual's actions and reactions affect others with whom they interact. These views on contextual interactions link well with Eccles' ideas of '*goodness-of-fit*', where individual – environment compatibility leads to successful change (Eccles *et al.*, 1993). Such theoretical frames are important conceptual structures in my interpretations of findings presented below.

d) *Transitional Challenges:* Bronfenbrenner and Valsiner have been important in highlighting the processes and mechanisms of human change. 'Challenge' and 'transition' have certainly appeared in the literature for some decades now as established parts in these developmental processes. Yet, with my co-researcher, Professor Marion Kloep, we have stressed that these concepts are somewhat 'under-emphasized' in their writings; and, I believe, our recent expansion of the role and function of these elements have given a new, fresh focus to this theoretical perspective.

e) *Perceptions and Perspectives:* Another aspect of my theorising has been to illustrate the 'adultist' perspective of adults' relationships with adolescents and their stated intentions for young people's development and education. Then, by allowing the same context to be perceived 'through the eyes of youth', illuminating similarities and differences of viewpoint emerged and could be used as a starting-point in planning programmes for – or better still – with, young people.

f) *Dynamic Systems Theory:* At this juncture, it is difficult to claim whether my interest in multi-directional effects and influences led my own thinking towards *Dynamic Systems Theory* or whether Dynamic Systems Theory began to *shape* my perspective and ways of considering development. Of course, both are true, and this is consistent with Dynamic Systems theoretical stance on multi-directionality! Hence, these themes, in combination, took me towards the theoretical perspectives, which became key parameters in my published works.

Resources, challenges and risks: Hendry and Kloep's Lifespan Model of Developmental Change

In my career I systematically and carefully broadened my research interests from studies on young people's competitive sports involvement, to investigations of the school context and teacher and pupil relations, adolescents' leisure pursuits, their family relations, parenting styles, youth workers and young people, mentoring, youth unemployment and youth training schemes, and adolescent health behaviours. This shifting focus of research interest also absorbed contextual implications such as rural living, early school leaving, and, at times, had cross-cultural perspectives. However, for a time, I was not fully aware of how the pieces of my 'developmental jigsaw-puzzle' fitted together, until the Lifespan Model 'emerged'. Together with Professor Marion Kloep, we constructed a lifespan model, derived from our discussions and not *consciously* influenced by other academic viewpoints, only to discover that other academics were moving towards a similar 'paradigm shift' albeit using a slightly different vocabulary. Ours highlighted the concepts of 'challenge', 'risk', and 'resources' and emphasized processes and mechanisms (see Hendry and Kloep, 2002).

The parameters in our simplified model emerged from the idea that human beings are both similar in their development – and, conversely, different. On the one hand, all normal babies learn to walk and talk, become adults, and eventually grow old and die. Yet, some will become parents, others not; some will be outstanding intellectually, others not; some will end up in prison, others in suburbia or an urban slum.

Here, I want to briefly describe the various components of the model (Hendry and Kloep, 2002) because it contains the building-blocks that emerged from my earlier writings, though I was less aware then of the importance of an interactive perspective than now.

First, we distinguished between three kinds of 'developmental shifts' that occur during the life course:

1 'Maturational-biological shifts', such as physical growth, puberty and ageing. They account for human similarities.
2 'Normative-social shifts' (e.g. school attendance, military service, retirement), prescribed by the individual's culture, often by law, religion or social norms. Because of these, individuals within the same culture are more similar to each other than members of a different culture.
3 'Non-normative shifts' – changes that do not occur for everyone, but vary, making every individual unique.

Second, these shifts present the individual with many different challenges as they adapt to new life situations, and coping with these challenges demand a whole range of changing 'resources' over the lifespan. Many of these resources are innate, such as genetic dispositions. Others are learned. Still others are structurally determined, such as nationality or social class. Thus, the individual's 'resource system' is an open system that consists of a variety of interacting resource-elements, which can vary at any moment, and over the lifespan, and as new resources are added, others disappear, and some elements become resources while others lose that quality. Just as certain potential resources exist for everyone from the very first moments of life in the womb, so too does the inequality in their distribution.

Third, there is no boundary between 'individuals' (and their resources) and 'environment' (and its challenges). Any characteristic can be a potential *resource* (e.g. being tall as a high jumper), *irrelevant* (being tall and trying to solve a mathematical problem) or a *disadvantage* (being tall and trying to sit comfortably in an Economy class transatlantic flight). In other words: these potential resources only become *actual* resources *in interaction* with the kind of task or challenge that has to be met.

Thus, fourth, the idea of 'goodness of fit' comes into play. While the task determines what resources *may be needed*, the number and kind of the individual's potential resources determine whether or not a particular task met turns out to be a routine chore, a challenge or a risk. A challenge can be a clearly positive experience, or it may contain negative elements that nevertheless lead to growth. For instance, something as undesirable as having a physical handicap can be the antecedent for enormous personal growth. On the other hand, something as apparently desirable as a large lottery win can be disastrous for people unable to cope with new-found wealth. Another important aspect affecting 'goodness of fit' between resources and challenges is the number of different challenges the individual faces *at the same time*. The 'goodness of fit' between potential personal resources and certain challenges is different *between* individuals, but also *within* individuals, because of situational factors: Something that is easy for one person is not necessarily easy for another; something that was too difficult yesterday might be relatively easy tomorrow. So, dealing with a challenge can add to a person's resources and lead to further development. Or it can be 'risky' and drain resources, making it more difficult to deal with future challenges.

Fifth, if an individual assesses his or her resources as being inadequate for meeting a challenge, anxiety will arise, and the individual will attempt to avoid the challenge. On the other hand, if the resource system is perceived as sufficient to the task, this will enhance feelings of security and efficacy. Hence, if the resource-system is relatively 'full', a state of contentment, a feeling of security is reached. However, after some time this can lead to feelings of boredom and the individual might set out to find new challenges and gain new resources. Such challenges sought when 'boringly' secure, can be anything from small *daily tasks*, to *sensation-seeking*, to real '*life shifts*' like emigrating.

Thus, in trying to find a balance between security and boredom on the one hand, and anxiety and risk on the other, a *dynamic and accumulative process* occurs: The more and better potential resources individuals possess, the more willing they are to seek out new tasks, and if meeting them successfully, adding even more resources. Similarly, a downward spiral can occur. The fewer and weaker resources individuals have, the greater will be their anxiety when confronted with new tasks and the lower the probability that they will voluntarily seek out new challenges. Their capacity to solve future tasks will further decrease.

Hence, sixth, 'developmental stagnation' is a period of time where no new resources are added. An individual can stagnate developmentally at any phase of the lifespan, if potential resources do not match up to challenges. Additionally, it is possible to stagnate in one life-domain while continuing to develop in others: Resources can be almost completely drained within one life-domain (e.g. being unskilled in sports), be sufficient to be happily stagnated in another (e.g. in social life) and continue developing in a third (e.g. occupational career). There is no steady-state in open dynamic systems, so these different resource-states are temporary, and can be reversed at any time. Rather, there is a continuous, ever-changing interaction within the system's elements.

Before concluding this book, we will return to and briefly re-assess the Lifespan Model and its various component parts, since various building blocks of the model appear in different guises within the extracts presented below.

Brief introductions and selected extracts

Since I was starting out academically in an era when personality theory within psychology was 'centre stage', so-to-speak, and Eysenck and Cattell were the theoretical leaders in the field, not too surprisingly, I utilised their measurements as the instruments for my earliest investigations, where I was interested in young elite swimmers and their coaches, and published the first two papers of my career in an international research journal: Hendry (1968) and Hendry (1969).

The findings essentially showed that elite swimmers, *in general*, possessed personality characteristics that tended towards introversion and neuroticism and sought security and dependency, while coaches *in general* were confident, driving individuals, and a blend of 'father-figure' and aggressive adult mentor. It is possible to suggest how such different 'types', with individual variations, might well be suited to be competitive partners, even at the risk of a somewhat restricted general socialization.

However, true to my critical self, even then, I felt somewhat dissatisfied with explanations of behaviour only in terms of underlying traits, and so added new personality measures of my own to attempt to gauge inter-personal perceptions. Additionally, I used Cluster Analysis to measure personality similarities and differences among different sports teachers and coaches in various sports; by methodologically adopting a technique that would enable a degree of disaggregation to be shown in the findings (see e.g. Hendry, 1974). This 'tinkering' with existing frameworks of grand theories can be simply described as Scottish stubbornness; or perhaps couched more academically in terms such as 'critical scepticism'.

Perhaps being something of a teenager at heart, even now – and a advocate of *real* recognition for young people in society – another aspect of these preliminary explorations was realising that in my writings I was attempting to present the young person's perspective, empathetically, though hopefully non-judgementally. This led to a rather provocatively titled journal article which was published in 1971 ('Don't put your daughter in the water, Mrs Worthington?'). This article received considerable media attention because it revealed a *darker* side to competitive sport and of coach/athlete interactions. The personal and social 'costs' when young people allowed coaches to dominate and decide how their lives and lifestyles, which would be designed and planned to maintain top-level competitive performances, left little time for these adolescents to have a varied leisure life and mix with other (non-sporting) peers. Then the effects such training regimes on these adolescents' social lives and interpersonal development was somewhat problematic as they were almost always in the company of their (adult) coach rather than other teenagers. Moreover, when the athlete's performances enhanced or temporarily, at least, diminished the coach's reputation and status was always a stressful aspect in the relationship. The media's and general public's attention to these intense 'partnerships' with adult mentors appeared to centre around the ways coaches and trainers of all kinds (including music teachers, sports coaches, academic home tutors, as young people mentioned and recounted) played particularly dominant and influencing roles in young people's lives. These ideas led me towards researching varying contexts of adolescent life – in school and in leisure – and exploring their perceptions and relationships.

References

Arnett, J.J., Kloep, M., Hendry, L.B., and Tanner, J.L. (2011) Debating Emerging Adulthood: Stage or Process? Oxford University Press: New York.

Blastland, M. and Dilnot, A. (2009) *The Numbers Game: The Commonsense Guide to Understanding Numbers in the News, in Politics and in Life*. New York: Gotham Books.

Coleman, J.C. (1974) Relationships in Adolescence. Routledge and Kegan Paul, London.

Eccles, J.S., Midgley, C., Whigfield, A., Buchanan, C.M., Reuman, D., Flanagan, C., and McIver, D. (1993) Development during adolescence: The impact of stage-environment fit on young adolescents' experiences in schools and families. *American Psychologist*, 48, 90–101.

Hendry, L.B. (1968) Assessment of personality traits in the coach–swimmer relationship, and a preliminary examination of the father-figure stereotype. *Research Quarterly*, 39, 3, 543–551.

Hendry, L.B. (1969) A personality study of highly successful and 'ideal' swimming coaches. *Research Quarterly*, 40, 2, 299–304.

Hendry, L.B. (1971) 'Don't put your daughter in the water, Mrs Worthington'. *British Journal of Physical Education*, 2, 3, 17–29.

Hendry, L.B. (1974) Coaches and physical education teachers: A comparison of the personality dimensions underlying their social orientation. *International Journal of Sports Psychology*, 5, 1, 41–53.

Hendry, L.B. and Kloep, M. (2002) *Lifespan Development: Challenges, Resources and Risks*. London and New York: Thomson.

Hendry, L.B. and Philip, K. (1996) Young people and mentoring: Towards a typology? *Journal of Adolescence*, 19, 3, 189–201.

Hendry, L.B., Shucksmith, J., Love, J. and Glendinning, A. (1993) *Young People's Leisure and Lifestyles*. London: Routledge.

Hendry, L.B., Glendinning, A., Shucksmith, J., Love, J. and Scott, J. (1994) The developmental context of adolescent lifestyles. In Silbereisen, R.K. and Todt, E. (eds) *Adolescence in Context: The Interplay of Family, School, Peers, and Work in Adjustment*. New York and Berlin: Springer.

Hendry, L.B. and Kloep, M. (2010) How universal is emerging adulthood? An empirical example. *Journal of Youth Studies*, 13, 2, 169–179.

Nisbet, J.D., Hendry, L.B., Stewart, C. and Watt, J. (1980) *Towards Community Education*. London: Elsevier Science.

Philip, K. and Hendry, L.B. (2000) Making sense of mentoring or mentoring making sense? Reflections on the mentoring process by adult mentors with young people. *Journal of Community and Applied Psychology*, 10, 211–223.

Whitehead, N. and Hendry, L.B. (1976) *Physical Education in England and Wales. Description and Analysis*. London: A. & C. Black.

Whiting, H.T.A., Hendry, L.B., Hardman, K. and Jones, M.J. (1973), Personality and Performance in Physical Education and Sport. Henry Kimpton, London.

*References appearing here refer to work quoted in the Personal Introduction and to introductions to various extracts presented in the remainder of the text.

1 Aspects of the 'hidden curriculum'

This paper outlines certain conflicts inherent in the Physical Education teacher's role both for pupils and for teachers themselves and alerted me to giving consideration to the young person's perspective of life-events rather than only taking an 'adultist' stance as in the case of many research studies. The article gives insights into what has come to be known as 'the hidden curriculum', by considering the advantages, disadvantages and conflicts established within physical education teacher-pupil relationships and how these 'spill over' to influence their school experiences and future life. Here, I was interested in discovering whether or not, within a non-examinable subject (as Physical Education was then), there existed a 'hidden curriculum' whereby the ways teachers and pupils perceived each other, and how well teachers 'knew' their pupils, created an unintentional climate of differential treatment and variations in pupil-achievement as pupils approached the end of their compulsory schooling. These educational interactions created perceptions that teachers treat pupils differently, revealed pupil-ratings of teachers' 'good' and 'bad' qualities, and showed a wide range of pupils' involvement (or non-involvement) with school's activities.

When one looks into the school context, findings also beg the question of the influences of other developmental contexts on young people's lives. This became an important strand in my research. I examined, from the viewpoint of adolescents themselves, several social contexts, both formal and informal, where young people interact with adult mentors – school, home, youth centres, other leisure settings. Since I have always been interested in young people's own perceptions of life and growing up, I was able to show aspects of adolescent lifestyles in a somewhat different light from that usually portrayed in the research literature – a perspective that matched well with my own 'critical scepticism'.

ASPECTS OF THE HIDDEN CURRICULUM

Teachers' and pupils' perceptions in physical education

L. B. Hendry and Jennifer Welsh

Introduction

The "hidden curriculum" has been described as the unplanned and often unrecognised values taught and learned through the process of schooling (e.g. Apple, 1971; Bidwell, 1972; Dreeben, 1968; Henry, 1966; Jackson, 1968; Overly, 1970; Silberman, 1971; Snyder, 1971). Various writers (e.g. Dreeben, 1968; Hargreaves, 1967; Holt, 1964; Illich, 1970; Jackson, 1968) have offered somewhat different versions of the "hidden curriculum", but all of them have indicated that it interpenetrates with, and is communicated alongside, the official curriculum in teacher-pupil interactions, and can be as highly structured and organized, detailed and complex as the formal curriculum.

It has been suggested that the "hidden curriculum" teaches the pupil norms and values necessary for transition to, and integration into, the adult world (e.g. Dreeben, 1968; Haller and Thorsen, 1970) and so an emphasis on socialisation — order, control, compliance and conformity — has been persistently reported (e.g. Adams and Biddle, 1970; Jackson, 1968; Leacook, 1969; Rist, 1970). On the other hand, some writers have criticised these implicit qualities as stressing consensus and cocial orientations not in the best interests of the individual (e.g. Apple, 1971; Friedenberg, 1963; Henry, 1963; Silberman, 1970). Further, the "hidden curriculum" has been described as a vehicle for a possibly unjustified differential treatment of pupils often on the basis of race, academic ability, social class or sex (e.g. Apple, 1971; Frazier and Sadker, 1973; Hargreaves *et al.*, 1975; Illich, 1970; Rist, 1970; Willis, 1977).

Most research on the "hidden curriculum" has used intensive naturalistic observations in a small number of classrooms (e.g. Cowell, 1972; Jackson, 1968; Rist, 1970; Keddie, 1971). Because of this, and the lack of statistical analyses, findings are not easily generalised to other situations (of Hargreaves, 1967). Additionally, cause and effect can be hard to disentangle, and delayed effects in pupils difficult to trace. One way of avoiding some of these limitations is to examine the cumulative differential effects of the "hidden curriculum" by investigating pupils towards the end of their compulsory schooling and to consider how these possible influences are manifested in the way in which teachers and pupils view each other. This is the approach taken in the present study, although it is acknowledged in turn that a general examination of differential perceptions obviates value inferences at the level of daily classroom (or sports field) interactions.

Eggleston (1977) argued that the "hidden curriculum" and official curriculum are, in fact, two perspectives of the total curriculum, in that the official curriculum is predominantly a teacher perspective and the "hidden curriculum" is predominantly a pupil perspective. This interpenetration of curriculum-interactions between teachers and pupils, inferred from consistencies in class organization, teacher behaviours and procedures, have been assumed to have a powerful impact on the values, norms and behaviour of pupils.

Various elements of the school system can combine to differentiate pupils in terms of their attitudes toward teachers, their self images, and their scholastic success. Hargreaves (1972), for instance, has offered a theoretical framework for studying the social processes and school relationships linked to academic attainment. He suggested that the teacher's conception of a pupil's ability, the pupil's own conception of his ability, and whether or not the pupil values the teacher's approval, all have a part to play in bringing about an educational self-fulfilling prophecy. Empirical support for such social processes is available (e.g. Hallworth, 1966; Hargreaves, 1967; Keddie, 1971; Nash, 1973; Rich, 1975; Silberman, 1969). Hurn (1978) has also argued that the teacher's expectations, which are shaped by ascribed characteristics of pupils, are translated into differential treatment of pupils, and these treatments in turn have powerful effects on subsequent student learning. In this connection it may be important to note that school sports participants tend to produce better academic results than non-participants, and have higher educational aspirations (e.g. Schaffer and Armer, 1966; Schaffer and Renberg, 1970; Spreitzer and Pugh, 1973). As Start (1966) has postulated, pupils who play for school sports teams also tend to accept the academic pupil role so that sport becomes another manifestation of school culture. Thus it can be hypothesised that a "hidden curriculum" within school sport may exist in British schools (of Jackson, 1968).

Hargreaves (1972) has pointed out that in evaluating pupils in the classroom, the teacher gives approval to those pupils who conform to his expectations. Further, Nash (1973) has written: "The most important point to understand about this evaluation is that it is not wholly (or even mainly) about academic matters ... Teachers are concerned about their pupils' liveliness, sociability, and simply how likeable they are."

The labels which teachers may use in "Getting to know" their pupils have been outlined by Hargreaves *et al.* (1973): (1) Appearance; (2) Conformity (or its opposite) to discipline role aspects; (3) Conformity (or its opposite) to academic role aspects; (4) Likeability; and (5) Peer group relations.

Similarly, a number of researchers have demonstrated the effect of pupils' physical attractiveness on teachers' expectations and evaluations (e.g. Clifford and Walster, 1973; Dion, 1972; Dusek, 1975; Rich, 1975), even when teachers have been made aware of teaching bias (Foster *et al.*, 1975). It can be hypothesised that conformity, attractiveness and skill could be major factors in the teacher's expectancies of pupils' performance especially (but not only) in practical subjects like physical education. Physical education teachers may use certain perceptual impressions of pupils to construct an overall evaluation of their physical ability and personal qualities, which is conveyed to pupils, setting up matching self estimations in these pupils as part of the differential effect of a "hidden curriculum" within school sports. Hence in the present study, by attempting to tease out possibly differing perspectives of teachers and pupils within a non-examinable subject, more general insights into the differential effects of the "hidden curriculum" may emerge. The present paper is, therefore, concerned with four issues:

1   How do physical education teachers perceive competitive, recreative and non-participant pupils?
2   How do pupils view physical education teachers?
3   How do pupils perceive their own abilities and enthusiasm for physical education?
4   What elements of pupils' self-estimations and of physical education teachers' perceptions best distinguish sports participants from non-participant pupils?

Procedure

The sample consisted of 2,619 (93%) fifteen-sixteen year old pupils attending 12 comprehensive schools in an area in Central Scotland, together with their physical education teachers ($N = 75$).

Pupils were classified on the basis of their involvement in extracurricular school sport as: (a) active competitively: (and voluntarily) in physical activities or sports at school, i.e. the pupil was actively involved and represented the school in games, sports, or physical activities ($N = 310$ boys, 227 girls); (b) active recreatively: i.e. the individual took part in physical activities or joined sports clubs extracurricularly for reasons such as enjoyment or health but not for representative competition ($N = 215$ boys, 211 girls); (both these groups have covered a wide range of overlapping sports and physical activities, and did not represent different forms of activity); or (c) non-participant: i.e. the individual had no voluntary extracurricular involvement in school sports or physical activities ($N = 683$ boys, 973 girls).

The present study attempted to gauge teachers' perceptions of pupils, and pupils' perceptions of teachers, and to assess the general framework on which their separate "definitions of the physical activities" situation may be based.

Teachers rated their own pupils on bipolar descriptive terms chosen from Hallworth's (1966) study, and in the light of Nash's (1973) comments about the use by teachers of constructs of pupils' sociability and attractiveness. Items such as competitiveness and physical ability were added by the researchers (after piloting) as being relevant to physical education. The items used for teachers' perceptions were as follows: General physical ability in sports; enthusiasm for physical education; sociability; friendliness; popularity; social anxiety; competitiveness; reliability; personal appearance (i.e. attractiveness) — all 5 point scales (1 — high; through 3 — average to 5 — low). Teachers' assessments of pupils' home background (good home — poor home) was rated on a 6 point scale.[1]

Teachers (who learn something of somatotyping during their teacher training) were also asked to assess pupils on a seven point scale for muscularity (7 — high; 1 — low), similar to scales devised by Sheldon (1940). As a check on the validity of teachers' ratings, in one randomly selected school, three skinfold measures of pupils were taken, namely triceps, subscapular, and suprailiac (see Tanner, 1964[2] for details) and compared with teachers' estimates. Correlations were: (a) for boys. $r = +0.79$ ($N = 60$); (b) for girls, $r = +0.70$ ($N = 70$).

Pupils' attitudes toward teachers were assessed by a number of statements which pupils perceived as being important to the physical education teachers' role. These were taken from a previous study by Hendry (1975). Pupils were asked to respond to these items on an agree-disagree basis. In addition, pupils were asked to assess their own physical ability level, enthusiasm for physical education, the amount of attention they received from physical education teachers and their desire to improve their physical skills — all on 3 point scales. Further, pupils were asked to give their perceptions of the physical education programme by responding to a number of "open-ended" questions.

Because of the large number of pupils involved physical education teachers' perceptions of pupils' characteristics were analysed using ANOVA, while pupils' views of teachers and of themselves in relation to physical education were analysed by Chi-Square. Data on teachers' and pupils' perceptions were also treated by a series of discriminant analyses. Essentially discriminant analysis is a technique carried out to examine trends in the combination of selected associated variables which best distinguish between criterion groups.

Results

1. Generally, physical education teachers' perceptions of pupils revealed differential views of active and non-participant pupils, with teachers having more favourable attitudes towards extracurricular sports participants. Of the three groups, competitors were seen by teachers to be most enthusiastic, friendly, popular, reliable, and of attractive appearance, as well as being highly skilled physically and highly muscular. Additionally, women physical education teachers considered competitive schoolgirls to be the most socially poised group of girls and to be more likely than other groups to come from a "good" home background, although no differences were found among the three groups of boys in these characteristics.

2. In their turn, pupils who were participants in extracurricular school sports had more favourable opinions of physical education teachers than non-participants; yet the majority of pupils, regardless of participation category, perceived physical education teachers as even-tempered, friendly and approachable, able to get on well with pupils and to establish good relationships with pupils. At the same time they were seen by most pupils as competitive individuals, giving differential treatment to pupils by paying more attention to the more highly skilled and by being less interested in pupils who were not especially enthusiastic about school sports. Additionally, based upon the Chi-Square analysis, there were interesting differences in the way teachers were perceived by the three groups of pupils. For instance only competitive boys, in any major way, regarded the physical education teacher as a "counsellor", while recreatives and non-participant girls seemed more acutely concerned with teachers' differential attention and time devoted to high skilled pupils than competitors. Further, there were more consistent differences among the girls' group than among boys in their views of

physical education teachers. Additionally, teachers were perceived as more friendly and approachable, and better able to give pupils confidence firstly by competitors, then by recreatives, then by non-participants.

3. In the light of such varying perceptions it is perhaps not surprising that pupils' self-evaluations revealed a rather similar pattern, with active pupils having greater self-esteem than non-participants.

In physical ability, enthusiasm, desire to improve physical skills, and in perceptions of the attention given to them by the physical education teacher, a greater percentage of competitive pupils possessed highly positive views of their own personal qualities, talents and interests than in the other two groups. Nevertheless, it should be noted that around 70 per cent of non-participants, as well as a high percentage of participants, wished to improve their personal physical ability level. At a more impressionistic level, non-participant pupils reported feelings of neglect and isolation from physical education teachers, within the learning procedures adopted in school sports programmes.

4. A series of discriminant analyses showed that teachers' evaluations of pupils' physical ability, enthusiasm for sports, competitive drive, reliability (for girls only), together with pupils' perceptions of their own enthusiasm for sports, and (for girls only) physical education teachers' attention best distinguished school sports competitors from both recreatives and non-participants. The standardized coefficients from these analyses were relatively small, however, and should simply be regarded as trends.

Discussion

Since more than half the boys and almost seventy per cent of girls in the sample were completely non-participant in voluntary extracurricular school sports it might be asked if there were any clues to be discovered about such widespread non-participation in the relationships and perceptions between physical education teachers and pupils?

On the face of it, there would seem to be less need within physical education for a teaching bias or for pupils to seek the teacher's approval as in the classroom (cf. Silberman, 1969). Physical education teachers are associated with a fairly popular and wide-ranging subject — or so it would appear from a report into attitudes and preferences of fifteen year old pupils (e.g. Morton-Williams and Finch, 1968). Sixty-four per cent of boys, and fifty-six per cent of girls thought physical education interesting, which placed it well ahead of art, crafts and music in terms of popularity with pupils. Taking a different view, however, Hendry (1978) has suggested that there may be a much greater affinity between the physical education teacher and muscular, physically skilled competitive children who reveal similarities to the teacher in both physique and behaviour; and by implication, there may be a neglect of children who do not conform to this "desired" social image: a "hidden curriculum" of sport.

In the present study, the fact almost every assessment of pupils' characteristics by teachers showed a significant difference in evaluation among pupils' groups may be particularly noteworthy. Women physical education teachers appeared to possess more clear-cut differential perceptions than their male counterparts. Teachers of physical education select the pupils who represent schools in competitive sports activities, and not unnaturally such pupils were rated by teachers as having a very high level of skills ability and muscularity. Physical ability and physique were not, however, the only important differentiators among competitive pupils, recreative pupils, and non-participants. Enthusiasm, sociability, popularity, competitiveness and reliability were other characteristics which made competitors outstanding. The discriminant analyses also showed that the elements which distinguished competitors from other pupils revolved around an amalgam of physical education teachers' and pupils' evaluations of perceived abilities and qualities.

In rather the same way as classroom teachers, certain personal characteristics may be used by physical education teachers as part of the basis for differential treatment of pupils. When questioned, a large number of non-participant pupils indicated feelings of isolation and neglect within the compulsory time-tabled programme. By far the most frequent comments were directed towards physical education teachers' decisions about teaching procedures and choice of activities without any real pupil understanding of reasons behind these decisions. Whitefield (1971) has referred to this as "curricular trade secrets", where pupils are excluded from knowledge of what is happening to them in terms of changes in behaviour. When sports groups were formed teachers appeared to give much of their attention to skilful athletes, so that other pupils felt there was a lack of opportunity to be helped in making personal progress. In other words, many felt they were being ignored by teachers and received little coaching as a result. While physical education teachers might well justify their actions in terms of learning strategies, the important point is that from the pupils' perspective, their main concern may be about the social context of learning.

The evidence suggested that the differential perceptions of teachers, and the perceived differential treatment of pupils can create a "hidden curriculum" of school sports potentially every bit as divisive as one operating within classroom subjects (e.g. Hargreaves, 1967; Willis, 1977).

What is being argued here is that the interactions between the teacher and pupils, either in the classroom or on the games field, may be crucial in conveying "messages" of praise or disapproval (Jensen, 1969), and attention or neglect, which subsequently influence different pupils' attitudes, interests and performance in school activities; and if such self-fulfilling prophecies do arise in educational contexts, then perhaps greater research attention should be given to the mechanics and processes involved in the encounters of teachers and their pupils.

Of course it can be argued that other factors may influence the pupils' involvement or non-involvement in extracurricular sports: out-of-school interests; perceived lack of ability; parental discouragement; part-time jobs and so on. But Hendry (1978) has reported that active sports participants are as frequently engaged in part-time employment as non-participants which suggests that interested pupils are able to arrange employment to fit in with their sports commitments. Further, Hargreaves (1967) and Sugarman (1968) have claimed that it is pupils who are disillusioned with, and alienated from, school that turn to pop oriented leisure interests. Such a division of interests might be seen as additional evidence for a divisive "hidden curriculum" within school sports (e.g. Hendry and Thorpe, 1977).

Pupils' views of physical education teachers confirmed a pattern of differential perceptions operating within the school sports context, seeing their teachers as friendly and approachable, yet highly competitive and giving greater attention to highly skilled pupils. Interestingly, competitors were not particularly concerned about teachers' attention and time, and they had a more favourable view of physical education teachers generally, suggesting they were well aware that they had a good relationship with their teachers. In addition, the self-evaluations of these adolescent pupils revealed the possible existence of a positive feedback system within the "hidden curriculum" which can lead to differentiations in pupils' behaviour, participation in and attitudes to school sport. Obviously favourable responses from teachers across the school years can encourage certain pupils to continue successfully in sports participation. Yet this same system may depress the self-image of a large number of pupils in relation to sports.

Notes

1 Not all teachers were prepared to evaluate pupils on this item (Nash, 1973).
2 The researches wish to thank Professor J. M. Tanner for his advice regarding the anthropometrical measures used in this study.

References

Adams R. and Biddle B. J., 1980, *Realities of Teaching*, Holt, Rinehart and Winston, New York.
Apple M., 1971, *The Hidden Curriculum and the Nature of Conflict*, "Interchange", 2, pp. 27–43.
Bidwell C., 1972, *Schooling and Socialization for Moral Commitment*, "Interchange", 3, pp. 1–27.
Clifford M. M. and Walster E., 1973, *The Effect of Physical Attractiveness on Teacher Expectations*, "Sociol. Educ.", 46, pp. 248–258.
Cowell R. N., 1972, *The Hidden Curriculum: A Theoretical Framework and a Pilot Study*, Doctoral dissertation, Harvard University.
Dion K., 1972, *Physical Attractiveness and Evaluation of Children's Transgressions*, "J. Personality Soc. Psychol.", 24, pp. 207–213.
Dreeben R., 1968, *On What is Learned in Schools*, Addison-Wesley, Reading, Mass.
Dusek J. B., 1975, *Do Teachers Bias Children's Learning?*, "Review of Educational Research", 45, pp. 661–684.
Eggleston J., 1977, *The Sociology of the School Curriculum*, Routledge and Kegan Paul, London.
Foster G. G., Ysseldyke J. E. and Reese J. H., 1975, *I Wouldn't Have Seen It if I Hadn't Believed It*, "Exceptional Children" (April), pp. 469–473.
Frazier N. and Sadker M., 1973, *Sexism in School and Society*, Harper and Row, New York.
Friedenberg E. Z., 1963, *Coming of Age in America*, Random House, New York.
Haller E. J. and Thorsen S. J., 1970, *The Political Socialization of Children and the Structure of the Elementary School*, "Interchange", 1, pp. 45–55.

Hallworth H. J., 1966, *Perceptions of Children's Personalities by Experienced Teachers*, "Educ. Res.", 19, pp. 3–12.

Hargreaves, D. H., 1967, *Social Relations in a Secondary School*, Routledge and Kegan Paul, London.

Hargreaves D. H., 1972, *Interpersonal Relations and Education*, Routledge and Kegan Paul, London.

Hargreaves D. H., Hester S. K. and Mellor F. J., 1975, *Deviance in Classrooms*, Routledge and Kegan Paul, London.

Hendry L. B., 1975, *The Role of the Physical Education Teacher*, "Educ. Res.", 17, (2), pp. 115–121.

Hendry L. B., 1978, *School, Sport, Leisure: Three Dimensions of Adolescence*, Lepus, London.

Hendry L. B. and Thorpe E., 1977, *Pupils' Choice, Extracurricular Activities: A Critique of Hierarchical Authority?*, "Intern. Rev. Sports Sociol.", 12 (4), pp. 39–50.

Henry J., 1963, *Culture against Man*, Random House, New York.

Henry J., 1966, *Jules Henry on Education*, Random House, New York.

Holt J., 1964, *Why Children Fail*, Pitman, London.

Hurn C. J., 1978, *The Limits and Possibilities of Schooling*, Allyn and Bacon, London.

Illich I., 1979, *Deschooling Society*, Harper and Row, New York.

Jackson P. W., 1968, *Life in Classrooms*, Holt, Rinehart and Winston, New York.

Jensen A., 1969, *Review of Pygmalian in the Classroom*, "American Scientist", 51, pp. 44A–45A.

Keddie N., 1971, *Classroom Knowledge*. In: Young M. F. D. (ed.), *Knowledge and Control*, Collier-Macmillan, London.

Leacook E. B., 1969, *Teaching and Learning in City Schools*, Basic Books, New York.

Morton-Williams R. and Finch S., 1968, *Enquiry 1: Young School Leavers*, H.M.S.O., London.

Nash R., 1973, *Classrooms Observed*, Routledge and Kegan Paul, London.

Overly N. (ed.), 1970, *The Unstudied Curriculum: Its Impact on Children*, Association for Supervision and Curriculum Development, Washington, D.C.

Rich J., 1975, *Effects of Children's Physical Attractiveness on Teachers' Evaluations*, "J. Educ. Psychol.", 67 (5), pp. 599–609.

Rist R. C., 1970, *Student Social Class and Teacher Expectations: The Self-Fulfilling Prophesy in Ghetto Education*, "Harvard Educational Review", 40, pp. 411–51.

Schafer W. E. and Armer J. M., 1966, *Participation in High School Athletics and Academic Achievement*, Proceedings of the International Sports Congress, Madrid.

Schafer W. and Renberg R., 1970, *Athletic Participation, College Expectations, and College Encouragement*, "Pacific Sociol. Rev.", 13, pp. 182–186.

Sheldon W. H., Stevens S. S. and Tucker W. B., 1940, *The Varieties of Human Physique*, New York, Harper, London.

Silberman M. L., 1969, *Behavioural Expression of Teachers' Attitudes Towards Elementary School Students*, "J. Educ. Psychol.", 60, pp. 402–407.

Spreitzer E. and Pugh M., 1973, *Interscholastic Athletics and Educational Expectations*, "Sociol. Educ.", 46, pp. 171–182.

Start K. B., 1966, *Substitution of Games Performance for Academic Achievement as a Means of Achieving Status among Secondary School Children*, "Brit. J. Sociol.", 17 (3), pp. 300–305.

Sugarman B., 1968, *The Social System of the School*, Brit. Sociol. Assoc. Annual Conference.

Tanner J. M., 1964, *The Physique of the Olympic Athlete*, Allen and Unwin, London.

Whitefield R. C., 1971, *Disciplines of the Curriculum*, McGraw-Hill, London.

Willis P., 1977, *Learning to Labour*, Saxon House, Farnborough.

2 Constructed case studies in a school context

Typologies are a method whereby social scientists allow findings to give some picture of sub-group or sub-cultural variations. In this extract from an earlier book, I went a step further and attempted to reveal both typological differences and individual differences within 'types'. Findings show the vast array of individual differences that lie hidden beneath the figures of reported means and standard deviations. As I stated earlier, I was never a believer in one-variable answers to questions about human behaviour, and this led to explorations of influencing forces in adolescent change. It is evident that many aspects of life – relationships, environmental contexts, perceptions and so on – affect the developing adolescent. Further, my critical and inter-disciplinary mind asked why, when personality theory was about individual differences, were results almost always reported as group means and standard deviations? Were there ways of disaggregating findings? One early resolution to this query was the employment of mixed methods in my own doctoral research, devising a research approach which could demonstrate both general trends and individual variations and illustrate individual differences within sub-groups. I 'invented' a method, which I called 'Constructed Case Studies', where I extracted typical cases from a sample. What I liked about my method (despite its possible weaknesses) was the way it revealed a whole variety of individual 'stories' within the framework of sample findings. Disaggregating results offer insights into individual differences, and provide an illuminating range of 'colour' to our social sciences' rainbow. These case studies offer a series of human stories that can be understood, importantly, within a framework of statistical results and typologies.

CONSTRUCTED CASE STUDIES

Individual views of school and sport

Leo B. Hendry

It does seem as if pupils who are actively involved in sports are differentiated by a number of qualities, attitudes, and interests from those who are non-participants.

There are also differences in their self-esteem, and in teachers' perceptions of their qualities and abilities. Yet these variations are essentially general descriptions, and it is only by considering alternative approaches that a way forward can be found in offering a more complete explanation of the effects of these differences on the individual pupil.

Recently educational research has begun to change emphasis from a strictly hypothetico-deductive model, and has moved towards a more sociological-anthropological paradigm in an attempt to understand the social processes involved in teacher-pupil encounters. Illuminative studies of this kind try to uncover the nature of what has happened in social situations (e.g. Glaser & Strauss, 1968).

Within physical education this means using illuminative approaches, and by concentrating on a small number of schools or just one school, studying in detail the whole physical education process. A useful beginning has been made in this direction in the work of Ward and Hardman (1973), and Carroll (1976). This chapter describes one such method of understanding individual pupils' views of school and school sports, by attempting to interpret and construct meanings from the comments of teachers and pupils themselves. In this way the writer takes on the role of a social biographer. The author makes no claim that the evidence here is presented fully from the pupils' perspective, simply that it provides certain insights into individual pupils' standpoints.

The previous chapter [of the original publication] revealed that general and consistent trends exist in the characteristics which distinguish between adolescent sports participants and non-participants (although the author's own investigations—Hendry, 1975—suggested that some overlap of scores was apparent in most variables). In case these general findings appear to create an over-simplified picture of the findings, five schools were studied in greater detail.

Five schools in focus

Three of the selected schools provided a fairly representative view of suburban, urban, and new town schools in terms of the number of pupils who were competitive, recreative or non-participant in each school. Two other schools were selected because they had 'deviant' characteristics; one urban school had limited opportunities to offer a range of extracurricular sports recreatively; one new town school served a fairly wide geographical area, and reported difficulties in having pupils stay on after school for extracurricular activities (i.e. transport problems). It also had poor facilities. In both cases physical education teachers claimed that the timetable was built round academic teaching and that sports were 'fitted in' thereafter.

The representative schools all had wide extracurricular provision for sports and facilities were good, though there was an element of restriction on pupil participation by teachers' discretion or teachers' estimate of pupils' ability level to gain membership to a sport club or activity.

The 'deviant' schools revealed some difficulties either of provision or facilities for physical activities, and it was clear that in these schools there were problems in maintaining pupil attendance at extracurricular sports activities.

Despite these diverse trends the characteristics of teachers in the various schools were similar, and the qualities and opinions and attitudes of pupils' groups in each school followed a fairly common pattern.

Taking teachers first, it can be stated that irrespective of school provision, their programme's aims are geared towards skills learning, leisure time interests, self and social awareness, and organic development. Enjoyment satisfaction, social understanding and general physical development are the expected pupil effects. Further, they consider that ideally physical education teachers should be knowledgeable of children and their subject, able to communicate their ideas and to win respect.

If physical education teachers share general commonalities of attitude, ideology and teaching approach (perhaps as an outcome of their teacher training experiences: Hendry, 1975) these attitudes of dedication, ability, enthusiasm, and selection may be transferred to their pupils. Certainly the previous chapter [of the original publication] highlighted the important association between teachers' perceptions and sports participation.

Pupils also showed a similarity of personal qualities, background and opinion irrespective of school. Within the three groupings (competitive, recreative, non-participant), pupils were remarkably alike in their general pattern of responses in each school. In physical skills and qualities, in their psychological make-up, and in teachers' perceptions general findings were confirmed. It was only in response to questions concerning physical education teachers, and about encouragement and having better facilities that pupils in the two 'deviant' schools and particularly non-participants, indicated more intense opinions: they were concerned about better facilities, more encouragement from teachers, and were more critical of physical education teachers than pupils in the three representative schools.

Constructed case studies

While there was little firm evidence of significant differences among schools, common sense tells us that individual schools *do* possess a distinctive ethos and social context. Thus if such differences can be detected by an observer (or by more 'objective' evidence) yet subjectively pupils do not perceive great differences in the total physical education process, and if their responses to teachers are roughly comparable among schools then clearly this state of affairs warrants closer research.

It may be most useful however to concentrate on two extreme groups: competitive and non-participant adolescents (although a small number of recreatives are included). It was reasoned that whatever forces were operating on these pupils would show up more powerfully or more frequently than in the recreative group. The results from the statistical study showed that the average scores and ratings for recreatives do indeed fall between those of the other two groups in almost every case.

The selection and construction of case studies centred on four types of pupils:

1   those who competed in and out of school;
2   those who did not participate in sport either in or out of school;

3   those who participated in school sport, but did not participate out of school;
4   those who did not participate in school sports but who participated out of school.

Fifty-five adolescents were scrutinised and picked out by the author to demonstrate aspects of the various classifications. The case studies finally written totalled twelve, of which eight are presented in the text. To provide a theoretical framework a number of questions were posed, and by concentrating on two of the five schools used for more detailed examination it was possible to gain some further understanding of the influence of teachers, school and community on the adolescent.

An attempt was made to seek answers to such questions as:

Why does this pupil compete for school but does not even participate recreatively in sports out of school?

What advantages does the pupil see in staying on at school after the compulsory leaving age?

What are the pupils' attitudes to physical education, extracurricular school sport, leisure pursuits?

How are the most popular boys and girls in class perceived (in four or five words).

What sort of spare time activities are followed beyond homework or housework.

General self-image, and so on.

Thus an extensive and coherent picture of the adolescent in the context of his school and community was developed. These descriptions, constructed in the manner of a biographer, are here called case studies although the term is being used in a rather unusual sense. It should be pointed out that, as far as possible, the words used in the case studies were those used by the pupil himself. Additionally case studies were used to look at teachers' perceptions of pupils and pupils' reactions to the physical education programme in an attempt to tease out the interactions between teacher, pupil, and physical activities at an individual level: an attempt to interpret and construct meanings (cf. Douglas, 1967). These case studies are used to illustrate in more personal terms some of the points argued in earlier chapters of this book.

Case 1 Janet: non-participant; recreative; urban

According to her physical education teacher, Janet is a girl of great athletic ability who likes games. Yet she does not take part in any school sports at all. The teacher describes her as extremely physically able, strong, muscular and reliable, and as more enthusiastic and competitive than average; she is attractive in appearance and comes from a 'good home'. All in all a very complimentary picture, but is it accurate?

Janet describes herself as very enthusiastic; her brother is also very keen, and both parents encourage her. Although she watches little television, she does watch sport, especially athletics, show jumping, swimming and football; and she enjoys physical education classes, the most important thing about them being the satisfaction she gains from being good at games. Of the sports that school provides she likes dance, gymnastics, swimming, indoor and outdoor team games, tennis and

Table 2.1 Categories of the twelve case studies

Number	Pseudonym	Sports participation in school	Physical recreation out of school
*1	Janet	Non-participant	Recreative
*2	Marianne	Competitive	Competitive
3	Angela	Non-participant	Competitive
4	Geraldine	Recreative	Non-participant
*5 and	Anna and	Non-participant	Non-participant
6	Marie	Competitive	Non-participant
*7	Tommy	Non-participant	Non-participant
*8	Stephen	Competitive	Non-participant
9	Charlie	Non-participant	Recreative
*10	George	Non-participant	Competitive
11	Alan	Recreative	Recreative
*12	Jimmy	Competitive	Non-participant

*denotes case studies described in text.

badminton. Able and enthusiastic are certainly accurate descriptions of Janet: but Janet is not competitive. Her scores on the attitude to physical activity inventory are remarkable: on four dimensions—social, health, aestheticism and catharsis—they are well above average, well above even the average for competitive girls, but on the other two, and especially vertigo, they are low. Sport to her is a social activity, graceful to watch, and useful as a relaxation and relief from the rest of life and a way of keeping fit. Excitement, risks, strenuous activity and competition do not appeal to her. She is adamant that she plays all sorts of games at the youth club for 'just fun and enjoyment'. She goes because 'I enjoy going to be with my friends', and her reasons for enjoying physical education are again being with her friends and keeping fit and healthy. It is sociability and fitness, not competition and excitement that she seeks from sport.

Other children (Stephen, Case 8, for instance) represent the school despite not being particularly competitive by nature. Why does Janet not even participate for 'fun and enjoyment'? She does not like school. School is boring, monotonous, useless; the teachers treat them like kids, she's fed up with being told what to do and finds the teachers disinterested in individual children: the sooner she can leave and start working the better. Not surprisingly, she is not expected to get any O-levels (guidance teacher's rating). The enthusiasm her physical education teacher noticed is strictly limited—it is enthusiasm for sports, but not for school or teachers or even physical education teachers. She is scathing in her criticism of the latter—they are, like all the others, not interested in pupils except the very able ones, not sympathetic or approachable and short-tempered into the bargain. Personally she gets less attention than other pupils from teachers. She doesn't like school sports primarily because of the teacher: 'It does not get taught right. The teacher takes you to play rounders, then just goes away because she has no time for the pupils'.

26   *Constructed case studies in a school context*

Janet seems to see school solely as a place to learn things (despite her low academic ability and negative school attitude, she sees staying on at school as an advantage because you can 'do O-levels') and she seems to resent not being taught games. She is quite happy playing games just for fun at the youth club, but seems to expect more from school—it seems unlikely that her physical education teacher, who has such a high opinion of her, is at all aware of her resentment. Without an improvement (in accordance with her ideas) in the teaching of physical education, it seems that no amount of enthusiasm for games and sports will make Janet take part in school clubs.

The next case study is of another enthusiastic girl, but this time the pattern of activity is very different.

Case 2 Marianne: competitive; competitive; urban

Marianne competes both in the school and outside it. Is she then a girl whose behaviour is determined primarily by high athletic ability? Her teacher describes her as extremely strong and above average in ability and enthusiasm for physical education and games, and her 600 yard time of 139 seconds confirms this; although not outstanding, she is good. She describes herself, perhaps a little modestly, as of average ability but as very enthusiastic. This she certainly is and her enthusiasm is catholic—on television she watches swimming, football and athletics, in school she plays netball and hockey; out of school she competes in athletics and dancing and after leaving school she hopes to continue dancing and to play ladies' football! In all this she is supported by the undivided attention (she is an only child) and strong encouragement of both parents. The importance of her dancing to her is evident in the attitude to physical activity inventory, where her score on the aesthetic dimension is the highest in the school. She is very interested in graceful sports like skating and dancing and feels very strongly that school should place more importance on them. On the other hand, she states that she very strongly prefers quiet activities like swimming to noisy ones and her score on the vertigo dimension is correspondingly low. When asked why she takes part in all her various activities, it is always the competitive element and having 'complete control of my body' that she stresses.

Marianne identifies strongly with the school—she looks forward to going, finds lots of interesting things going on and does not complain of being treated like a kid. She wants to stay on to try for O-levels; she is in no hurry to start work and feels that the money is less important than having a job you like. Not surprisingly, her attitude to physical education teachers is also very favourable; they are friendly, approachable, fair and interested in all their pupils.

This enthusiasm for school, perhaps deriving from her enthusiasm for sport, leads Marianne to describe herself as a good pupil; cheerful, dependable, friendly, hardworking, clever and eager to learn, and with all this it is not surprising to find that her physical education teacher believes her to come from a 'good home'. What is perhaps surprising is the report of her guidance teacher: Marianne is not very bright, being expected to get no more than one or two O-levels. In addition she comes from an unskilled working class home. It seems that her enthusiasm for sport, and hence for school, and the favourable response she meets from her teachers have given her a slightly inflated estimation of her academic ability.

The last two girls in this section make an interesting comparison, and are dealt with in a combined case study.

Cases 5 and 6 Anna: non-participant; non-participant; new town
Marie: competitive; non-participant; new town

Two girls ran 600 yards several seconds faster than any other girl tested in the school. One of them represents the school in athletics; the other does not participate in any sport in or out of school. What are the differences between Anna and Marie that account for the former's greater involvement in physical activity?

In fact, the two girls are surprisingly alike. This study will first describe their similarities, then look more closely at Anna, and finally compare Marie with this picture.

They are both small girls—Anna is only 4'9" tall, while Marie, at 5'1", is still below average height. They are both just over 6 stone, about 2 stone below the average weight. Not surprisingly, the physical education teacher describes Marie as one of the thinnest girls in the school, whereas Anna's shorter stature compensates for her lightness and she is rated about normal, neither fat nor thin.

Both girls view physical activity largely as a way to keep healthy and are not much attracted by the social aspects of sport. When asked to select the most important things about physical education, they both included 'health and fitness' and 'timing and co-ordination' in their four responses. Neither girl scores highly on the attitude to school questionnaire and their attitudes to physical education teachers are similar—Anna is heavily critical while Marie is a little more favourable than average. Neither takes part in any of the school's non-sporting activities—Anna seems unaware that the school runs a youth club, although many of her classmates attend it—and neither girl intends to continue with any sporting activities after she leaves school.

The analysis so far shows the girls to be alike in many ways, but does indicate a difference in degree; while Marie is rather neutral in her identification with the school and its activities, Anna is strongly antagonistic. She is not expected to get any O-levels and sees staying on at school as 'a waste of time'. She would rather start work as soon as possible, get into the adult world and earn some money. She is not in the least interested in sport and would not go to physical education classes if she had the choice. Her brother and her three sisters are not very keen either, but she says her father encourages her strongly to take part in physical activities. She watches a good deal of television, but it is old films, westerns, comedies and variety shows that she watches, never sport. When not watching television, she goes to the cinema, listens to pop music or goes dancing with a friend. Of all the school activities listed in the questionnaire the only one she admits to liking is dancing. Her boyfriend, pop music and 'having a good time' are very important in her life. Personal appearance is important. Anna is described as an attractive and popular girl. She wishes she were more beautiful, believes that physical education will improve her 'cleanliness, dress and posture' and describes the most popular girls as 'brainy and pretty'. Perhaps she thinks that if she were more pretty she might have more good times and be less bored than she is.

Anna is academically poor, but even without sports involvement of any kind after school hours she can run 600 yards as fast as anyone. If the alternative route to status, through sport rather than study, does operate, there is surely no-one for whom it would be more appropriate than Anna.

Marie is not really a sporting type either: her attitude to physical activity, as already said, is particularly oriented to health and fitness but she also enjoys the ascetic aspects of strenuous exercise and the excitement and thrills of sport more than most girls. On the other hand, her score is extraordinarily low on the social and cathartic dimensions of the inventory. Her actual choice of sports bears out these scores. Athletics is her favourite, the only sport she watches on television, and she also enjoys gymnastics and swimming: but nothing else—no team games, no tennis, no skating, or horse-riding. She chooses the individual 'fitness' activities, the ones whose principal component is fitness and sheer effort, and at the same time the 'solitary' ones. Not only are they not team games, but even in competition a runner or a swimmer or a gymnast hardly needs to interact with the other competitors; they are rivals rather than opponents.

Marie describes herself as of average sporting ability but very enthusiastic, and says her two brothers and five sisters are quite keen too. She would be better at sport if given any encouragement. It is interesting that Anna, who is not at all enthusiastic, describes her father as very encouraging, while Marie, who is very keen, says her parents give her no encouragement. It seems that these girls are perhaps assessing parental encouragement relative to how much they want rather than how much they get: Anna is over-encouraged and Marie under-encouraged. Marie spends her leisure time with a group of girls, plays games and watches a great deal of sport. She does not spend much time watching television or at the cinema; pop music, discotheques and boyfriends are not important in her spare time, but she is seldom bored. Where Anna described the most popular girls as 'brainy and pretty', Marie puts 'brainy, strong, kind and pretty'; she relegates 'pretty' to fourth place, and is herself one of the few girls described as unattractive by the teacher.

Her attitude to school score is higher than Anna's, but is still no more than average. She is expected to get a few O-grades, but not many, and she wants to stay on to take them. She wants a job she will like and starting it soon is not important. School is useful and most subjects are interesting too, but the teachers treat her like a kid, and she is not sure whether she would rather be in school or out working.

Here then we have the two fastest girls in the school. One is not interested in school, not interested in sport and does not participate in physical activities, preferring coffee-bars and discotheques. The other is fairly happy in school, very keen on physical exercise and runs for the school, though she participates only in school and will stop when she leaves. It is unlikely that Anna would run for a school team even if she fully identified with the values of the school, such is her dislike of physical activities. It is difficult to doubt that Marie's relatively favourable views on school and physical education teachers are partly the result of the school providing the facilities and the encouragement to indulge her interests that she feels she lacks at home.

The other case studies are of boys. The first of these deals with a boy who, in many ways, is like Anna.

Case 7 Tommy: non-participant; non-participant; new town

Tommy does not take part in any games in or out of school, yet he can run very fast—only four of the boys in his school are faster over 600 yards. Why then does he not at least participate in sports?

It might be expected that Tommy dislikes sports, but in fact, he says that he does like them, mentioning athletics, gymnastics and football in particular. To understand his behaviour it is necessary to look more closely at his attitudes to physical education and games in school, and to school itself.

He does not like school. He is fedup with it and welcomes any excuse to stay away (he is, in fact, frequently absent). English is the only academic subject that he ever finds interesting (and that is only sometimes) but his school ability is high, as can be judged from the fact that despite his very low motivation he is nonetheless considered to be a potential A-level candidate. The only other subject he likes is woodwork. He longs to start working and earn money and is not in the least concerned about getting a job that he will like. His opinion of physical education teachers is not very flattering—they are not friendly, and are only interested in the sports teams, having no time for boys like himself who have little interest in games, and thus accord him little attention. His physical education teacher has assessed him as average on every single personality trait, although his ability is clearly high and his enthusiasm clearly low, which suggests that the teacher may have no clear picture of this boy who stays away from school whenever possible and would not go to physical education if he could avoid it.

In his spare time, Tommy watches a lot of television. He enjoys watching sport, especially football, but receives no encouragement to play. He is often bored, spending much of his time with a group of boys who, like himself, play no games. But he seems to be rather a lonely boy—he particularly dislikes the social aspects of games, he does not like dancing and does not think that girl friends matter much, and does not think it is important to have friends to go around with. Family and earning money are the only really important things in life.

Thus it is not a dislike of physical activity, but a distaste for the organisation of school or club that keeps Tommy away from sport—he is able and interested but unrecognised and unencouraged. His physical education teacher apparently has not realised that he is one of the most athletically able boys in the school; his parents give him no encouragement. His own opinions of himself and of his abilities seem depressed by these poor opinions that others hold of him—he believes he is no better than average athletically, he does not realise how fast he can run, he feels restricted and awkward in his movements. Manifestly school has failed in this case; Tommy is not developing his potential, academically or physically.

30   *Constructed case studies in a school context*

Case 8 Stephen: competitive; non-participant; new town

Stephen swims competitively for the school, but is not involved in any activities unconnected with the school. He enjoys school, likes and respects his teachers and wants to go to university and get a 'good job'. Here clearly is one subject who contributes greatly to a positive correlation between loyalty to the school and involvement in its sporting activities. What does a closer look reveal about his reasons for competing and not participating?

He is of average height, well-built and, as he puts it himself, 'no weakling'. His physical education teacher considers him average in athletic ability, but not especially enthusiastic. And Stephen agrees with this assessment, more or less, describing himself as fairly vigorous and very fast (in fact, his running speed and agility are very slightly above the average for all boys). He would like to be more vigorous and better at games, but not if this means hard training and athletics. 'I don't enjoy the really strenuous PE classes.' All the same, he would not give up physical education if it was optional, recognising the need of some exercise to keep fit. But this exercise he gets adequately from swimming, and recreatively from hill-walking and occasional games of badminton, and the simple reason why he does not participate outside the school is 'I find adequate exercise at school with swimming, climbing, and I do cycle'.

His identification with the school is really in more intellectual ways—his academic ability is high and he is a member of the debating society and the geology club and plays a horn in the school orchestra. He sees himself as clever, hard-working, dependable, friendly and popular, and believes in the 'sensible' things in life—family, appearance and a good job rather than dancing, pop music, or starting work as soon as possible. To be popular, a boy should be amusing, helpful, intelligent and sensible, just as he sees himself, in fact.

In short, Stephen is a 'good pupil', embodying the academic and social values of school. His physical activities are individual rather than team games, undertaken for fitness and enjoyment, not for ascetic or competitive reasons. But he is a good swimmer and does compete for the school when asked to—a sharp contrast with the 'delinquescent' Derek, also a good swimmer, quoted by Hargreaves (1967) as saying 'I wouldn't swim for this bloody school'.

Case 10 George: non-participant; competitive; urban

An urban working class boy, assessed by teachers as coming from a poor home and having very low academic ability. George plays for a football team in the youth club he goes to. Why does he not play for a school team?

He seems to have physical prowess: according to his physical education teacher he is above average in ability, enthusiasm, reliability, friendliness, competitiveness and in appearance, and is extremely strong. His attitude to sport is remarkable for his very high score on the ascetic dimension—strenuous training and competition—only three boys in the school scored higher. He is also attracted by the social aspects of sport, but not by excitement and risks. His running speed is fairly fast, though not exceptionally so; he describes himself as average in ability, but fairly enthusiastic and would like to be much more vigorous and skilful.

In contrast to his physical ability and enthusiasm, his academic ones are low. He will not be presented for any O-levels, school is utterly boring, and he would rather be working; 'You never get taught anything in the fourth year'. But he is prepared to admit that woodwork and metalwork are useful and interesting while english and maths are useful, and physical education is interesting. School is worthwhile only where it prepares him for work.

It seems that George's negative attitude to school is sufficient to explain his non-participation in school sport. But some other items do not fit this picture so well. Just as his physical education teacher gave a fairly complimentary picture of him, so does he in turn of them. They do not concentrate too much on the good pupils and their teams, but they are friendly, approachable, sympathetic, even-tempered, inspire confidence and he is given reasonable attention by them. Physical education classes are important because of the satisfaction and enjoyment he gets from them, and because they develop team spirit and interests in and out of school—the last two seem a little odd for a boy with such an anti-school attitude. He enjoys physical education classes because 'I enjoy the thrills, speed and excitement of the action'. He enjoys watching football, wrestling, swimming and cricket, and after school he plans to play golf; he also is a member of the school chess club. One last point, when asked which school sporting activities he particularly enjoyed, George only answered yes to swimming: not football, although it seems to be his favourite sport out of school, and although he has an extremely high score for asceticism and hard training.

Case 12 Jimmy: competitive; non-participant; urban

Jimmy is the captain of the school football team; out of school he has no sporting interests. To what extent does he espouse the 'school values' for life in general?

Just over average height and almost a stone below average weight, Jimmy is particularly strong and a very fast runner, while his general ability and enthusiasm are described as above average. It is his enthusiasm that sets him apart. He has three older brothers, none of whom are very keen on sports (once again, as with Maria and Anna, Cases 5 and 6, this probably means 'compared to me'), but he gets strong encouragement from both his parents. Football is naturally enough his favourite sport, but he also swims for the school, and plays badminton and table-tennis recreatively. He likes pretty nearly every kind of sport; athletics, dance, gymastics, swimming, football, tennis badminton, table-tennis, cycling, wrestling and golf all get a mention somewhere in his answers.

The important things he gets from physical education are that it keeps him fit and gives him enjoyment and more satisfaction than he can get from other school subjects. He likes the classes mainly for the excitement, but it is the chance to do his best and compete that he finds most compelling in sport after school hours. He does not go to any non-sporting school clubs, or to any out-of-school clubs, saying 'don't know anybody in clubs'; his friends all come from school. An extravert, Jimmy is described as friendly, assertive and competitive, very popular, and he claims to get a lot of attention from teachers. He describes himself as popular, fair and honest, a bit of a bully, a good sport but a bad loser—sounds like the ideal competitive team captain!

Along with the enthusiasm for sports goes a positive attitude to school; it is enjoyable, interesting, adult and he would rather be there than out working. All his subjects are interesting, and he is happy to stay on at school 'because you learn a bit more'. It comes as a bit of a surprise to find that he will not be presented for any O-levels at all!

Academically Jimmy is very poor, but his enthusiasm for sport has been harnessed by the school, making him football captain, and producing in him a strongly positive attitude to school. For once, at least, the alternative to status has certainly worked.

Concluding comments. Observational studies examine real-life situations looking for causal relationships and influences, while statistical correlational research need not necessarily mean that causal connections exist. A weakness of observational research, however, is that the original statistical correlations or significant differences are often not established at all. Observers frequently admit that different researchers might well derive different events or aspects of events to record and interpret.

The constructed case studies were extracted, as it were, from a larger statistical study, so that the use to which the case studies can be put is intimately bound up with the overall results of that investigation. It seems possible to suggest that constructed case studies (corroborated by a statistical skeleton) can provide theoretical insights of their own by forcing the researcher (and reader) to concentrate on individuals, and perhaps especially the 'atypical' ones.

In conclusion case studies remind us in very personal terms that school sports can serve a useful function for some adolescents, but also serve—in conjunction with the school system generally—to drive some adolescents to seek out other leisure interests. They also raise questions about both the teaching of physical education and teacher-pupil relations. This may be considered to be important by some if there is an intimate association between school sport and physical recreation: and if, when the 'pupil' role is discarded it is substituted by a 'pop' or 'street corner' role in adolescence.

References

Carroll, R. (1976) Evaluating lessons. *Brit J. Phys. Educ.*, 7, 6, 202–203.

Douglas, J. D. (1967) *The social meaning of suicide.* New Jersey: Princeton University Press.

Hargreaves, D. H. (1967) *Social relations in a secondary school.* London: Routledge & Kegan Paul.

Hendry, L. B. (1975) School, sport, leisure: a study of personal social and educational factors. Report to the Scottish Education Department, Edinburgh.

Ward, E. & Hardman, K. (1973) The influence of values on the role perceptions of men physical education teachers. An investigation for the N. W. Counties Physical Education Association.

3 Educational pathways and interactive factors

Is it possible to devise a picture of the various 'pathways' that lead to pupil-involvement in school activities? I used Cluster Analysis (a relatively new technique in the UK in the early 1970s) to disclose the differential, interactive 'power' of a large array of various psycho-social, anthropometrical and environmental factors in answering research questions about school attainment, involvement in extracurricular school sports, leisure, and how these aspects of adolescent lifestyle might be associated: Whilst essentially a descriptive model, for its time, it was an extremely insightful way of demonstrating the vast array of variables that impacted on and were associated with adolescent socialisation. The diagram might well serve as an early example of Bronfenbrenner's ecological model and of the way Dynamic Systems Theory would like us all to study development. There were a host of influencing factors from somatic and psycho-motor aspects, through teacher–pupil relationships, to social and material/environmental ones, all interacting in concert to affect young people's attitudes to school and schooling, their scholastic attainment and their sports participation at school and at leisure. However, what I was not aware of, then, was the possibility of bi-directional influences, that is, young people's effects on all these variables. That insight would come later.

As is evident from the examples of my writings and my comments so far, I was already interested in the theoretical frameworks of authors like Bronfenbrenner. The next two reported studies reveal how varying influences can direct individuals toward different leisure-styles and how differing perceptions can lead to different choices being made.

ACADEMIC ATTAINMENT, SCHOOL SPORT AND TEACHER-PUPIL RELATIONSHIPS

A typological approach

L. B. Hendry and A. J. B. Anderson

Introduction

While the social and psychological correlates of academic attainment have been carefully studied and commented upon (e.g. Wiseman, 1964; Douglas, Ross and Simpson, 1968; Beech, 1963; Ridding, 1966; Warburton, 1969; Entwistle, 1972) involvement in school sports has been less well considered from either a social or psychological viewpoint (though see, for example, Hendry, 1970; Emmett, 1971.) Yet within the school context the most persuasive influence on sports involvement would appear to be academic success (e.g. Start, 1966; Hargreaves, 1967; Nichols, 1971). Reid (1972) has also pointed out that the more socially "favoured" and academically able pupils were over-represented in extracurricular pursuits such as school choirs and sports teams. Thus there have been general claims that school sports reinforce academic superiority (Hargreaves, 1967). In this light sports might be seen not only as an opportunity for pupils' recreation but also as an occasion for demonstrating a wide range of social skills and further identification with school's values (Spady, 1970). As Start (1961) has shown, pupils who play for school teams also tend to accept the academic-pupil role, so that sport becomes another manifestation of school culture.

Hargreaves (1972) has offered a theoretical framework for studying the social processes and school relationships linked to academic attainment. He suggested that the teacher's conception of a pupil's ability, the pupil's own conception of his ability, and whether or not the pupil values the teacher's approval, all have a part to play in bringing about an educational self-fulfilling prophecy. Empirical support for such social processes is available (e.g. Hallworth, 1966; Hargreaves, 1967; Silberman, 1969; Keddie, 1971; Nash, 1973; Garner and Bing, 1973; Rich, 1975). Hargreaves (1972), for instance, believes that teachers' perceptual bias is unintentional, but that such differences among pupils as exemplified in speech, appearance, values, attitudes and behaviour in the classroom, are used by the teacher as a part of the basis for estimating pupils' intelligence, ability and future potential. In the same way physical education teachers may use certain perceptual impressions of pupils to construct an overall evaluation of their physical ability and personal qualities, which is conveyed to pupils, setting up matching self-estimations in these pupils. There are ample opportunities in the varied educational settings in physical education for processes of teacher-bias to arise: from fleeting impressions, labelling of pupils and the "halo effect", which are undoubted features of assessments in the classroom. What is being argued here is that the interactions between teacher and pupils, either in the classroom or on the games field are crucial in conveying messages of praise or disapproval, which subsequently influence pupils' attitudes, interests, and performance in school activities.

Yet participation in school sports (like academic achievement) may be related to a variety of personal, social and educational factors, and it would be simplistic *not* to acknowledge some of them. At the conclusion of a cross-cultural study of involvement in, and attitudes towards, physical activity, Kenyon (1968) wrote: "A variety of behavioural, dispositional and situational variables were significantly related to ... different forms of involvement. Involvement tends to be the result of a rather complex set of factors." Kenyon's quotation makes clear the fact that the relationship pattern of various factors to the adolescent's involvement in school physical activities is not a simple one.

Firstly, previous investigations have shown that personal attributes such as personality, attitude, physique, skill, and level of fitness are connected with the individual's involvement or non-participation in sport: and, for example, there appears to be a relationship between emotional stability, extraversion and general movement ability (see Hendry (1978), for an overview).

Secondly, in examining social factors, both Sillitoe (1969) and Emmett (1971) have shown that individuals from a middle-class background are more active in physical activities. Emmett (1971) has also demonstrated that adolescent boys are more sports-loving than girls. In this connection, games may be seen as "miniature achievement models" reflecting particular upbringing, sex roles and lifestyles (Sutton-Smith et al., 1963). The family appears to be a significant influence on participation in sport (Orlick, 1972). In adolescence, however, its effect is dissipated somewhat by the influence of the peer group (Emmett, 1971).

Thirdly, within the educational system itself the influence of academic attainment or involvement in school sports has already been discussed.

Further, a Scandinavian study has shown how pupils' interests and involvements in physical activities were bound up with their teachers' preferences and influences (Heinila, 1964).

Such findings beg consideration of the school situation, the physical education programme, how such personal attributes as have been found to be important in previous studies affect teacher-pupil perceptions, and the whole range of social interactions from class lessons and school clubs to representative teams, undergone by pupils together with their physical education teacher. To date little is known of the processes involved in the encounters between the physical education teacher and pupils. It might be asked, for example, what assumptions are made by teachers about the differentation of pupils according to perceived physical abilities?

Many studies concerned with predicting academic success have attempted to describe associated variables by a single profile or equation, yet Entwistle and Brennan (1971) have argued that the assumptions underlying such an approach can be patently false.

Similarly there have been no typological analyses of pupils' involvement in school sports even although McIntosh (1963), for instance, pointed out that "in sport ... human motives are never simple." Correlational analyses, followed by factor analyses or multiple regression techniques, have been previously applied to data in attempts to describe or predict the characteristics of sports participants (e.g. Kane, 1968). Implicit in this approach is the assumption that the conditional distribution of scores on the involvement variable is normal, or that the scatter of points in multidimensional hyperspace formed by all the variables included in the analysis is multivariate. In addition, such studies suggest that involvement can be described by a single profile of attributes or predicted by a single regression equation. Such assumptions may certainly not be justified. Experience with sports participants would suggest that there are a variety of paths leading to involvement or non-participation. Hence, we should expect not *one* regression equation or *one* profile, but a series of equally useful descriptions of *types* of pathways leading to participation in physical activities. A statistical procedure which follows this "typological" approach is cluster analysis, and this has been applied to the findings reported below.

Methodology

(a) Sample

The study was based on over 3,000 pupils aged 15–16 years (87% of the total year-group) and 75 physical education teachers in 15 comprehensive schools in central Scotland. These pupils were classified on the basis of their involvement in extracurricular school sport as: competitors (i.e. they represented the school in some form of games or sports or physical activities[1]), recreatives (i.e. they participated non-competitively in school sports clubs) or non-participants (i.e. they did not take any part in extracurricular school sport).

The general aims of the investigation were to describe the main personal, social and educational differences among the three designated groups of pupils, together with an examination of pupils' leisure interests; and to consider the factors which were most closely associated with sports participation and which distinguished between participants and non-participants.

Data were collected by questionnaires and inventories; from teachers' ratings and assessments; and by direct measurement, observations and recordings. The information thus available about pupils and the variables on which pupils and teachers in the study were assessed included:

(A) Inventories:
Eysenck Personality Inventory: Attitude to Physical Activity; Embedded-Figures Test; Body-esteem; Self-esteem.
(B) Measures:
Height; weight; ponderal index; cardio-vascular fitness.
(C) Teacher-Ratings:
  i. Physical education teachers' perceptions of pupils; general ability in physical education and games; enthusiasm for physical education and games; sociability; popularity; general social nervousness or anxiety; competitiveness; reliability; personal appearance (i.e. attractiveness);

home background; attendance at physical education; representational standard of physical activities; physical disabilities.
  ii. School assessments of: (1) socioeconomic rating based on father's occupation; (2) predicted scholastic attainment.

(D) General questionnaire:
  i. Social Aspects: family size and position; family encouragement in physical activities involvement; television viewing frequency and choice of programme; social attitudes.
  ii. Educational Aspects: interest in and value of school subjects; attitudes to school and to the raising of the school leaving age; school clubs membership; school status.
  iii. Physical Education: perceptions of personal abilities, enthusiasms and interests in physical activities; outcomes of the physical education programme; perceptions of physical education teachers; voluntary attendance and enjoyment; reasons for liking timetabled physical education; reasons for liking extracurricular physical education.
  iv. Leisure: perceptions of school — community recreative links; post-school recreation; active or passive leisure; peer groupings; reasons for leisure sports involvement.

(E) Further, observations were carried out in each school together with informal interviews with teachers and pupils to get some understanding of the particular ethos of each school and to gauge impressions of teaching styles and teacher-pupil interactions.

(F) Dependent variable:
pupils' involvement in school physical activities in extracurricular time; (in addition, pupils' involvement in physical activities in own leisure time away from school was similarly assessed).

Teachers also completed a questionnaire about: activities available to pupils at school; publicity given to school sport; objectives of physical education; teaching styles; teachers' involvement in extra-curricular activities; club membership; pupil-effects from physical activities participation; teacher-characteristics; factors influencing physical education teachers' work; facilities; assistance from classroom colleagues; attitude to physical activity inventory.

Thus the general intention of the present paper is to describe data by two types of cluster analyses on the basis of fairly clear cut differences in personal, social and educational factors among competitive, recreative and non-participant pupils.

(b) Method of analysis

Associations among the one hundred and fifty variables of Hendry's (1975) data on 3,000 adolescents were studied using the method suggested by Hills (1969) for the inspection of large correlation tables. A two-dimensional picture is produced such that points representing highly correlated variables appear close together whereas those relating to uncorrelated or negatively correlated variables are relatively far apart. Separate analyses were made for each group of variables described as "personal", "social" or "educational". Groupings for both boys and girls were sufficiently clear-cut to warrant attention in a selected composite analysis of 41 variables.

Each pupil in the sample can be described in terms of a particular combination of scores on these 41 variables. As Entwistle & Brennan (1971) have suggested, any sample can be thought of as a distribution of points in hyperspace analogous to stars in physical space.

In a dual way, the variables can be described as points on a unit hypersphere, the cosine of the angle between two radii being equal to the correlation between that pair of variables. We are entitled to project such a hypersphere into a two-dimensional approximate representation (as in Hills' procedure) or to apply methods of cluster analysis, preferably agglomerative.

Just as matter is not equally distributed throughout the universe but condenses into stars held together in galactic formations of varying shapes, so points in psychological space may produce regions of high or low density. There may be large volumes of relatively empty space and others of considerable density corresponding to groups of variables that are highly inter-connected (Entwistle and Brennan, 1971).

The shape of such clusters is to some extent a function of the definition adopted for inter-cluster distance (see, for example, Anderson, 1971). For example, the distance between clusters A and B might be related to the greatest correlation between two variables, one from cluster A and one from cluster B, as in single link clustering; or it might be defined as the variance between clusters A and B as in minimum variance clustering. Where distinct variations in density occur, the clusters are likely to be clearly defined whatever clustering procedure is adopted and this was found in the present study.

We have employed two methods for representing the clusters of variables that emerge, superimposed on the intercorrelation diagrams.

(i) The "minimum spanning tree" presents a picture topologically identical to that of single link cluster analysis. Such a tree, based on "distances" between variables, has the properties that there are no closed loops and the total length of the links is minimal. We can create single link type clusters by breaking links in descending order of length. It should be noted that distances may have been artificially shortened by "missing" variables i.e. variables not included in the study but nevertheless of crucial importance. For example, what might "fill in" a link between social class, academic attainment and fitness (endurance run)?

(ii) The main groupings produced by a minimum variance cluster analysis can also be represented diagrammatically, the emphasis there being on the joint inter-relations of all variables in the cluster, rather than on a "stepping stone" type of connectedness.

Results and discussion

Since more than half the boys and almost seventy per cent of girls in Hendry's (1975) original study were completely non-participant in voluntary extracurricular physical activities, and since there were consistent trends of descriptive differences among competitive participants, recreative participants and non-participants it might be asked if there are any clues to be discovered about school sports involvement from the present analysis?

Firstly, it should be noted that a fairly coherent pattern emerged for both boys and girls with only minor differences between them.

Secondly, a number of paths were associated with participation in physical activities, supporting McIntosh's (1963) and Kenyon's (1968) view that reasons for sports involvement are complex. Thus at an intuitive level the present cluster analysis makes sense, and reinforces the idea that a single path analysis for such complex interactive phenomenon can be misleading. Six distinct clusters were identified for boys and girls and these have been tentatively labelled by the researchers, according to the groupings of variables as: 1. Social Values; 2. General Attitudes to Sport; 3. Social Class and Academic Attainment; 4. Physical Education Teachers' Ratings; 5. Teacher-Pupil Relations; and 6. Miscellaneous (which included pupils' self-estimates, personal attributes and social factors).

Although six groupings were in evidence nevertheless one constellation of factors predominated. For both boys and girls a clustering of physical education teachers' perceptions and pupils' self estimates in relation to physical activities were seen to be most closely linked with school sports involvement, together with a number of physical and physiological components (see Figure 3.1).

Within a second area of constellated variables it can be noted that there is a relatively "mixed" range of items linking "*home factors*" such as parental encouragement, watching sport on television (i.e. secondary participation according to Kenyon, 1968); "*social aspects*" like leisure sports involvement, intentions to continue sport after leaving school; "*relational considerations*" such as perceptions of and attitudes about physical education teachers; and "*personal factors*", for instance, extraversion, attitudes to sport, body esteem and so on. Further, the pattern for boys and girls does show some variation at this level.

It is important, at this stage, to draw attention to a number of "super stars" in our hyperspace. An examination of the "minimum spanning tree" shows that certain variables are crucial centres linking the various elements of a psycho-social constellation. "Enthusiasm for sports", "physical ability", and "involvement in school sport" all reveal several avenues converging on those variables. These may serve as aspects of concern for further investigation. Again the track between "fitness" (distance run) and "academic attainment" is fascinating because it raises questions about possible "missing" variables — perseverance, motivation, achievement needs and such like.

Social class, academic attainment, and favourable attitudes to school are shown to be closely linked — supporting incidentally a vast array of research findings — but a little distanced from school sports participation, which might

40 *Educational pathways and interactive factors*

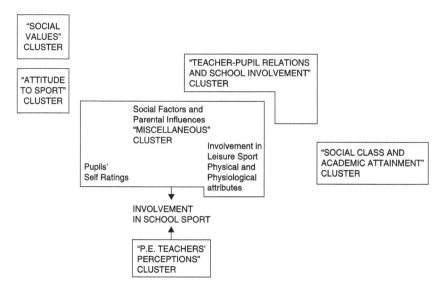

Figure 3.1 Minimum variance cluster analysis: diagrammatic representation of adolescent pupils' involvement in physical activities.

raise important questions about the influences of comprehensive education on pupils' extracurricular activities.

Because of the nature of Hendry's (1975) investigation and the various ways in which data were collected it was *not* possible to classify certain items that *may* be important to sports involvement; for example, perceptions of sports participants by non-participants and of non-participants by participants were not ascertained simply because the researcher did not wish to make pupils consider possible differences between themselves and others within the school setting except in a very general way. It might be adduced from Hendry and Simpson's (1977) study of a sports and community centre, however, that adolescent groups are reasonably accurate in estimating differences (as they perceive them) between sports participants and non-participants, and clearly such perceptions may be important in reinforcing attitudes, interests, and involvements in both school and leisure.

Nevertheless, given these limitations a plausible general picture is evident which is reasonably consistent for both adolescent boys and girls. On examining Figure 3.1 (which is a simplified diagrammatic representation of the minimum variance cluster analysis) it may seem a little puzzling at first sight to note that the "Teacher-Pupil Relationship and School Involvement" cluster is somewhat distanced from the "Physical Education Teachers' Perceptions" cluster. The explanation for this lies in the various components which make up the two clusters.

The "Teachers' Perceptions" cluster comprises evaluations of pupils' abilities and qualities in relation to school sport, whereas the other cluster is constructed of a mixture of teachers' and pupils' views about aspects of the school physical education programme. This may also help to highlight why the "Attitude to Sport" cluster is also at some distance from "Involvement in School Sport". These variables actually represent sub-scales of a questionnaire about attitudes to sport generally (Kenyon, 1968) and not school sport specifically.

In any case it should be remembered that in the figures all the individual variables were found to be associated with "School Sports Involvement" and we are, therefore, basically looking at the relative positioning of clusters and variety of pathways in relation to school sport.

Teachers of physical education select the pupils who represent the school in sports activities, and not unnaturally such pupils were rated by teachers as having a very high level of skills ability. Enthusiasm, sociability, popularity, competitiveness and reliability were other characteristics which were closely clustered with school sports involvement. It is possible to suggest that if a pupil shows high ability in sports, then he is usually enthusiastic about physical activities. Thus selection may reinforce possession of certain qualities in pupils; being chosen to represent the school confirms the value of such personal characteristics in pupils' eyes. There is no suggestion, however, that one quality leads on to another — simply that they tend to cluster together.

Translated into adolescent socialization and in relation to school sport this paper has tried to explore the "dynamic interplay" between the individual and situational adjustments by considering the various qualities and characteristics which adolescents "bring" into the school setting and the processes involved in their encounters with various members of the school community — particularly physical education teachers. From such situations, which are embedded within a series of interactions carrying their own rules and meanings, patterns begin to emerge concerning the way particular adolescents conceive of themselves, their attitudes to others, their identification with the school, their areas of abilities and competence, their interests in and reaction to sports and extracurricular activities.

Towards a typology

In an attempt to move towards a typology the author used the technique of cluster analysis. As Entwistle and Brennan (1971) have previously suggested any sample can be thought of as a distribution of points in hyperspace, analogous to stars in physical space. Just as matter is not equally distributed throughout the universe but condenses into stars held together in galactic formations of varying shapes, so points in psychological space may also produce regions of high or low destiny.

There are likely to be large tracts of relatively empty space populated by rare or unlikely kinds of pupils. Just as certain regions are empty, so others may be dense. Such high density regions may be regarded as continuous swarms of points (the galaxies of our cosmic analogy). The shape of the cluster is determined by the boundary conditions imposed by the computer programme on membership of a cluster. These limitations may be based on minimising the variance of the cluster, or on exploring variations in the density of points in hyperspace. Where distinct variations in density occur, the clusters are likely to be clearly defined whatever clustering procedure is adopted.

Cluster analysis was used to aid classification, and it was hoped to create a backcloth of evidence from which smaller scale 'illuminative' research investigations might be developed. The chief value of large scale research, in the author's mind, is to offer general evidence of possible trends or typologies which can then be studied at a more particularised level.

From the author's data on 3000 adolescents a separate cluster analysis for each group of variables designated as personal, social and educational factors was carried out for both boys and girls. In all this amounted to about 150 variables. Groupings for both boys and girls were sufficiently consistent and clear-cut to demand attention and consideration by a selected composite analysis (Figs. 5–7). For these composite clusterings two particular kinds of cluster analysis were employed:

1. Minimum spanning tree, which considers 'distances' among the 41 variables represented as points, and shows the pathways joining the (correlated) points. (It should be noted that there are *no* close loops, and the total length of the pathway is the minimum possible.) Thus it can 'say' something about clustering, if the measurement of the distance between clusters is taken to be the distance between the two nearest neighbours from two separate, i.e. different, clusters (Fig. 5). Further, we can break linkages (i.e. the first to be broken is the largest length, and so on) to create clusters. Those broken linkages lead us on to the second type:

2. Minimum variance cluster analysis. As with principal component analysis the distance between clusters is based on the sum of squares of the multidimensional planes (like multidimensional scaling, thus providing a 'cosmic' picture of galaxies and clusters (Fig. 6).

A number of points should be noted in relation to these diagrams or scatterplots. Firstly that the variables presented assume importance in relation to each other—in the diagram all is relative! Secondly, since the clusterings are shown two-dimensionally there is of necessity some pictorial distortion. Lastly, the 40 or so items presented were selected from the separate analyses because of their relative proximity to the 'sports participation' variable. The negative side of the picture, so to speak, is seen more clearly in the separate scatterplots (Figs. 2–4), where associations with non-participation are presented pictorially as diametrically opposed to school sports participation.

That said, a reasonably coherent pattern begins to emerge in the diagrams. For both boys and girls a grouping or clustering of physical and physiological components linked to physical education teachers' perceptions and pupils' own self estimates in relation to sports are seen to be most closely associated with school sports participation.

Within a second circle of constellated variables it can be noted that there is a relatively 'mixed' range of items linking 'home factors' such as parental encouragement, watching sport on television (secondary participation, Kenyon,

1968); 'social aspects' like leisure sports involvement, intentions to continue sport after leaving school; 'relational considerations' such as perceptions of and attitudes about physical education teachers; and 'personal factors', for instance, extraversion, attitudes to sport, body esteem and so on. Further, the pattern for boys and girls does show some variation at this level.

Social class, academic attainment, and favourable attitudes to school are shown to be closely linked—supporting incidentally a vast array of research findings— but a little distanced from school sports participation. This may raise important questions about the continuing influences of comprehensive education on pupils' extracurricular activities.

It is important at this stage to draw attention to a number of 'super' stars in our hyperspace. An examination of Figure 5 shows that certain variables are crucial centres linking the various elements of a psycho-social constellation. 'Enthusiasm for sports', 'physical ability' and 'involvement in school sport', all reveal several avenues converging on those variables. These may serve as aspects of concern for further investigation. Again the track between 'fitness' (distance run) and 'academic attainment' is fascinating because it raises questions about possible 'missing' variables—perseverance, motivation, achievement needs and such like. Further, a number of paths were associated with participation in physical activities, supporting McIntosh's (1963) and Kenyon's (1968) view that reasons for sports involvement are extremely complex.

Because of the nature of the author's investigation and the various ways in which data were collected it was impossible to classify certain items that may be important to sports involvement. For example, perceptions of sports participants by non-participants, and of non-participants by participants, were not ascertained simply because the researcher did not wish to make pupils consider possible differences between themselves and others within a school setting except in a very general way since the association between the author and the 15 schools continued for more than a year and there was some concern about possible shifts in 'self-esteem', and 'perceptions of others' during the actual investigation.

Adolescent groups seem reasonably accurate in estimating differences (as they perceive them) between sports participants and non-participants (see Hendry & Simpson, 1977) and such perceptions may be important in reinforcing attitudes, interests, and involvement in both school and leisure. Further, the author suggested that sports participants at this particular age and level of involvement were provided with a wider network of social roles involving peers and adults—other sports participants, sports officials, friends, parents, and so on. Elsewhere it has been argued (Hendry, 1971; Tattersfield, 1971) that at a relatively high level of participation social roles are very much restricted to other athletes, coaches and sports administrators, with little time or opportunity to engage in a range of relationships with a variety of adolescent peers. If this is so it provides a restricted and narrow socialization process with limited access to 'appropriate' role models. It would be interesting to ascertain a 'cut off' point where the versatility of role possibilities proposed by the author in relation to sports participants ceases and the level of competitive sport precludes 'normal' adolescent socialization because of the commitment and dedication necessary for success. Nevertheless, given these limitations, a plausible general picture is evident which is reasonably consistent for both adolescent boys and girls.

If the offered general typology has any credence then a number of questons need to be asked about adolescents. What are the important links among physical ability, physique, and teachers' and pupils' perceptions in relation to pupils' personal characteristics and sports participation? What *practical* applications can be derived from the evidence that a number of links exist? Within comprehensive education there is still a strong association among social class, attitudes to school, attitudes to raising the school leaving age, and academic attainment: what are the reasons for this? Why are attitudes to work, to earning money, and to pop culture opposed to both scholastic attainment and sporting endeavour? Would studies of single schools reveal this same pattern? Would case studies and an 'illuminative' examination of teachers' and pupils' definitions and perspectives bring us closer to causal explanations?

It may be suggested that adolescent socialization into sport appears to 'fit in' with theories of the development of self by absorption of the perceptions and expectations of others. In this way self is seen as a social product. The adolescent's self identity develops in relation to the expectations and reactions of other people so that he reacts to himself as he perceives others reacting to him. Cluster analysis, in providing some move towards a typology, provides a broad outline and leads us to further important questions, most crucial of which perhaps is consideration of an analytical framework which encompasses the individual adolescent, and his self-esteem, in interaction with the various aspects of his culture (and subcultures) so that resultant socialization processes can be explored.

Obviously we must search for some kind of interpretative framework. More than this there is a need to progress from what is given—that is the behaviour, attitudes, involvements, perceptions of these adolescents, towards theory, to a set of predictions, explanations, interpretations and applications.

Note

1 Participation in school sports can range from individual sports such as golf and swimming, through team activities (e.g. hockey) to outdoor pursuits like canoeing and orienteering. It would have been interesting to study different patterns of participation (i.e. outdoor activity participants; team participants; individual pursuits participants) but on examination the pattern was extremely complex, so that while certain pupils could be clearly categorized as "outdoor", "team" or "individual" participants, the majority of sports participants exhibited cross-involvement (e.g. golf, soccer, canoeing) over the school year. Because of this, a broader sports classification of "competitive" and "recreative" participation, and "non-participation" was used.

References

Anderson, A. J. B. (1971) Numeric Examination of Multivariate Soil Samples. *Maths. Geol.*, 3, 1–14.

Beech, F. (1963) Investigation into the effects of personality factors on progress in english and maths, Adv. Dip. Educ. Dissert. Univ. Manchester.

Douglas, J. W. B., Ross, J. M. and Simpson, H. R. (1968) *All our future*. London. Davies.

Emmett, I. (1971) *Youth and Leisure in an Urban Sprawl*. Manchester.

Entwistle, N. J. (1972) Personality and academic attainment. *Brit. J. Educ. Psychol.* 42, 137–151.

Entwistle, N. J. and Brennan, T. (1971) Types of successful students. *Brit. J. Educ. Psychol.*, 41, 3, 268–276.

Garner, J. and Bing, M. (1973) Inequalities of teacher-pupil contacts. *Brit. J. of Educ. Psychol.*, 43, 5, 234–243.

Hallworth, H. J. (1966) Perceptions of children's personalities by experienced teachers. *Educ. Res.* 19, 3–12.

Hargreaves, D. H. (1967) *Social relations in a secondary school*. London. Routledge and Kegan Paul.

Hargreaves, D. H. (1972) *Interpersonal relations and education*. London. Routledge and Kegan Paul.

Heinila, K. (1964) The preferences of physical activities. In Jokl, E. and Simm, E. (eds.) *International Research in Sport and Physical Education*. Springfield, Illinois: Thomas.

Hendry, L. B. (1970) Some notions on personality and sporting ability: certain comparisons with scholastic achievement. *Quest*, 13, 63–73.

Hendry, L. B. (1975) School, sport, leisure: A study of personal, social and educational factors. Report to S.E.D. Edinburgh.

Hendry, L. B. (1978) *School, sport, leisure: Three dimensions of adolesence*. London. Lepus.

Hendry, L. B. and Simpson, D. O. (1977) One centre: two sub-cultures. *Scott. Educ. Studies*, 9, 2, 112–121.

Hills, M. (1969) On looking at large correlation matrices. *Biometrika*, 56, 249–253.

Kane, J. E. (1968) Personality in relation to physical abilities and physique. Ph.D. Thesis. University of London.

Keddie, N. (1971) Classroom knowledge. In Young, M.F.D., (ed) *Knowledge and Control*. London. Collier-Macmillan.

Kenyon, G. S. (1968) Values held for physical activity by selected urban secondary school students in Canada and Australia, England and the United States. U.S. Office of Educ. Contract S-376. University of Wisconsin.

McIntosh, P. C. (1963) *Sport in Society*. London. Watts.

Nash, R. (1973) *Classrooms observed*. London. Routledge and Kegan Paul.

Nichols, A. K. (1971) The field dependence-field independence personality dimension and games attainment in schoolboys. *Bull. of Phys. Education*. 8, 6, 10–16.

Orlick, T. D. (1972) A socio-psychological analysis of early sports participation. Ph.D. Thesis. University of Alberta.

Reid, M. (1972) Comprehensive integration outside the classroom. *Educ. Res.* 14, 2, 128–134.

Rich, J. (1975) Effects of children's physical attractiveness on teachers' evaluations. *Jour. Educ. Psychology*, 67, 5, 599–609.

Ridding, L. W. (1966) An investigation of the personality measures associated with over-and under-achievement. Unpublished M.Ed. Thesis. University of Manchester.

Silberman, M. L. (1969) Behavioural expression of teachers' attitudes towards elementary school students. *J. Educ. Phychol.*, 60, 402–407.

Sillitoe, K. K. (1969) *Planning for Leisure*. London, H.M.S.O.

Spady, W. (1970) Effects of peer status and extracurricular activities in goals and achievements. *Amer. J. Sociol.* 74, 630–720.

Start, K. B. (1961) The relationship between games performance of a grammar school boy and his intelligence and streaming. *Brit. J. Educ. Psychol.*, 31, 2, 208–211.

Start, K. B. (1966) Substitution of games performance for academic achievement as a means of achieving status among secondary school children. *Brit. J. Sociol.*, 17, 3, 300–305.

Sutton-Smith, B., Roberts, J. M. and Kozelka, R. M. (1963) Games involvement in adults. *J. Soc. Psychol.*, 60, 1, 15–30.

Warburton, F. M. (1969) Personality and attainment. Unpublished memorandum. Dept of Educ. University of Manchester.

Wiseman, S. (1964) *Education and environment* Manchester University Press.

Appendix

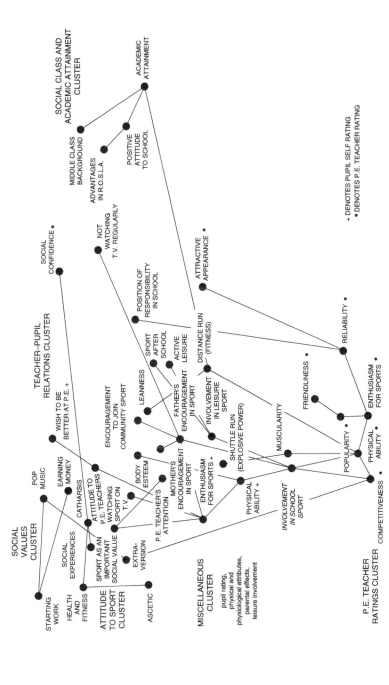

Figure A1 Minimum spanning tree cluster analysis: involvement in physical activities (boys only).

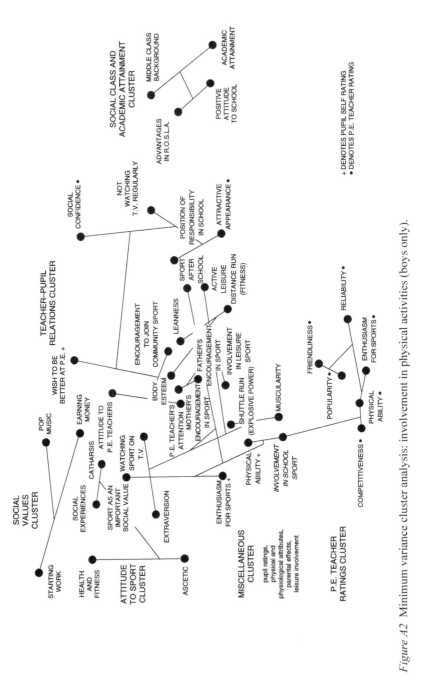

Figure A2 Minimum variance cluster analysis: involvement in physical activities (boys only).

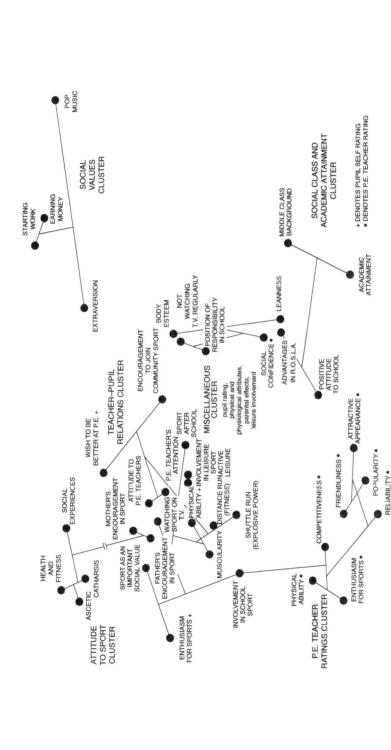

Figure A3 Minimum variance cluster analysis: involvement in physical activities (girls only).

4   Differing perceptions

This project was carried out in order to gain a multi-layered, intensive analysis of one leisure facility for young people by utilising a questionnaire survey, interviews and non-participant observations of the centre over a period of several months. This first extract shows that among the adolescents who attended a youth centre there were two distinct sub-groups, with individual variations within each grouping, possessing quite different motives for their attendance at the centre, and exhibiting quite different modes of behaviour whilst in the building. Additionally, the context, the organisation of various sections of the centre, and the types of professional adults running the different activities, created varying responses from the two adolescent sub-groups. Having taken part in the procedures of the study myself, it is interesting to report that when one was present in the sports area one did experience certain feelings of 'alienation'. For example, sports participants wore training gear, were skilful and eager to improve their performances, were on very friendly terms with the coaches and could handle the equipment easily. By contrast, the community area seemed 'relaxed', like a coffee-bar, was not 'demanding', dress was casual and the emphasis was on socializing. As a follow-up on completion of the investigation and based on our findings, centre staff devised less formal sessions once-a-week in order to encourage community members to participate in sporting activities.

In the light of my results from over three decades ago, Mahoney, Stattin and Magnusson's (2001) more recent findings, for example, seem disappointingly over-generalized in claiming an association between criminality and youth centre attendance, and do not show the finer-grained shadings of my earlier investigations. Our more varied research approach was able to demonstrate that quite different sub-groupings existed and participated differentially in the centre's activities. Further, from our findings we were able to offer some interpretative explanations for their choices that provided possible guidelines for those professionals who work in youth and leisure centres.

During the early 1990s the Scottish Office commissioned me to carry out a national assessment of the role of youth work in young people's lives. This second (short) extract provides only findings from one aspect of the research though the overarching design of the whole study involved multi-level methodologies and case studies. Nevertheless, it provides important 'messages' about the objectives of professional services for adolescents and asks questions about whether or not these aims are seen to be achieved in the actual delivery of youth engagement and participation.

ONE CENTRE: TWO SUB-CULTURES

L. B. Hendry and D. O. Simpson

Introduction

> Whatever the views held about leisure, there is general recognition that for individuals and communities its mode of use is an indicator as well as a powerful determinant of the quality of life they enjoy . . .
> (Scottish Standing Consultative Council on Youth and Community Service, 1968)

By examining one community centre in some detail the present study attempts to consider leisure, and draws attention to "its mode of use" by comparing two groups of adolescents who attend this centre regularly for quite different leisure purposes.

At a time when leisure facilities are available on a considerable (if not extensive) scale in Britain, it is pertinent to ask how far such leisure proposals represent preconceptions and value-judgments of those who are in positions of influence, since much of what is written about leisure rests on the assumption that certain leisure pursuits are more "rewarding" and "worthwhile" than others. In discussing education for leisure Scarlett (1975) stated:

> Hopefully if children are given a model throughout their formative years which is a constructive one, rather than a passive one of merely sitting round the TV, they will later on seize the opportunities which are available . . .

Although Scarlett's findings on the leisure patterns of Scottish youth have been criticised as being "biased and superficial", and the sample can hardly claim to be representative of Scottish youth, there is agreement with Jephcott's (1967) earlier findings. One reason young people in both studies gave for not attending youth groups was that they were too closely linked with school, either because of the pattern of authority and discipline, or because school premises were used. Scarlett also commented on the "non-constructive" aspects of Scottish youngsters' leisure. She argued that working class children were less likely to make "constructive" use of available leisure opportunities than middle class children, since they have had less encouragement at home to teach them how to use their leisure. It may be, therefore, that when facilities are available locally, adolescents choose leisure activities because of different sub-cultural values and life-styles based on social class. In common with Jephcott, Scarlett found that a considerable proportion of leisure time was not spent on any definite activity, and that youngsters often announced that they were bored. Many of those who complained of boredom made very little effort in their leisure to take part in any specific activity.

There is little doubt that discos, coffee bars and some other forms of commercial leisure provision are popular with some sections of young people, possibly due to the independent status such places usually confer on them. If we accept the premise that young people should be allowed to determine for themselves their own leisure provision, it appears that competitive commercial provision fulfils this condition. This is often illusory, however, since commercial enterprises are only interested in providing for activities with wide profit margins, and to the extent that clubs or coffee bars achieve a virtual monopoly in any area, the young people have to accept what is offered with little opportunity for their own views to be taken into account.

The widely prevalent view that "sport is good for one's physical health" has resulted in an expansion in the provision of sports facilities. This argument about the positive health values of sport is endorsed by Smith (1973) who maintained that the government, in a recent, more positive policy of leisure for youth, "has generally found it easier to proceed on the firm ground of sport and physical recreation". The other argument for the provision of sports centres is that they form a vital part of community life. It is claimed that sport and physical recreation are essentially social activities, and that the main attraction for many people is the friendship and companionship found in them (Sports Council, 1968). Indeed, Taylor (1970) predicted that the programme of sports centre development would fail unless ordinary people with little or no sporting skill used these centres frequently, and that if centres became "expensive clubs for experts", then sooner or later they would have to be closed, as constituting an unjustifiable expenditure of public money. When users in five sports centres were classified into socio-economic groups by occupation, however, it was found that 68 per cent of all the users were in non-manual occupations and only five per cent came from the unskilled or semi-skilled groups. The remaining 27 per cent were skilled manual workers. (Sports Council, 1971). Emmett (1970) has argued that such factors as social class, sex, type of school attended and the teenage sub-culture generally influence youngsters' behaviour in many ways and affect their view of the world which may, or may not, include certain leisure activities. Emmett's view is that the identity of the adolescent sub-culture depends on it posing itself against adults, and that "with-it" adolescents do not participate so much in sport, not only because they are too involved with pop music, dance, dress and so on, but also because adults say that sport is one of the things young people should do with their leisure! The results from Emmett's study showed that sport and physical recreation play a less important part in the lives of young people than is often assumed. The purpose of the present investigation, therefore, is to consider two groups of young people who made regular but different use of a large Community Centre in an attempt to draw comparisons between them.

Method

The centre under study was a modern, purpose-built Sports and Community Centre consisting of a large, well-equipped sports hall, and on a separate, upper level, facilities originally designed as a youth and community centre and including a coffee bar with observation windows overlooking the sports hall. The investigation, concerned only with the use made of the facilities by young people aged 12–20 years, was carried out by a questionnaire, informal interviews and observation over a period of three months.

130 members, comprising adolescents who attended the centre on average more than twice a week and could therefore be considered as representative of the regular attenders completed the questionnaire; 72 were regular members of the Community Area (35 boys and 37 girls) and 41 of the Sports Area (19 boys and 22 girls). A further 17 were recorded as having dual membership, more than half of whom were under 14 years of age.

Completion of questionnaires was voluntary and anonymity was respected. Of those members approached, only three in the Community area and one in the Sports area refused to participate. For the purpose of this study, questionnaire items were designed to obtain data for educational attainment (1 = leaving school at minimum leaving age, 2 = leaving after O-Grades, 3 = leaving after Highers), and for social class by intended or actual occupation (1 = manual, 2 = non-manual). Members were also asked to state whether they took part in extra-curricular clubs at school, represented their school in a sports team or represented their school in a non-sporting activity. Information was also collected relating to use of centre facilities, leisure patterns outside the centre and attitudes towards leaders and other users of the centre.

Informal interviews, involving 23 members and nine leaders, were also conducted as opportunities arose. These interviews were semi-structured, as a means of checking the validity of responses to questionnaire items and to stimulate critical appraisal of the facilities and opportunities available.

Visiting the centre, on average twice a week for a period of three months, the investigators were able to observe what actually took place and compare their observations with the reports and claims of the members and leaders.

Results

Observation of the centre suggested that young people were divided into two main groups — those who only attended the sports area (boys, N = 19; girls, N = 22); and those who only attended the community area (boys, N = 35; girls, N = 37) — with a much smaller group of younger children with dual membership (N = 17).

1. More than 92 per cent of Community members lived within 15 minutes walking distance of the centre, whereas only 36 per cent of sports area members lived within the same locality. Thus sports area members attended from a much wider radius, with the definite purpose of participating in a sporting activity; while community area members were more likely to see the community centre as a meeting place in a neighbourhood lacking alternatives (Table 4.1).

2. As an extension of the previous finding, there were highly significant differences between groups in their use of the centre's coffee bar. Only 13 per cent of sports area members made some use of the coffee bar*, whereas *all* community

54 Differing perceptions

Table 4.1 Reasons for attending the Community Centre[1]

	BOYS		GIRLS		X_2^2
	Sports Area N = 19	Community Area N = 35	Sports Area N = 22	Community Area N = 37	(a) For Boys (b) For Girls
Enjoy the activities	15	9	20	2	(a) 14.4***
Meet people	1	8	—	17	(b) 48.1***
No alternatives in the neighbourhood	—	9	—	17	

d.f.2   *** denotes P < 0.001
[1] Number discrepancies noted above represent "don't know" or "no response" from subjects.

area members used it — although 65 per cent of sports area members indicated that the coffee bar *was* important and a useful part of the centre.

3. As their main reason for joining the sports and community centre, male community members reported self interest — "to find out what it was like" — significantly more often than male sports members. It should also be noted that "self" together with "friends" were the most important reported influences on all groups in joining the centre except for male sports members who indicated a variety of influences. Further, friends were influential for *all* groups in actual initial attendance at the centre (Table 4.2).

4. Sports and community members differed in the following ways:

(a) Sports members were more likely to stay on at school to obtain "Highers", while the majority of community members considered "O" Grade to be the peak of their academic attainment — many leaving school at the minimum leaving age;
(b) Sports members were more likely than community members to be involved in school based clubs and activities and to be members of school sports teams; sports girls were also more involved in non-sporting activities like school choir;
(c) Sports members were more likely than community members to choose non-manual occupations. (Table 4.3).

5. In an attempt to investigate possible differences in attitude (rather than in behaviour) between the two groups of users, the 130 adolescents were asked to indicate whether they agreed or disagreed with certain descriptions of sports leaders and community group leaders in the centre, and with certain descriptions of themselves. Generally speaking community and sports members showed no significant differences in their views of community leaders in terms of their sensibility, strictness, interest in young people, or about their age-range. There was general agreement about sports areas leaders only in terms of their sensibility.

Table 4.2 Original Influences to Join and Introduction to the Centre

	BOYS		GIRLS		X_1^2
	Sports Area $N=19$	Community Area $N=35$	Sports Area $N=22$	Community Area $N=37$	(a) For Boys (b) For Girls
Original Influence to join centre					
Self	5	26	11	22	(a) 12.6***
versus	v	v	v	v	
Others (combined, d.f.1)					
i.e. Friend,	5	8	8	15	
Teacher,	4	—	1	—	
Activity,	5	—	2	—	
Family	— 14	8	— 11	15	(b) 0.05
	—	—	—	—	
Introduction					
Friend	12	18	10	32	(a) 12.6***
versus	v	v	v	v	
Others (combined, d.f.1)					
i.e. Self or	4	16	7	5	
Family	2 6	1 17	5 12	— 5	(b) 11.3**

** denotes P < 0.01   *** denotes P < 0.001

Where significant differences did occur, however, boys attending the community area were less certain than sports area boys about the trendiness, sympathy, and lack of interference of community leaders. With regard to sports leaders, community boys considered them to be older and more interfering than sports boys, while more community girls perceived them as being stricter, less trendy, less sympathetic or interested in young people than did sports girls (Table 4.4).

6. All groups perceived themselves in a reasonably favourable light, though there was general agreement (i.e. no significant differences) between sports and community groups that community users were *not* well behaved, active or particularly sensible: on the other hand community users regarded sports users as being unfriendly and not particularly modern; additionally, community girls stated that sports area users were rather immature and lacking sense.

7. In their leisure time spent outside the centre the pattern of commercial leisure involvement of both groups was somewhat similar, with disco dancing, casual swimming, ice rink skating, ten-pin bowling, cinema and theatre going, attendance at football matches and public houses being mentioned. Yet in their membership of youth organisations and participation in sports teams not connected with school there were considerable differences: 42 per cent of male sports members and 23 per cent of girls belonged to youth organisations by comparison with five per cent of community area boys and 13 per cent of community girls; and 52 per cent of sports area boys, 41 per cent of sports area girls played for sports teams whereas only 28 per cent of community area boys and 13 per cent of girls played for teams.

56 *Differing perceptions*

Table 4.3 School and Occupational Differences between Groups

	BOYS		GIRLS		X_2^2
	Sports Area N = 19	Community Area N = 35	Sports Area N = 22	Community Area N = 37	(a) For Boys (b) For Girls
Leaving School (d.f.2)					
16 years	4	20	—	16	
"O" levels	6	11	8	20	(a) 11.8**
"Highers"	9	3	14	1	(b) 30.6***
Extracurricular* Clubs/Activities (d.f.1)					
1. Club member	10	5	12	6	(1a) 9.03**
2. Represents school in sports teams and	9	3	14	3	(b) 9.56** (2a) 10.72**
3. Non Sports Activities (e.g. School Choir)	3	3	9	4	(b) 20.74*** (3a) 0.65 (b) 7.58**
Occupations (d.f.1) (Actual or Intended)					
Manual or don't know	7	32	2	29	(a) 18.3***
Non manual	12	3	20	8	(b) 26.6***

** denotes P < 0.01   *** denotes P < 0.001
* X^2 calculated separately for each of 1, 2 and 3 by comparison with remainder of the group (e.g. 1. Club member: 10 out of 19 were members; 5 out of 35; 12 out of 22; 6 out of 37, etc.)

Table 4.4 Community and sports area members' views of centre leaders[1]

		BOYS		GIRLS		X^2
		Sports Area N = 19	Community Area N = 35	Sports Area N = 22	Community Area N = 37	(a) For Boys (b) For Girls
Community Leaders						
Sensible	Agree	11	28	17	36	(a) 0.01
	Disagree	3	7	1	1	(b) 0.3
Not Strict	Agree	8	20	13	23	(a) 0.01
	Disagree	6	15	4	13	(b) 0.8
Modern/Trendy	Agree	13	22	16	30	(a) 96.9***
	Disagree	1	11	2	6	(b) 0.3
Interested in	Agree	14	26	13	32	(a) 4.0
Young People	Disagree	0	8	4	5	(b) 0.8
Sympathetic	Agree	10	10	9	16	(a) 7.6**
	Disagree	4	25	9	20	(b) 0.2
Young	Agree	12	24	8	22	(a) 1.2
	Disagree	2	10	8	14	(b) 0.6
Do not Interfere	Agree	14	19	13	30	(a) 9.5**
	Disagree	0	16	4	6	(b) 0.4

Sports Leaders

Sensible	Agree	17	21	20	25	(a)	3.6
	Disagree	2	11	0	8	(b)	6.6
Not Strict	Agree	6	6	12	7	(a)	1.0
	Disagree	13	25	8	26	(b)	10.2**
Modern/Trendy	Agree	15	17	18	17	(a)	4.6
	Disagree	3	15	1	16	(b)	10.2**
Interested in	Agree	14	18	19	19	(a)	1.2
Young People	Disagree	5	13	1	14	(b)	8.6**
Sympathetic	Agree	14	12	16	10	(a)	6.2
	Disagree	5	20	3	23	(b)	14.0***
Young	Agree	16	14	11	10	(a)	8.6**
	Disagree	2	16	7	22	(b)	4.2
Do Not Interfere	Agree	17	14	18	21	(a)	9.2**
	Disagree	2	16	1	12	(b)	6.2

[1] Number discrepancies noted above represent "don't know" or "no response" from subjects.
** denotes P < 0.01   *** denotes P < 0.001
* The nature of the sports activities themselves and the coaching and teaching programmes further restricted the use of the coffee bar by sports area members.

Discussion

There is no doubt that in this single, purpose-built Sports and Community Centre, two distinct and separate sub-cultures existed. There was little, or no, rapport between the two groups of members. Sports members were content to stay in the Sports area and apparently saw nothing to attract them to the Community area. Further there was limited opportunity for either groups to interact with leaders from the other area: thus Community leaders, for instance, were not well known to sports users.

Although the two groups remained isolated in this way, a middle group of young people did exist which frequented both areas. By the time they reach the age of 14 years, however, most of this dual membership group will have opted for one area or the other. It appears to be a largely one-way movement — to the Community area. This would seem to contradict Scarlett's (1975) suggestion that one of the reasons for non-participation in "constructive" leisure pursuits is a lack of information, since Community members appear to have ample knowledge about what is available to them in the Sports area and reject it.

Two questions arise then. Firstly, where do most of the Sports members come from, if not from the dual membership group? Secondly, why do most of the dual membership group choose the Community area rather than the Sports area? The first can be readily answered from the results of the study. As the results made clear, the majority of Sports area members came from a wider radius than the Community members, and attended to take part in specific activities for which the centre catered. The dual membership group thus appears to be "local kids" who enjoy anything that is being offered, but when they outgrow this youthful vitality they tend to adopt the values of local adolescents, the majority of whom are largely anti-Sports area.

This brings us to the second question. Why do the majority of young people in the neighbourhood of the centre choose not to attend the Sports area? Many of the young people in studies by Scarlett (1975) and Bone (1972) complained about the lack of facilities for sport, yet in this study, children who were well catered for seemed unwilling to make use of the facilities on offer, yet, perhaps surprisingly, still complained of boredom.

One possible reason which suggests itself is costs, but there was little evidence of a shortage of money in the Community area, judging from the sales at the coffee bar counter and the extremely high incidence of smokers among members.

Many of the Community members, particularly the boys, complained that there were too many rules in the Sports area, and that it was too strict. The results showed that an overwhelming majority of the sample in the Community area regarded Sports area leaders as being strict and unsympathetic, and a substantial proportion felt they interfered too much. Surprisingly perhaps, they agreed with the necessity of rules and tight discipline in a sports hall (mainly for the prevention of accidents and damage to equipment) and were not therefore advocating a Sports area without rules. Instead, rather than subject themselves to the discipline and the rules, they preferred not to attend.

The findings by Jephcott (1967) that many youngsters do not attend activities because they are too closely linked with school — either because of the pattern of discipline, or because school buildings are used — seemed to fit the Sports area under study. In discussion, Community members in general did not seem to accept school values to any great extent; and as results showed most of them leave school early, and few are involved in school activities, so any linkage of the school with the Sports area would tend to make the Sports area a less attractive source of leisure provision for them. Girls, in particular, presented age as a reason for not taking part in Sports area activities, and a common feeling was that, "You get too old for jumping about like that". Several of the girls who were interviewed had been members of the gymnastics club, one of the most popular activities in the Sports area, but felt that they were too old "to make a fool of myself" any longer. The girls in question were only 15 and 16 years of age.

Regular attenders at the Sports area who were "serious" users of the facilities were easily identifiable by their "uniforms" of tracksuits, specialised clothing and equipment, and often identical sports bags. In addition, as Emmett (1971) discovered, a sub-culture may exist, which does not accept the values of sport (this may be class orientated, or associated with "with-itness"), and such attitudes may have prevented many young people from attending the Sports area. Girls, in particular, dressed and generally behaved, in a way obviously meant to attract the male members of the Community area, and many of them, in interview, admitted to attending only with this aim in mind. In such cases, sport did not fit into the picture at all.

Murdock and Phelps (1973) pointed out that adolescent sub-cultures provide a social and psychological context for the development of leisure "styles" where the individual is supported and reinforced in his behaviour by like-minded peers. They further suggested that these particular sub-cultures are concentrated within social classes, which operate through various leisure activities. Present results showed clearly that two quite separate sub-cultures existed side by side. Differences were such that many members could see for themselves — "It's the brainy ones who go downstairs (Sports area), the ones up here are all mental", remarked a 17-year-old girl in the Community area.

Similarly, aspirations were very different. Evidence from studies such as the Sports Council (1971) had suggested that Sports Centres are predominantly middle class havens with few working class users. What the present results showed was that Sports members tended to be middle class aspirants. The majority of them chose non-manual occupations, a considerable proportion of which were professional, most notably teaching. Community members were more likely to choose manual occupations, the boys choosing trades while the girls chose mainly office work of some description. Community members maintained that the young people in the Sports area were snobs, and though impossible to substantiate, what is important is that they perceived a difference between themselves and those in the other group. By contrast, fewer Sports members were able to suggest differences of such a kind between the groups and most claimed to know none of the Community area users on which they could base an opinion. One 14-year-old girl who *did* have an opinion, and who was completely frank, declared confidently that Sports members were more sensible and intelligent and that Community members were "rough, always swearing, smoking, fighting and getting into trouble".

It is clear that not all children consider sport as part of their school or leisure life, and as this study suggests mere encouragement will not necessarily produce more sport-loving people.

In the present study the two groups proved to be different in their attitudes towards the centre, and what they expected to get out of it. For Sports members, attendance at the centre was for one reason — to take part in an activity, or more than one activity, which they enjoyed, or happened to be good at. To do this, they were willing to travel fairly long distances and spend considerable sums of money on transport, so presumably considered the efforts worthwhile. A 14-year-old girl in the Sports area spent over £1 each week on bus fares, but considered it better spent that way than sitting in a coffee bar.

Community members were less united in their motives for attending the Community area, enjoyment of activities being only one. For most of them, it was a place for meeting and talking with friends, not to meet new friends but to continue their established friendship patterns in a relaxed, fairly comfortable, cheap and convenient meeting place. The results confirmed that for many of them, especially the girls, the centre was only somewhere to go, since they had nothing else to do. One boy gave as his reason for attending, "I come here to get out of the house". Others unenthusiastically claimed, "It's better than sitting at home". Complaints and criticisms seemed to be part of their "enjoyment" of the centre and it was observed that every member who was interviewed in the Community area had at least one unfavourable comment to make about the centre. For example, two 16-year-old girls admitted they only attended for "the talent" but complained that "the talent" was hopeless!

Coupled with complaints were pleas for more organised activities, especially among the girls, who felt neglected (cf. Bone, 1972). Yet when asked to be more explicit, they were unable to say exactly what they wanted. This seemed to be an important difference between the two groups — the Sports members knew what they wanted, and made an effort to attend to achieve their desires, whereas Community members were often unable to say what they wanted or to communicate their needs, and made little effort to change things.

Concluding remarks

Sport is only one way a young person can occupy his leisure time and the need for sport does not exist in equal amounts in all young people, and in some, it does not exist at all. The need to meet and form relationships with other young people is a generally felt need, however, and sport is only one (perhaps not very satisfactory) way of fulfilling this need. In their attitudes towards the centre, it was clear that for Community members, the centre was the hub of their leisure time, around which their leisure lives revolved. For most of Sports members, the centre was only one of the places they attended where they met like-minded young people engaged in the same kind of activity. In effect, the centre provides a meeting place for two separate sub-cultures – a Community area which is patronised by the local young people, and a Sports area which is patronised by a wider based, sports loving community. Overall the present study may indicate that not all young people enjoy sport, and the provision of facilities will not necessarily ensure their participation. Not all young people can be encouraged or persuaded to enjoy sport, and certainly not on other people's terms. Possibly these findings described above may not be generalisable to other centres in Britain but nevertheless they may be of value in setting up hypotheses or suggesting other lines of future enquiry.

References

Bone, M. (1972) *The Youth Service and Similar Provision for Young People*. HMSO, London.
Emmett, I. (1970) Sociological research in recreation, in T. L. Burton (ed.), *Recreation Research and Planning*. Allen & Unwin, London.
Emmett, I. (1971) *Youth and Leisure in an Urban Sprawl*. Manchester University Press.
Jephcott, P. (1967) *Time of One's Own*. Oliver & Boyd, Edinburgh.
Murdock, G. and Phelps, G. (1973) *Mass Media and the Secondary School*. London, Macmillan.
Scarlett, C. L. (1975) *EuroScot: The New European Generation*. The Scottish Standing Conference of Voluntary Youth Organisations, Edinburgh.
Smith, C. S. (1973) Adolescence, in MA. Smith, S. Parker and C. S. Smith (ed.), *Leisure and Society in Britain*. Allen Lane, London.
Sports Council (1968) *Planning For Sport*. Central Council of Physical Recreation, London.
Sports Council (1971) *Indoor Sports Centres*. HMSO, London.
Standing Consultative Council on Youth and Community Service (1968) *Community of Interests*. HMSO, Edinburgh.
Taylor, G. B. (1970) Quality in recreation, in T. L. Burton (ed.), *Recreation Research and Planning*, Allen & Unwin, London.

Like research into youth clubs, studies of youth workers and other adult mentors for young people seldom take into account the varying perspectives of participants or attempt to seek the range of forces and factors that may determine alternative social strategies. Importantly, these findings raise questions for professionals who work with young people concerning their ways of assessing whether or not they really succeed in what they set out to achieve in the process of participating with youth.

Now, we explore a variety of contexts and relationships 'through young people's eyes'. The following three extracts offer a range of adolescents' views of various aspects of their lifestyles and illustrate ways in which their perspective may differ from adults and why.

YOUTH WORKERS AND YOUTH PARTICIPANTS

Two perspectives of youth work?

John G. Love and Leo B. Hendry

Introduction

From a recent historical perspective, the findings of the Albemarle Report (1960) in England and the Scottish Kilbrandon Report in 1973 gave a boost and new direction to a youth work focus within community education in Scotland. Henceforth, it was proposed, youth work should emphasise informal education and the personal and social development of young people. These laudable, if unspecific, aims originally manifested themselves in vague policy statements: encouraging 'personal growth'; the 'development of character'; 'association' and 'challenge'. Later, in the early 1980s, under increasing pressures to demonstrate the effectiveness of youth work, policy makers within community education were encouraged to spell out its aims more clearly. Accordingly Strathclyde Regional Council, the largest local authority in Britain, produced a somewhat more explicit statement of its aims for youth work, in which the community education service was called upon to be *responsive to the personal educational needs of the individual whether social, intellectual or recreational and within a community development context, so that it is concerned with the individual's role in relation to the wider society and his or her active participation in it (Strathclyde Regional Council, 1984).*

Grampian Regional Council (1988) offered further details and suggested that community education should attempt to

support young people to gain self-confidence... and to make informed choices. (Also) to make the process of learning as important as reaching the goals.

More recently national statements have reflected similar views:

Youth work is essentially educational and interventionist. It has as its aims the personal and social development of young people. While it must adapt to meet changing needs, there are certain unchanging principles which form the core of youth work. Youth work must always help young people in:

> *the formation of attitudes to life*
> *the formation of standards*
> *the testing of values and beliefs*
> *the development of skills for involvement in society (SSCYO, 1989).*

If then, as these statements propose, youth work is about informal education for personal and social development, it is important that those involved in youth work reflect upon the processes and outcomes associated with particular methods in practice in working with adolescents. Claims made across a variety of types of youth provision, from uniformed groups through to detached youth work programmes deserve careful consideration and scrutiny. These can be usefully evaluated from two main perspectives; from youth workers as informal educators and from young people as users of, and participants in, the service. The present paper offers some Scottish insights into this dual perspective, based on a research project 'Measuring the Benefits of Youth Work' (Hendry et al, 1991)[1]. It is important to note that in this paper the term 'Youth Worker' is used to refer to people who work with adolescents. In Scotland this may include people whose job title is community education worker, or community worker.

Six main areas were examined which allowed for comparison to be made between what youth workers *claimed to be doing* in a variety of settings and what they considered to be important factors associated with youth work and what young people *claimed to experience* in different youth work settings and (equally) what young people considered to be important. The six areas were (1) reasons given for attending youth groups; (2) the content of group activity; (3) the learning claimed in different settings; (4) the attraction of youth groups; (5) the qualities needed in youth workers, and (6) decision-making in youth work settings.

Discussion

Reflecting on the findings it is perhaps most instructive to highlight the similarities and differences in attitudes, beliefs and experiences among youth workers and young people in youth groups. Looking firstly at reasons for attending youth groups the findings suggest that workers and young people bring with them different expectations to such settings. As proposed in most official regional and national documents in Scotland, youth workers rationalise their involvement in terms of youth work being variously described as informal teaching and learning in order for adolescents to develop personal, social and inter-personal skill[2]:

... self-confidence, the ability to talk to/form relations with others
... (an) ability to test, build and sustain relationships ...
... acceptance of others ...
... the ability to get on with others, particularly their peer group ...

Hence the vast majority see 'meeting friends' as a major attraction of youth groups for youth participants. It has been known for some time however that although most young people are introduced to youth groups through the influence of friends – Bone & Ross (1972) discovered 87% of young people went to a group in the company of others – meeting friends is not the main attraction of youth groups for many adolescents. Indeed in the Bone & Ross study the chance to meet friends ranked third behind the opportunity to pursue a particular interest and (more negatively) of having nothing better to do. The fact therefore that just over half the young people questioned in the present study claimed to attend youth groups in order to 'meet friends' and that the majority do so to 'enjoy' themselves, raises the possibility that youth workers and young people perceive quite different values for participating in youth groups. The implications of such differing perspectives may be far reaching. If young people can get by on having fun – seeing youth work settings as an alternative leisure outlet – whither youth work? Alternatively, of course, the differences in expectations may in part reflect the contrasting values found in any 'professional adult-adolescent' relationship, wherein complementary rather than identical motivation underpins the learning context. For instance, the school teacher's desire to instil a thirst for knowledge may be effected through the pupil's desire to pass exams; either way a habit of study is promoted. For youth work, however, concerned as much with process as with the outcome of learning, is there a need to make its aims and purposes more explicit to its youthful participants?

In a critique of the youth service, Jeffs (1979) concludes rather pessimistically that provision which originated as a leisure facility for working class young people in the 19th century has changed little over the past century and remains essentially recreational. Similarly youth work as a form of 'alternative' leisure – adult organised and led – is hinted at again in the present findings on the content of youth work activity. While youth workers may be ideologically committed to providing contexts in which personal and social 'issues' (eg poverty, discrimination, the environment) can be discussed, the delivery of such opportunities to young people is missed if the reported experience of young people is to be believed. It was the minority of young people across a diverse range of youth groups (ie uniformed, youth club, activity group and after school group) who reported 'discussing issues' as a component part of their youth group experiences. Indeed 'discussing issues' was the least reported activity out of five activities asked about. By contrast, playing games and sport was the most reported activity experienced by young people attending youth groups. Once again youth work is equated with recreational activity by young people.

The findings on 'learning claimed' in youth groups reinforces the impression that youth workers and young people may perceive themselves to be engaged in different enterprises. Consistent with the rationale of informal education and the development of interpersonal skills the most reported learning outcome claimed by workers was '(learning) to get on with others'; 93% of youth workers considered this to be important. However, amongst young people only between a quarter and (less than) a half of those who attend a range of youth groups, claimed that learning 'to get on with others' was an outcome of involvement in youth groups. Learning 'to enjoy oneself' was the most consistently reported experience across the various groups. Youth groups appear – at least on the surface – to be about fun and leisure for those young people who attend.

The differing perceptions held of youth work by youth workers and participants can be seen further in the response to a series of questions about the attractions of youth groups. While the majority of youth workers cite a variety of positive attributes such as the 'chance to meet friends' (95%), the 'good atmosphere' (84%), a 'place to go' (76%), only between a third to a half of young people concur with such beliefs. As such far fewer adolescents can see what workers perceive to be the benefits of youth work. Once again this raises the issue of the extent to which the beliefs and views of youth workers and young people *should be* in agreement. It may be that young people can still benefit from the context provided by youth workers in the various groups, without explicitly recognising the informal social learning opportunities afforded them. The possibility of 'parallel agendas' operating as a 'hidden curriculum' within youth work settings is an attractive explanation of this phenomenon for the providers of such services and this was further evidenced in the responses of a number of workers to a question about the major benefits of youth work to society.

> *... keeps them off the streets and allows them the chance to take part in activities and mix.*
> *... keeping trouble off the streets – social control.*
> *... keeps them off the streets, away from their parents, gives them the opportunities to enjoy themselves ...*
> *... can be an agent of social control. It should allow young people to discuss issues affecting society and thus foster a better understanding.*

Nevertheless the suspicion remains that the differing perspectives of workers and youth participants about the aims, practices and processes of youth work reflect a lack of clarity and true understanding about its role and purposes in present day society. It raises the question of whether or not youth work aims should remain implicit or be made more explicit and put 'up front' so that as young people grow older within youth organisations they are enabled to develop an understanding of the underlying objectives of the activities they engage in and are given greater awareness of the social control function of youth work described above as 'Keeping trouble off the streets'! This stresses the importance of 'reflection on learning processes' aimed at developing young people's strategies to discriminate, and assess values within youth work's hidden agenda: it enables choice rather than conformity.

Asked directly about the valued qualities of youth workers the difference in perception between young people and adults about the nature of youth work, becomes clearer. In their national study of the youth service in England and Wales, Bone & Ross (1972) report high levels of satisfaction among adolescents with respect to adults who run clubs for young people. However, although 88% felt that their youth workers were interested in their (young people's) ideas, around a quarter (22%) felt workers were bossy and a third (32%) believed that the workers attempted to 'push' their own ideas at adolescents. A study by Hendry, Brown & Hutcheon (1981) also looked at the attitudes of young people who attended youth groups to their youth workers. Hendry *et al.* found that although perceptions were 'mixed', young people tended to hold favourable rather than unfavourable views of these adults. It was concluded that these 'clubbable' adolescents were basically conformist and related positively and well towards adult workers and had a willingness to accept their rules, regulations and authority. The present study showed that youth workers and young people apparently valued different qualities in a youth worker. Thus, although both young people and professionals value 'trustworthiness' in a youth worker, many fail to appreciate the importance to young people of workers being 'friendly', 'good at dealing with trouble' and (not surprisingly in the light of evi-dence cited earlier) being 'good at sport'. Accordingly the 'enthusiasm' and 'interest in members' which ranked highly with some workers, may be insufficient in themselves to satisfy the needs of those adolescents for whom youth work is provided. The characteristics prized by youth workers reflect a desire to become affectively involved with young people, a desire rooted in the paradigm of social development and community involvement, yet the instrumental and practical skills looked for by young people may derive from a different set of priorities linked to a desire for a safe recreational environment in which to pursue a variety of leisure activities.

The last area of youth work activity looked at in this study was decision-making. In a national community education report on aims and objectives of youth work in Scotland (SCEC, 1989), stress was laid on the importance of shared responsibility and joint decision-making in youth work settings. The evidence on decision-making from the present study however suggests that much is still to be achieved in this area. Indeed the findings simply confirm the perceptual mismatch of workers' beliefs and young people's reported experiences in this crucial area of youth work practice. While young people perceive themselves to be involved in the decisions surrounding the planning of events and fundraising – with workers agreeing about joint decision-making in these areas – in the other areas of decision-making (ie spending money, making rules, enforcing rules and appointing leaders) young people considered adults to be solely responsible for the decision-making. In two of the latter areas, spending money and making rules, youth workers disagreed with young people's perceptions and claimed that joint decision-making *was* practised. However, the agreed absence of areas where young people themselves take responsibility for decision-making calls into question the extent to which adolescents perceive and are made aware of a genuine commitment to informal education and empowerment within youth groups. This awareness and knowledge of purpose are vital if adolescent participants are to be 'enabled' to act on their own behalf and to develop self agency. After all claims were made by youth workers in the present study that youth work:

> *... encourages young people to develop their full potential ... (in order to) make a more meaningful contribution to the society in which they live.*
> *... is an essential investment to produce responsible, participating citizens.*
> *... (develops) young people who are well-balanced and have a stable outlook on society.*
> *... (encourages) young people to learn to live within a community and become a part of the community rather than against it.*
> *... allows young people to participate in projects in the community and giving them the skills to enter into life outside school ... as responsible adults.*

Yet it would appear from this research project that in some aspects of its operations, as reflected by the perceptual mismatch of workers and participants, youth work may be falling short of providing for adolescents the social relationships which allow them to challenge, engage and question the forms and substance of the informal learning process in which they are involved.

Notes

1 The authors gratefully acknowledge the project grant given by the Scottish Office Education Department and the research support of colleagues on the project team, especially Ian Craik, Deputy Director of Education (Community Education), Grampian Region, John Mack, Community Education Team Leader (East Gordon Team), Grampian Region, Greta Weir and Wendy Jamieson, research officers, but wish to make it clear that views expressed in this paper are entirely their own.
2 All quotations in the Discussion section are taken from the five qualitative 'Case Studies'.

References

Albemarle Report (1960) *The Youth Service in England and Wales*, London, HMSO.
Bone, M. & Ross, E. (1972) *The Youth Service and Similar Provision for Young People*, London, HMSO.

Grampain Regional Council (1988) Education for the Community: *a review of community education in Grampian Region*, Aberdeen, Grampian Regional Council.

Hendry, L. B., Brown, L. & Hutcheon, G. (1981) 'Adolescents in community centres: some urban and rural comparisons', in *Scottish Journal of Physical Education*, Vol. 9, No. 1, pp. 28–40.

Hendry, L.B., Love, J. G., Craik, I. & Mack, J. (1991) *Measuring the Benefits of Youth Work*, A report to the Scottish Office Education Department, Edinburgh, Scottish Office.

Jeffs, A. J. (1979) *Young People and the Youth Service*, London, Routledge & Kegan Paul.

Kilbrandon Report (1973) *Royal Commission on the Constitution* 1969–1973, cmnd 5460, Edinburgh, HMSO.

Scottish Community Education Council (1989) *Youth Work in the Community Education Service*, Edinburgh, Scottish Community Education Council.

Scottish Standing Conference on Voluntary Youth Organisation (1989) *Youth Work Curriculum*, Edinburgh, SSCYO.

Strathclyde Regional Council (1984) *Working with Young People*, Glasgow, Strathclyde Regional Council.

5 Young people's views on people and places

We know in general that peer groups play an important role in adolescents' transitions toward adulthood and here we consider not only different adolescent peer-groups but also the influences of setting and context to take account of ecological factors. It is a description of leisure peer-groupings and how these identities and activities shape their behaviour and perceptions of their own and other groups. The article is extracted from a larger, funded study and offers multi-level insights into relations among various local peer-groups, the variations that occur dependent on context, and the inter-play of youth and adult perceptions when 'space' and 'territory' are involved. The ways 'context' operates within young people's lifestyles provides interesting insights into the interacting factors that determine their peer group allegiances.

YOUNG PEOPLE TALKING ABOUT ADOLESCENT RURAL CROWDS AND SOCIAL SETTINGS

Leo B. Hendry, Marion Kloep and Sheila Wood

Introduction

For some time now, scholars have been interested in understanding the influences on adolescents' development of peer groups in various social settings (for example, Dunphy, 1972). From a psychological perspective, research on the influence of social contexts on social identification until recently has been concentrated mainly on family settings, small friendship groups, and on social aspects of the school context (Kroger, 2000). However, beyond self-chosen groups based on interaction and friendship, there are at least two other types of adolescent groupings, which should be considered for their possible effects on identity.

First, there is the widest category of same-age and same-gender peers; and within this, there is a broad categorization of 'types' or (sub-cultures) such as 'skinheads', 'punks', 'gothics', or 'rastas'. These peer groups set the general styles and patterns of adolescent behaviour for those who are attracted to identifying with their values, and who perceive—and receive—their norms, not necessarily face-to-face, but perhaps also 'at a distance' via media 'images'. On the local level, members of these groups exert pressures towards conformity to their group norms, and young people who want the necessary 'entrance ticket' to a particular group, by and large, accept these. Thus, membership of sub-cultural groups is to a large extent self-chosen.

Second, and more locally based, are the peer groups that are more akin to Brown et al.'s (1994) definition and description of adolescent 'crowds'. Crowds are 'collections of adolescents identified by the interests, attitudes, abilities and/or personal characteristics they have in common', but that are *reputation*-based rather than interaction-based (Brown et al., 1994, p. 121). Their belonging to a certain crowd is largely defined by other teenagers, who perceive subtle yet distinctive markers (e.g., dress, hairstyle, accent and behaviour) that help to identify and label different crowd members.

Given that pupils in large high schools cannot know all of their peers individually, crowds help clarify the 'rules of engagement' with peers (for example, Brown, 1996). Thus, crowds reflect wider peer norms in the local community. Again, while these crowds may not be always known through *direct* face-to-face contact, they are visible within the local 'scene' by the establishment of 'reputations'. So, by contrast to sub-cultural groups, membership of crowds happens through stereotyping by others and the categorization of others into labelled peer affiliations that can serve as a reference point for defining one's own identity by social comparison. Most often, these 'out-groups' are described in negative terms, and this maximizes, comparatively, the positive distinctiveness of one's own peer affiliation (for example, Hogg & Abrams, 1988).

This is not the whole picture. Young people are further embedded in a wider social network that extends from family members, through friends of siblings, to adults who organize local clubs and activities, to adult mentors, to 'significant' adults in the community, and so on. Additionally, there are huge influences from a globalized media culture offering various role models and lifestyles for young people to copy. To some extent, adolescents have a certain degree of choice and agency regarding the groups and peer contexts they choose that might affect the processual aspects of their social identification. At the same time there will also be constraints on choices, based, for example, on the availability of peer groups and crowds, places in which to display sub-cultural styles and values, and the tolerance level and controls exerted by wider (adult) society.

From a sociological perspective, research on adolescents in various social settings has a long history. Studies can be traced from Jahoda et al.'s (1933) and Foote Whyte's (1943) classic explorations of 'street corner' societies during the 'Great Depression' to more modern studies of 'violent gangs' (for example, Yablonski, 1962; Patrick, 1973; Mungham & Pearson, 1976); from an examination of different types of British youth sub-cultures (Brake, 1985) to youths in school settings (for example, Hargreaves, 1968; Willis, 1977). The idea of sub-cultures within a school setting is well illustrated by Brown & Mounts' (1989) study of multi-ethnic American high schools, where between one-third and one-half of minority pupils were in ethnically defined crowds—'rappers' (blacks),

Asians, Hispanics, and so on—while the rest of the pupils were classified as belonging to reputation-based groups such as 'populars' or 'druggies'.

Rapid social changes and 'globalization' have created new patterns of social groupings and social venues (for example, Hendry et al., 1993; McRobbie, 1994). Within this state of social flux, Maffesoli (1994) has suggested that the more permanent and 'visible' youth sub-cultures of the 1980s, described by Brake (1985) among others, have given way to other more transient and varied forms of youth gatherings and that many young people might 'dip into' various peer groupings and attend several different gatherings in one week, and these choices are both directed and constrained by media influences. Thus, for many young people, attending youth organizations of various types, supporting soccer teams, going to discos, pubs, night clubs, raves, and so on, represent the social networks of these youthful 'tribes'.

Over the past two decades or so, research has also considered teenagers 'hanging around' in the neighbourhood (Corrigan, 1979), and utilizing supermarkets and urban shopping malls for their own pursuits and activities (Giddens, 1991). Many locations serve as meeting points for urban adolescents. Popular venues are shopping malls and amusement arcades, although a street corner or park may also serve this function (Fisher, 1995). Groups of adolescents are a common sight around many streets, parks and other public venues. Thus, 'crowds' are highly visible to each other—and for adult society—and, from an adult point of view, these groups often become labelled as 'threatening' and 'dangerous' (for example, Davis, 1990).

Furthermore, these new forms of 'local leisure mobility' have led to young people contesting adults' rights to the use of public venues in the community. In a study by McMeeking & Purkayasta (1995), young people indicated that, regardless of location, a key issue was a concern about their inability to independently access leisure settings. Among the causes of frustration was the lack of accessible spaces as well as the social sanctions prohibiting the use of such spaces for unstructured social activities.

Obviously, then, the wider local context itself plays a significant role in which adolescent groups exist, how they can variously express specific patterns of behaviour to establish their distinctive reputation, how they perceive and label 'out-groups', and how different groups interact within the local 'scene'. Furthermore, Brown & Mounts (1989) have demonstrated some of the functional variables that underpin crowds—in particular, the impact of large urban schools on young people's social lives, contrasting this with smaller, more rural settings.

In a recent study on the social labelling of urban adolescents in Britain, Thurlow (2001) found a range of social type labels similar to American findings, but also some clear cultural differences. Moreover, he showed considerable differences even among the various schools within his sample, with some distinctive, highly localized groupings in evidence. Perhaps most notable of all, there were large individual differences in the perceptions of 'out-groups'. Over 50 per cent of his sample did not identify any major gangs or groups within their school setting; about one-third of them naming interaction-based friendship groups instead.

Since these differences exist in urban settings, it would be interesting to see how adolescents describe crowds and social venues in rural settings. For example, the possible lack of social facilities and venues for different groups to meet may be a problem for rural youth—in many cases, there is not even a street corner. Furthermore, there are other differences between urban and rural settings that might impinge on the formation of social groupings and their labelling by adolescents. Friends are spread over a wide geographic area, so the school or village green may become an essential meeting point—even though it may not be an ideal social context from the adolescents' perspective (for example, Kloep & Hendry, 1999), and parents and other adults exert a degree of social control on young peoples' dress and behaviour in more personal ways than in the urban setting, where, for instance, young people can join sub-cultures without parental awareness.

Given the richness of previous urban research, it is surprising how little we know about rural adolescents' meeting places, social groupings and 'out-group' labelling. In the light of this, the present paper sets out to explore the ways rural young people perceive their local peer crowds and social contexts, and the implications of when they 'contest' public settings with adults.

Methodology

Introduction

The data for the present paper is extracted from the Scottish Office study 'Lifestyles, Health and Health Concerns of Rural Youth, 1996–98' (Hendry et al., 1998). The overall aim of the funded project was to examine the health practices, health concerns and lifestyles of young people in a wide range of rural settings and communities in Northern Scotland (see, for example, Hendry & Reid, 2000, Hendry et al., 2002; Kloep et al., 2001; Kloep et al., 2003, in press). While the larger study (Hendry et al., 1998) consisted of both quantitative and qualitative methods, the present paper centres on a number of focus group interviews with young people.

Sampling

We defined 'rural locations', using Randall's (1992) classification of rural districts, as small communities located at least 40 kilometres from large urban settlements. Five locations were chosen to reflect a diversity of geographic locations—with regard to sociodemographic profiles, such as fishing, farming or tourism-based communities; inland, coastal or island areas; and settlement size. Thus, these sites reflected a range of rural settlements and local socioeconomic circumstances from a farming area in Perthshire (Angus), a large community in the Northern Isles dependent on an oil-related economy (Shetland), a rural community within commuter distance of a large city (Deeside), through a rural area in decline on the east coast of the country (Caithness), to a small coastal village in the Western Highlands dependent on tourism (Wester Ross). Each study site had a secondary school that served the local area.

In each of these locations, a small group of young women and a group of young men from two different age groups were interviewed. In all, 39 girls and 34 boys participated in focus group interviews amounting to almost 40 hours of interviewing (i.e., 15/16-year-old girls, $N = 20$ and 15/16-year-old boys, $N = 18$; and 17/18-year-old girls, $N = 19$ and 17/18-year-old boys, $N = 16$). In each of the five sites, one young person (from each of the age groups and of each gender) was invited by a teacher or community education worker to take part in the project. This procedure was carried out after the teacher/community worker had discussed with the researchers the type of characteristics to be represented in the sample (i.e., coming from a local family or being an incomer, and whether the young person lived in a rural town, village or the surrounding countryside). However, as we observed later, these young people came mainly from small rural townships, and few from the 'remote' areas of the surrounding countryside.

The approach of this interview study was entirely qualitative, which means we were interested in finding out the narratives of young people about rural groups and social contexts. It was not intended—and not possible with this small number of respondents—to find out generalizable differences between genders, age groups or dwelling areas.

On invitation, there were very few refusals to participate. The volunteer then asked three or four friends to be interviewed with him or her since it was considered to be important that the young people felt comfortable and supported in the interview setting.

Focus group interviews

The interview schedule was semi-structured; starting with one question, 'Tell me what you did last Friday night?', and (if required) followed up by a number of open-ended prompts by the interviewer. This approach was chosen after lengthy piloting of a number of methods because it led to wide-ranging discussions about young people's lives and lifestyles. The nature of the interviews encouraged young people to develop their own priorities as to what was important to them. From these a vivid picture was built up around young people's social groupings and leisure activities in rural settings.

Analyses

A framework of themes was derived after all of the interviews had been reviewed. All interviews were analysed independently by two experienced researchers in order to extract themes (Vaughn *et al.*, 1996) concerning adolescents' perceptions of social groupings, activities and venues in their local communities. These extracted themes were scrutinized for comparability, and a high level of agreement was found between the two researchers in their extractions of the themes.

Results

Introduction

Themes emerged around young people's perceptions of local crowds and contexts, and on adolescents' views of adult constraints on teenagers' uses of public 'space' in the local community, and the relevant findings are presented in five sections:

- group labelling in the school context;
- group labelling in the leisure context;
- conflicts between groups;
- youth groups in different venues; and
- conflicts between youth groups and adults.

Group labelling in the school context. School provides one particular and very influential setting for group differentiation and social labelling in rural settings. Each of the friendship groups interviewed readily described different categories of young people at school. The descriptions given are mainly in terms of 'out-group' labelling, and based on whether or not there is a desire towards association. The division between 'yokels' (young people from the country side) and others is interesting. For example, mid-adolescent girls described different groupings as, 'cool', 'medium', and 'sad' (i.e., pathetic or uncool), with this last category comprising those who are seen as 'childish', 'loners' or 'yokels':

—There's the 'cool' crowd, which think they're cool. And which no one else thinks that they are that cool.
—I don't know if they really are better off or richer like, but they all seem to have a lot more expensive clothes.
—Designer crew.
—And then there's the 'medium' lot.
—And the 'sad' bunch.
—The yokels.
—It's just the way they are.
—There's groups of people who just don't go out.

Interviewer: Are they academic?
—A few, but no, not necessarily really. They just stick to themselves, on their own. And this group is really childish.

(15/16-year-old girls)

Additionally, these different groupings were influential in various aspects of school life:

—The School Council? There's no point in going in for that. It's just a popularity contest.

—Everybody in the popular crowd, they've just got it. It's just like, did anybody else get a chance?
—And they're not going to be any use at it anyway.
—They just do it for the status, like they don't do it to do anything. It's just a mark about their name.
—All the 'cool' crowd.

(15/16-year-old girls)

Boys in all research locations reflected rather similar typologies of group differences.

Group labelling in the leisure context. When young people gathered in various leisure contexts there was also clear evidence of differentiation into crowds, even in fairly small rural communities. There were groupings that were differentiated according to their dwelling place (rural town/countryside), or because of par-ticular behaviours (e.g., those perceived as being involved in 'bad' or risky activities). Notably, the young people interviewed make a point of seeing themselves as 'normal' and clearly distinguished from the other groups they describe. In the various areas of the present study, the crowd names changed somewhat but they were recognizably similar to groupings in other areas. Additionally, group labelling was sometimes applied according to age and gender (see the final quote in this section):

Interviewer: Why is your Dad not keen about it [. . . the night-club]?
Because he thinks it's a drug hole. It is, if you are in that group, but they stick to themselves, and we stick to ourselves. So it's not that bad.

(15/16-year-old girl)

There's the drinkers, and the ones with the drugs, and there's us lot. There's the people hanging around on the streets, sitting on the benches, and waiting for the cars to go past and they jump in the cars and go spinning and that's just it. Some people are in one car and then in the other . . . it's like that the whole night until they go home.

(15/16-year-old girl)

Interviewer: Are there different groups here?
Yeh, there's the mangies and the toonies.
Interviewer: What are the mangies?
Mangies are the country boys.

(15/16-year-old boys)

Interviewer: Are there different groups here?
—There's cruisers and skaters.
—And there's the spivvy lot.
—They just stand about smoking fags. And there's us lot. We just stand behind the station.

—We're normal.
—We're the only sane ones around here.
—And there's the druggie-hippie lot.
—And then there's people like me who just stay at home and just watch TV.
—And there's the druggie lot and the cruiser lot, and they have big fights together.
—They hate each other.
—The cruisers are from about 15. Maybe 20 about the most.
—Yeah, they are from 15 to 17 or 18.
—Then the druggies are all like 18 till about 25, that's the oldest.
—The cruisers are mixed really, and ours is mixed. The druggies isn't. It's just lads.

(15/16-year-old boys)

One context in which gender is closely associated with labelling is when categorizations are based on physical attractiveness:

And all the boys of your age just sit in front of the TV and they're all boring and uninteresting. They're all sheep farmer's sons or football fanatics who don't care about girls. I think the ones you get on with are the ones that come up on holiday and stuff like that. They're nice. There are about 5 really nice good looking ones but every single girl in the school is after them. It's a cat fight, who is going to get off with them at the next dance. And it turns out to be nobody. Because they are off with someone from the next village!

(15/16-year-old girl)

We played football and went to the dance. I pulled an ugly dog. I pulled a dog. I went to the dance and had a few drinks. I got off with her on the bus on the way home. I fell asleep on top of her and Tim stabbed me with a fag and Sally slapped me. I think that was what happened to me. I can't remember. Ugly girls. There's not that many tidy birds at all. There's only about 6 in the whole school, if that. Even if there are no good looking girls you still get off with them at dances . . .

(15/16-year-old boy)

The next quote illustrates the connection between group labelling and the competition for 'space', where different tastes and interests could be expressed:

—Like discos. We'd love discos just for us, without like the druggies or the cruisers.
—Just like for us.
—But that's the problem . . . there is not a lot of folk like us here.
—There's a lot that's younger, but we don't want them.

(15/16-year-old boys)

Two groups spoke about how a local club with a reputation for drug-taking had been shut down. They were afraid that this simply meant that the 'druggies', whom young people also saw as a problem, would now invade other contexts where they themselves gathered and socialized, and that the drug problem, in turn, would become less 'visible' to the adult community.

Conflicts between groups. The transition from labelling 'out-groups' to actually coming into conflict with them did not seem difficult. Again, a main differentiation existed between town and country youth, where groups, congregating and hanging around recognized meeting places in the community, were often seen as a focus for conflict.

> *Interviewer*: Is 'pulling' someone part of what you are trying to do in town?
> —Well, fights as well.
> —With folk that come in from the country.
>
> *Interviewer*: So what are the fights about?
> —Toonies and the country boys.
> —Every time we go out to country discos, they always do it to us.
> (15/16-year-old boys)

> It's about the toonies and the country boys. It's the ones from [names communities outside the main town], and we don't want them. The boys [from one particular island] are supposed to be big and strong, and they always come and start fights, just because they're in the toon. The boys [from another island] normally get involved as well. It's a bit pointless, it just ends up happening.
> (15-year-old boy)

> It was just a boy [from an island]—he was about 19—there were seven boys from the town and they all just started picking on him, punching him. He went away and got a couple of his mates. So it was like seven on seven and they all started fighting. There was a guy standing with a bottle and he cracked it over one of the guy's heads. Then that was the end of it.
> (17-year-old boy)

It is possible to suggest that these scuffles are public demonstrations of community identification and cohesion on the one hand, and inter-community rivalry and contest on the other. This was not solely an issue for young males, as the comments of a group of young women reveal:

> —Just a drunk kind of thing. Drunk and they don't get on with one another and they just sort of argue. A lot of times it's usually . . . Yokels.
> —Yokels . . . Toonies and Yokels.
>
> *Interviewer*: So were you involved in one of these fights?
> [Laughter] Yes.

Interviewer: So what happened?
—I don't know. It was just some people started fighting with me. They just didn't like me. I was covered in bruises and my nose was bleeding.
—She lost a shoe . . .
—Somebody threw my shoes away on the roof. Somebody carried me home. I was drunk. But I don't usually get in fights.

Interviewer: So was it all girls?
—Yes.
—Somebody split it up.

Interviewer: So when you got home were you in a bad state? [Laughter from others].

My nose was all swollen. My mum didn't know until the next day 'cos I didn't go home to my own house until the next night. She wasn't very pleased.

(17/18-year-old girls)

Sometimes conflicts between groups led to the destruction of certain leisure venues, as in the example one group gave us about a local park, which had been a good facility for skate boarding but had been vandalized by other adolescents:

—We had a place in the park but it's been vandalized to bits.
—Just damaged, they took all the wood off it.
—There's people that go there that are really annoying. Drink and smoke and all that.

(15/16-year-old boys)

If groups transform the use of certain amenities, such as playgrounds and parks, to meet their own needs (for example, Giddens, 1991), others recognize these as places to avoid in order to prevent 'trouble':

—There's an adventure playground in the park and everyone used to go there when it opened but it's all 18-year-olds an a'thing and they've graffitied all over it an a'thing and they just go and drink and smoke an a'thing.
—That's where they sit an a'thing, they don't let anybody else on it. The police are a'ways doon there an a'thing.
—It's not safe to go down there at night in case like they attack you or anything.
—They just sit on the swings and drink an a'thing. If you just look, glance at them they'll do you!

(15/16-year-old boys)

However, from the young person's perspective, only a minority viewed 'gangs of youth' as representing a *serious* problem in the local area, and almost one-half

Table 5.1 Percentage reporting 'gangs of young people' as a problem by location (Hendry et al., 1998)

Gangs of young people seen as a problem	Selected locations				
	Wester Ross	Shetland	Deeside	Caithness	Angus
Females					
Serious	7	8	12	15	17
Minor	20	47	47	52	50
None	73	45	41	33	33
($n = 100\%$)	39	222	144	249	151
Males					
Serious	4	9	12	19	18
Minor	18	42	42	43	44
None	78	49	46	38	38
($n = 100\%$)	56	208	178	242	149

of the survey sample in Hendry *et al.*'s (1998) larger study did not see this as a problem at all (see Table 5.1).

It is interesting to note from Table 5.1 that perceptions did not vary by gender, although the level of concern differed by study location. Much less concern was expressed in smaller and more remote rural communities (such as Wester Ross) and correspondingly greater concern was evident in larger or more populated settings (such as Angus).

Youth groups and their venues. Leisure facilities and venues in the community were demarcation lines for different rural crowds. For young people living in more remote villages or in the surrounding countryside, there was often an acceptance that the youth club was an integral part of village life that required their support and commitment, and sports club involvement was often seen as central to a rural masculine identity. There was a sense of loyalty and obligation to attend these activities, even 17 and 18 year olds in some smaller villages continued to attend the local club. By way of contrast, 15 and 16 year olds in certain rural townships (which were larger and possessed some social and/or leisure facilities and amenities) saw this form of social activity as no longer relevant to their social lives, as previous urban findings have demonstrated (for example, Hendry *et al.*, 1993). Thus, in rural townships, the youth club was something most young people had attended in the past but, by age 15 years, few of those interviewed went to youth clubs, preferring more informal social activities or commercial leisure pursuits. These young people expressed a rather negative view of local youth clubs.

Furthermore, in the more rural settings, the point was often made about the leisure facilities being shared with the local community school, where a purpose-built leisure centre occupied the same site as the school that young people attended during the day. From the young person's point of view this may not be such an attractive option, desiring to see leisure time as clearly distinct from the rigours of school.

There are few settings in which youths can meet to share their leisure time, places where they can be with their own crowd and take part in their specific interests.

Given these constraints, one of the main social activities cited by young people in rural areas was meeting up 'doing nothing' and 'hanging about' in public spaces.

> We went into [the town] on Saturday night, just to hang about. We had a drink . . . It's OK as long as you look like you're drinking coke . . . After that we wandered around the street, and that, and went to this someone's house, and then to the [square] to hang about, and that.
>
> (15/16-year-old boy)

Young people from surrounding villages and the countryside were often keen to come into a rural town at weekends just to meet up at these gathering points, although there were also descriptions of 'hanging around' and 'getting into trouble' in the surrounding villages.

> Well there is only a few of us in the village, like friends, and we just go out and muck about which ends up in trouble.
>
> (15/16-year-old girl)

To take a detailed example from one town, 'the Square' was seen as a central place in the social life of local youth at weekends. Adolescents talked about it in relation to a wide variety of themes, including somewhere to go in a community when there was nothing else to do, as a setting for social interactions with friends and peers, as a focus in developing relationships, in terms of access to 'space' for young people, and in terms of perceived threats to community life and public order issues. But, even more significantly, it was portrayed as 'Where the action is'. Young people congregated there, and there was an air of unpredictability as to what might happen (for example, Corrigan, 1979). Fights that had occurred in 'the Square' were talked about both in general and from personal experience. It was *the* place to go at the end of a night out.

> —Yes. On Saturday I was working during the day, and then at [the night-club] at night, and then 'The Square'.
>
> *Interviewer*: Are there lots of young folk around at 'The Square'?
> —Yes, hundreds.
> —All the people from the night-club and the pubs.
>
> (15/16-year-old girls)

> —It's after twelve and it's pretty mobbed. There's a burger van and a baked tattie shop, so you can go and get something to eat.

> *Interviewer*: So do you all go there?
> —Yeah.
>
> (17/18-year-old girls)

For younger adolescents, particularly males, it was a place to hang around and, sometimes, drink illegally, although whenever possible young people preferred under-age drinking in pubs and clubs, if they were able to gain access (for example, Kloep *et al.*, 2001).

Conflict between youth groups and adults. However, public settings and venues were seen as a focus for conflict both between groups of youth and between adolescents and the local adult community.

As popular as 'the Square' is as a meeting point for young people, adults look less benevolently on this choice. The same reason that makes 'the Square' interesting for young people—giving them space to try out identity-related roles and behaviours without interference of adults—makes it a 'shock scenario' for parents. Some young people had to lie to their parents so that they could be at 'the Square' at the weekend.

> *Interviewer*: What did your parents think of all this [... going to 'The Square']?
> —They didn't know about it.
> —Yeah. We all went out at about one o'clock in the morning and came back in at about three.
> —I have secrets because I don't want them to find out what I'm doing.
> —I think some of it's about us growing up, and them not wanting to let go or something, and still wanting us to come in at 9 o'clock at night... [Giggles]
>
> (15/16-year-old girls)

Additionally, 'the Square' was seen as under threat from the adult community. At the time of the interviews there was much correspondence in the local press around this issue. Young people said that adults wanted to curb their presence there at weekends—it was seen by adults as 'local youth out of control, fighting, drinking and, some, using drugs':

> I wrote a letter in to the paper complaining because they were threatening to shut it down, and I said, 'Why?' Because it (the alleged drug problem) would just move on somewhere else, and it would be a bigger problem then. At least now they know where everyone is.
>
> (15/16-year-old girl)

'The Square' had an important symbolic meaning for adolescents as a place where they felt free from adult controls, despite a frequent police presence. On the other hand, they believed that adults in the community saw it as a threat to peace and order.

Similar problems were evident in the use of public spaces in other rural settings. A group of mid-adolescent boys in another rural setting said:

> Like in [another local township], we were told people started complaining because young folk started using the seafront but now they've got their own stuff there, like it's much better noo. [Here it's] Presto's car park, a lot of folk go roller blading in that. They go round the car park and there's just nowhere else for them to go. They just get thrown off by the manager. Young people have just been starting building their own places, and stuff, here, just wherever. They need to change the BMX track for roller blading. There's a petition going about it. A lot of people would go to the BMX track if they were to concrete it.
>
> (15/16-year-old boy)

These views were not restricted to rural townships. For another group from a smaller village—picturesque, historic, and a popular tourist location—the railway station platform, car park and approach road were seen as the best available spaces for skate boarding. Again, this group had been 'chased off'.

> —We just hang about, and do skate boarding and stuff.
> —The police, they're always round checking up what time you should be home.
> —The same is true for young people who simply walk up and down the street:
> —We just met up at the (village green) but people are telling you not to do things all the time.
>
> (15/16-year-old girls)

This experience was repeated in all of the study locations, and for some young people it was seen as an integral part of rural social life:

> —Most of the time we hang around the streets in the village, but recently we've been getting the blame from the police for all the things that have been going on when it wasn't us. Like on Saturday night there was trouble going on in the village and we were stopped and asked what happened and we didn't know.
> —It was just like other kids going about and they vandalize. We got the blame for it. And it wasn't us.
>
> (15/16-year-old girls)

Some young people talked of the difficulties that were associated with being part of a small community, and that the community was full of antagonistic adults, trying to prevent young people from being young and 'having fun'. They felt that they were simply seen as a problem by adults or ignored. Being labelled as an 'out-group' by adults, these young people 'stuck together' in response. Building up a reputation, gossip, criticism and blame were all seen as relevant to this picture.

82 *Young people's views on people and places*

—They all gossip about us.

Interviewer: Is that a pressure?
—I don't care.
—It doesn't really bother me if they talk about you.
—It's quite easy to get a reputation.
—Och, aye.
—I had one before I even came up here. I'm the bad one from [the city].
—Like some people are known to be really heavy drinkers, right the way across from one end and right the way down [. . . the coast].
—Yeah, it is easy to get a bad reputation.
—And you can't get rid of it.

(15/16-year-old boys)

Late-night gatherings, seen as an important feature of weekend social life by adolescents in rural townships, were viewed with some concern by local authorities and parents, with adults seen as actively campaigning to move young people from these public settings. Reflecting Davis' (1990) viewpoint that adults 'use' young people as a litmus paper for the current condition of society, it was claimed that adults blamed them for anything that was thought to be 'bad' in the community:

—Well there are only a few of us [in the village], like friends, and we just go out and muck about which ends up in trouble.

Interviewer: What kind of trouble?
—Well there are public toilets and they were badly vandalized last year and so we're not allowed anywhere near them, so there is nothing for us to do. There is nothing for youngsters to do here. That's how it has been provoked. That's it.

(15/16-year-old girls)

—Everyone hates us
—Nobody likes us hanging around the streets.
—My Grandmother said to me the other night, 'I don't like to see you hanging about the village, giving it a bad name'.
—They don't want you hanging around the streets and that.
—I was grounded for a month because I was caught up in the village with her.

(15/16-year-old girls)

Echoing such concerns of social control, even though there were only a limited number of shops and local businesses in the central town square of one of the rural townships, a strategically placed video surveillance camera was installed to oversee this public space.

Many young people spoke about identifying strongly with their local area, yet, at the same time, felt that they were seen as a threat in their own community.

Interviewer: How is it being young here?
It's a small village where everybody knows each other. I've lived here all my life. Yeah, well, people are telling you not to do things all the time.

(15-year-old boy)

Discussion and conclusions

Perceived groups

To sum up this picture of rural youth's affiliations—aside from obvious differentiations in terms of age and gender—there *are* recognizable crowds of young people in all five of the study locations.

In general terms, the friendship groups who participated in the present interview study regard themselves as 'normal' in their dress, interests and activities. By comparison, crowds are typically seen as either 'cool', 'bad' or 'sad' (Michell, 1997). These variations in labelling are often related to perceived peer status and, sometimes, to the pecking order within the wider peer population. A 'high status' group was identified in each location in the study, variously defined as 'cool' and associated with consumption, youth culture and expensive designer clothes.

Differentiation of rural crowds means that some, such as 'druggies', are regarded broadly by most as highly deviant. Other 'delinquent' behaviours are also seen as markers of crowd differences: some use cigarette smoking and/or drinking or fighting to describe different crowds. Perceptions of maturity are clearly important to this social differentiation, where these are tied to perceived boundaries of what represents 'appropriate' behaviour in young people.

Social activities and contexts also mark young people out from each other— going out to dances and to commercial nightclubs as opposed to hanging around late at night in public places. Against this backdrop of social and leisure activities, some young people are perceived as 'low status' and as being socially isolated or immature. This negative aspect of social differentiation is most often focused on whether the young person comes from an even more rural (i.e., country) location. There are few peer affiliations mentioned by those interviewed that can actually be labelled as 'sub-cultural' groupings (such as 'gothics', 'heavy metals' or 'punks'). Rather than differentiated sub-cultures as in urban findings, there is a strong division between town and country youth.

Perhaps more importantly, over all interviews there are no cases of self-identification with crowds (beyond descriptions of being 'normal'). Group labelling seems to be used not so much to *find* an identity, but rather to build up a self-image based on a 'negative identity', on identifications and roles that are seen to be undesirable. Maybe fewer young people in the rural setting perceive themselves as belonging to certain teenage crowds than both peers and adults estimate.

By comparison with Thurlow's (2001) urban findings, a large group of 'baddies' was also identified in the present study, and the labelling of a 'cool' group (or those who think they are 'cool') and 'normals' all show some parallels with

Thurlow's findings. Neither are there any 'sport jocks', supporting his view that this might be a unique feature of American teenage crowds.

Thurlow also questioned why he did not find the same peer orientations as in US findings, such as 'loners/outcasts'. Such a group does not appear in the Scottish rural context either. (Young people used the word 'sad' when characterizing a group as 'pathetic', 'uncool' or 'unpopular'.) This might be due to the fact that both British studies used 'other identification', and that a socially isolated group is simply so withdrawn from contexts where young people meet they are not usually labelled or commented upon.

In a quantitative study of Scottish rural youth, Kloep & Hendry (2000) used cluster analysis to categorize young respondents on the basis of their self-reports (on various measures such as a depression, self-esteem, perceived social support, relationships to parents, friends and teachers, views about rural living, drinking and smoking habits). They discovered four clear clusters, each with a male and female type possessing varying and different characteristics, namely: 'rural adjusted', 'peer oriented', 'lonely', and 'withdrawn' young people (see Table 5.2).

Table 5.2 Typologies from Kloep & Hendry (2000)

'Rural adjusted young men' ($N = 341$), with low depression, high self-esteem, good support from parents though with some conflicts, spending a lot of time with friends and very positive about rural life and its amenities; and *'Rural adjusted young women'* ($N = 324$) with low depression, high self-esteem, having good friends, no problems with peers, parents or teachers and very positive about rural life and amenities.

'Peer oriented young men' ($N = 285$) spending much time with many friends, smoking and drinking a lot, seeing 'fun' as important and being very negative about rural social life and amenities; and *'Peer oriented young women'* ($N = 316$) receiving little support from parents, spending much time with many friends, smoking and drinking and being very negative about rural living but not social life.

'Lonely young men' ($N = 268$) with high depression, low self-esteem, worried about appearance, some smoking and drinking occasionally, spending little time with few friends, receiving some support but having many conflicts with parents, and being somewhat negative about rural social life; and *'Lonely young women'* ($N = 231$) with high depression, the lowest self-esteem of any group, having a negative body image and worried about appearance, having few friends and no parental support, and a high level of conflict with their parents, thinking it is very important to have 'fun' but unable to access it, and negative about rural life and amenities.

'Withdrawn young men' ($N = 372$) who displayed a negative body image, but without caring about it, some parental support but also some conflicts, thinking 'having fun' is not important, not smoking or drinking, not caring about how friends look or dress, negative about rural social life, but positive about other rural characteristics; and *'Withdrawn young women'* ($N = 316$) with negative body image but not worrying about it, not many friends and little time spent with friends, no parental support but neither much conflict, don't think 'having fun' is important, don't drink or smoke, highly negative about social life in rural areas, but not negative towards other aspects of rural life.

These findings to some extent parallel other studies (Glendinning *et al.*, 1995; Glendinning & Inglis, 1997; Glendinning, 2002) of a national sample of Scottish adolescents, which also used self-categorization. Thus, if young people are grouped by their self-reports, the 'normal, adjusted, good' group emerges together with a conglomerate of 'bad', 'cool' and 'popular' types. However, two more groups appear, which do not emerge as clearly in the descriptions of others. These are the 'lonely' (which might partly reflect the 'sad, uncool, unpopular' crowd in the presently reported study) and the 'withdrawn'. The 'lonely' may have withdrawn so effectively that their existence is not prominent in the minds of other young people. It would be interesting to speculate whether some of those who did not name existing peer affiliations in their school in Thurlow's study might also belong to this 'invisible' crowd, not seen—but not seeing either!

Venues and conflicts

From the present findings it would seem that trying to establish and maintain a local 'identity' can lead to a powerful rivalry among different adolescent crowds, and may show, as do urban studies, that 'territory' is important to rural youth in their wishes to create clear-cut—if varied—community 'identities'. When young people gather in various social settings, they see other crowds as somehow 'different' in style of dress and behaviour, and at times threatening to give rise to 'trouble'. These variations appear to be associated with such factors as hedonism (i.e., smoking and drinking), 'trouble' (i.e., wanting to appear 'hard'), transformation (i.e., leisure as fun) or boredom. Within the context of the small rural townships studied, this creates a growing ground for conflict, as the different crowds are unable to avoid each other in the limited public 'spaces' available for meetings. It would be interesting to see how young people from the truly 'remote' country areas perceive their situation: on their home territory there *is* no square or street corner at which to meet, and if they commute into a rural township they are labelled and responded to as 'yokels'.

These gradations from (relatively speaking) larger townships to more and more rural settings with their attendant status differentials seem important to pursue in subsequent studies since they appear to express the whole question of symbolic and tangible territoriality in adolescents' attitudes, behaviours, social relationships and treatment of other reputation-based crowds.

However, the greatest competition for public 'space' does not necessarily come from other peer groups. It comes from adults. Adults represent a powerful group who already have ownership of most community 'space': home, streets, public buildings and social institutions. So, from a young person's perspective, why do they want to compete for all the public venues too? And, if they want to have these public spaces to themselves, why do they not provide more alternative venues for young people? There may be reasons of hegemonic power, concern for what adolescents do and the risks they take, or anxiety over public order, as Davis (1990) has suggested. In examining the possible contradictions between youth's need for 'space to develop socially and have meaningful leisure' and adults' desire for 'socialisation and control' as the power holders in society, we need to consider that there are strong forces in society that pressurize young people towards conformity from early life. From nursery school onward, leisure time is safeguarded and organized for young people—instead of by them. This continues into adolescence so that many feel the need to create their own leisure challenges away from parents but in adult society. This may conflict with society's values, and even at times with the law—thus confirming the horror picture some adults have of 'teenage monsters'. These images are currency for the mass media, following a long tradition of adult anxiety about the lifestyles of the young, and clearly rural youth are not excluded from all this.

At this stage, one could also pose the question of why this conflict does not arise in more southern cultures, where the Plaza Mayor is the daily meeting place for all generations and where they mix together amicably. Is it a reflection of the condition of British society, that adults promote apartheid rather than integration in their relations with young people? Thus, in attempting to look at social differentiation of groups from an adolescent perspective, it may seem rather surprising to conclude that, in the eyes of rural young people, the most powerful and menacing 'out group' of all are—adults.

Acknowledgements

The present paper is based on the results of the funded research project 'Lifestyles, Health and Health Concerns of Rural Youth, 1996–98', Department of Health, Scottish Office, Edinburgh. The Grantholders are Professor L. B. Hendry and A. Glendinning. The ideas and interpretations in the present paper, however, are solely those of the named authors.

References

Brake, M. (1985) *The Sociology of Youth Culture and Youth Subcultures* (London, Routledge & Kegan Paul).

Brown, B.B. (1996) Visibility, vulnerability, development, and context: Ingredients for fuller understanding of peer rejection in adolescence, *Journal of Early Adolescence*, 16, pp. 27–36.

Brown, B. & Mounts, N. (1989) Peer group structure in single vs. multi-ethnic high schools. Paper presented at the Society for Research in Child Development Conference, Kansas, April 1989.

Brown, B.B., Mory, M.S. & Kinney, D. (1994) Casting adolescent crowds in a relational perspective: caricature, channel and context, in: R. Montemayor, G. Adams & T. Gullotta (Eds) *Personal Relations during Adolescence* (Thousand Oaks, CA, Sage).

Corrigan, P. (1979) *Schooling the Smash Street Kids* (London, Macmillan).

Davis, J. (1990). *Youth and the Condition of Britain: Images of Adolescent Conflict* (London, Athlone Press).

Dunphy, D.C. (1972) Peer group socialisation, in: F.J. Hunt (Ed.) *Socialisation in Australia* (Sydney, Angus & Robertson).

Fisher, S. (1995) The amusement arcade as a social space for adolescents, *Journal of Adolescence*, 18, pp. 71–86.

Foote Whyte, W. (1943) *Street Corner Society: The Social Structure of an Italian Slum* (Chicago, IL, University of Chicago Press).
Giddens, A. (1991) *Modernity and Self Identity: Self and Society in the Late Modern Age* (Oxford, Polity).
Glendinning, A., Hendry, L.B. & Shucksmith, J. (1995) Lifestyle, health and social class in adolescence, *Social Science & Medicine*, 41, pp. 235–248.
Glendinning, A. & Inglis, D. (1997) Smoking behaviour in youth: The problem of low self-esteem? *Journal of Adolescence* (Special Issue), 22, 673–682.
Glendinning, A. (2002) Self-esteem and smoking in youth—muddying the waters? *Journal of Adolescence*, 25, 415–425.
Hargreaves, D. (1968) *Social Relations in a Secondary School* (London, Routledge & Kegan Paul).
Hendry, L. B. & Reid, M. L. (2000) Social relationships and health: the meaning of social 'connectedness' and how it relates to health concerns for rural Scottish adolescents. *Journal of Adolescence*, 23(6), pp. 705–719.
Hendry, L.B., Shucksmith, J., Love, J. & Glendinning, A. (1993) *Young People's Leisure and Lifestyles* (London, Routledge).
Hendry, L.B., Glendenning, A., Reid, M. & Wood, S. (1998) Lifestyles, Health and Health Concerns of Rural Youths, 1996–98. Report to the Department of Health, Scottish Office, Edinburgh.
Hendry, L.B., Kloep, M., Espnes, G. A., Ingebrigtsen, J.-E., Glendinning, A. & Wood, S. (2002) Leisure transitions: a rural perspective, *Leisure Studies*, 21(1), pp. 1–14.
Hogg, M.A. & Abrams, D. (1988) *Social Identifications* (London, Routledge).
Jahoda, M., Lazarfield, P.F. & Zeisel, H. (1933) *Marienbad: The Sociography of an Unemployed Community* (London, Tavistock).
Kloep, M. & Hendry, L.B. (1999) Challenges, risks and coping in adolescence, in: D. Messer & S. Miller (Eds) *Exploring Developmental Psychology* (London, Arnold).
Kloep, M. & Hendry, L.B. (2000) All men are different, but rural youths are more different than others? Towards a typology of rural adolescents. Paper presented at the XXVII International Congress of Psychology, Stockholm, Sweden, 23–28 July.
Kloep, M., Hendry, L.B., Ingebrigtsen, J.E., Glendinning, A. & Espnes, G.A. (2001) Young people in drinking societies? Norwegian, Scottish and Swedish adolescents' perceptions of alcohol use, *Health Education Research*, 16(3), pp. 279–291.
Kloep, M., Hendry, L.B., Ingebrigtsen, J.-E. & Glendinning, A. (2003) Peripheral visions?: Rural youths' perceptions of aspects of community life, *Children's Geographies* (forthcoming).
Kroger, J. (2000) *Identity Development: Adolescence Through Adulthood* (London, Sage).
Maffesoli, M. (1994) *The Time of the Tribes: The Decline of Individualism in Mass Society* (London, Sage).
McMeeking, D. & Purkayastha, B. (1995) I can't have my mom running me everywhere: adolescents, leisure and accessibility, *Journal of Leisure Research*, 27, pp. 360–378.
McRobbie, A (1994) *Postmodernism and Popular Culture* (Routledge, London).
Michell, L. (1997) 'Loud, sad or bad': young people's perceptions of peer groups and smoking, *Health Education Research*, 12, 1–14.
Mungham, G. & Pearson, G. (1976) *Working Class Youth Culture* (London, Routledge & Kegan Paul).
Patrick, J. (1973) *A Glasgow Gang Observed* (London, Eyre Methuen).
Randall, J. (1992) *Scottish Rural Life* (Edinburgh, Department of Environment, Scottish Office).

Thurlow, C. (2001) The usual suspects? A comparative investigation of crowds and social-type labelling among young british teenagers, *Journal of Youth Studies*, 4(3), pp. 319–334.

Vaughn, S., Schumm, J.S. & Sinagub, J. (1996) *Focus Group Interviews in Education and Psychology* (London, Sage).

Willis, P. (1977) *Learning to Labour: How Working Class Kids get Working Class Jobs* (Farnborough, Saxon House).

Yablonski, L. (1962) *The Violent Gang* (New York, Macmillan).

6 Young people talking

Here we look at the entwined roles of adolescent communication and leisure activities. It is often said that teenagers spend a great deal of their time doing 'nothing', just hanging around, talking with friends. In this extract we utilise quotes from a larger, cross-cultural, mixed method series of studies to give 'voice' to young people. Further, we argue that a great deal of learning happens in leisure – as well as in school – by using adolescents' own words in expressing their feelings about what they do in their spare time, how well they are prepared to cope with their leisure-time. In doing so, within the framework of our Lifespan Challenge Model, we conceptualise the various roles that conversation and leisure pursuits play in their lives.

Continuing with the theme of giving adolescents a 'voice' in attempting to gain an understanding of young people's psychosocial transitions to adulthood, another project I undertook was for the Health Education Board for Scotland, to investigate the views and needs of young people as they grow up. Although adolescents are reasonably well informed in many ways, they do experience concerns and pressures in relation to issues such as body shape, sexual behaviour and the safe use of drugs. By speaking out for themselves they reveal how health messages are absorbed, adapted, or even ignored, by today's youth.

'TALKIN', DOIN' AND BEIN' WITH FRIENDS'

Leisure and communication in adolescence

Leo Hendry and Marion Kloep

One of the misconceptions of modern times is that young people learn the really important preparatory life skills in school, although leisure is a time for relaxation, for recreation, and for fun. However, this point of view ignores the vast array of learning opportunities leisure can actually offer, not least the numerous occasions and various settings available for learning to communicate with others. Young people also use leisure to acquire many of their most valuable communication skills—because, in order to enjoy their leisure, they have to communicate with friends, peers, parents and other adults! As the quote in the title of our chapter shows, leisure and communication are intimately connected. Leisure plays an important part in human development, because, to a certain extent, it allows individuals to choose and pace the developmental tasks they encounter and the skills they learn. According to contemporary trends in developmental psychology theory, for example, development occurs every time an individual meets and overcomes a challenge that slightly exceeds their existing psychosocial resources (Hendry & Kloep, 2002). This adds new resources to their 'resource pool' and makes successful coping in the future more probable. Equally, if only a few new, challenging experiences are encountered, little (if any) new capabilities will be added, and a certain developmental stagnation occurs. Resources can also be lost when the individual is unable to cope with challenges, either because these challenges exceed existing resources or because there are too many challenges facing the individual simultaneously. Therefore, encountering challenges can be stimulating to the level of actually creating some anxiety in the individual, so that at times, if there is a choice, he/she avoids seeking challenges until feeling secure enough and believing that there are sufficient resources to cope. On the other hand, being underchallenged, though this provides security for the individual, can soon lead to feelings of boredom. Hence, people can stagnate and their development can be restricted and limited if their skills are not tested and their resource pool strengthened. Some of the most important sets of skills to master in the process of growing up are the skills of social relationships and interpersonal interactions, and some of the best opportunities for learning, practicing and trying out these skills are leisure settings of various kinds. Developmental resources can be of very different types: they may be a variety of skills, material advantages, enhanced self-esteem, biological advantages, social support, positive attitudes and so on—and what exactly makes them useful resources in a certain situation (and maybe not in another!) depends on the kind of challenge that individuals face. In other words, there is a dynamic interaction between challenges and resources, in which one defines the other. Hence, the same feature can be a resource in one situation and a challenge in another. If we consider, for example, communication skills and leisure, we can easily see that having a rich repertoire of leisure pursuits can provide excellent resources for making new friends. On the other hand, having friends and having good social and communication skills can serve as resources for coping with the challenges that leisure activities provide.

For many young people, adolescence is a time that offers many challenges. Apart from the onset of puberty and changes in body shape, schooling, examinations and career choices, and increasing adult rights and responsibilities, reconfigured social relationships with parents, peers and romantic partners all have to be negotiated. How do young people manage these challenges and maintain or even add to their 'resource pool' in the transition to adulthood?

Findings of one well-known study of adolescent relationships showed that attitudes to different relationships changed as a function of age, but more importantly the results also indicated that concerns about different issues reached a peak at different periods through adolescence (Coleman, 1978). This key finding led to the theoretical formulation of the 'focal model,' which provides one possible explanation for the successful adaptation of many young people to developmental demands. That is, they cope by dealing with one issue at a time, and spread the process of adaptation over a span of years, attempting to resolve first one issue and then the next. Different problems and different relationship issues come into focus and are tackled at different points in the adolescent developmental process, so that the stresses resulting from the need to adapt to new modes of behavior are rarely concentrated all at one time. The model suggests that at different phases, particular sorts of relationship patterns (relationships to peers, parents and romantic partners) come into focus, in the sense of being most prominent, though no pattern is specific to one phase only. Yet, even if a focal issue is not highly prominent at one specific point in the transition, it could still be critical for some individuals around that time. The focal model goes some way toward reconciling the apparent contradiction between the amount of adaptation required during the transitional process and the ability of most young people to cope successfully with the pressures inherent in that process. Results from studies in other countries (Kroger, 1985, in New Zealand and United States; Goossens & Marcoen, 1999, in Belgium) support this notion of different issues coming into focus at different times. As Goossens and Marcoen (1999: 65–80) state,

> The general pattern of peak ages for adolescents' interpersonal concerns provided support for the focal model. Negative feelings about being alone, relationships with parents, heterosexual relationships, small groups, and rejection from large groups do not all emerge all at once, but seem to be dealt with one issue at a time.

In a study of our own carried out in Sweden (see Kloep, 1999), we provided additional support for the notion that, where possible, adolescent developmental issues are dealt with one at a time, rather than all at once. In another series of studies (Hendry *et al.*, 1993; 1996; 2002), we and our colleagues used the focal model to provide a perspective on the way young peoples' leisure activities interact dynamically with their developmental needs in learning relational skills. These studies showed how young people move from one style of leisure involvement to another and one type of relationship to another as they progress through adolescence, demonstrating how there are a series of leisure transitions allied to these relational transitions. Young peoples' leisure patterns generally move through three transitional stages: 'organized leisure,' 'casual leisure' and 'commercial leisure.' These three transitions coincide with three relational 'shifts,' namely, developing a friendly/romantic interest toward the opposite sex, peer group acceptance, and gaining independence from parents. Such shifts and strategies ideally incorporate three phases of development, in each of which a consecutive set of new capabilities is learned, releasing young people step by step into the world of adult relationships.

Hence, this chapter looks at the dynamic interactions between leisure and communication in the psychosocial development of young people. We want to illustrate this association by presenting the voices of young people themselves, talking about their leisure pursuits and their leisure settings. When adults—be they academic theorists, researchers, youth professionals, policy makers or laypersons—consider young people's leisure, the adolescent's perspective is rarely included. Here we attempt to redress the balance by presenting what young people have said to us about various aspects of leisure in some of our recent research projects, and in particular what they have said about its role in creating and maintaining social relationships. We do this by extracting and interpreting what young people themselves have told us when we have talked with them about their lifestyles and leisure pursuits. The quotations we offer here are all taken from a number of fairly recent studies of young people that we have conducted in various regions of Sweden and Scotland. Our Scottish data comes from 20 focus group interviews (with 5-7 same age/sex young people in each group, N–80), and approximately 40 individual interviews with young people between 11 and 18 years of age from a study by Hendry *et al.* (1998). The Swedish data, on the other hand, is drawn from essays titled 'To be young in Jamtland,' written by 240 young people between 13 and 18 years of age (Kloep, 1998). This material—including that cited here—was translated by the second author, a bilingual speaker. (As you will see from the quotes, it is not unusual for many Swedish teenagers—and even a few Scots— to use the term 'one' instead of 'I' in their essays, as well as in their daily talk.) These qualitative studies were part of a larger research project investigating the lifestyles of young people in Scotland, Sweden and Norway, and some of the results are published in different journal articles (e.g., Hendry, Kloep & Wood, 2002; Hendry *et al.*, 2002; Kloep *et al.*, 2003).[1]

The stories young people have told us are presented in this chapter to show the complex process of developing communication and leisure skills throughout the teenage years. We start by looking at communication as a leisure activity, then go on to examine how leisure is used to learn relational skills, and conclude by giving examples of how leisure can be used more widely to communicate identity and 'style.'

Communication as leisure

Often, when asked what they do in their leisure time, young people will answer, 'Nothing—just hanging around with friends!' In fact, young people spend a great deal of their leisure time with friends (Flammer *et al*, 1999; Kloep, 1998), often 'not doing anything' but chatting, giggling and 'hanging out.' Indeed, many young people perceive 'fooling around' and laughter as among the most fulfilling of activities (e.g., Csikszentmihalyi & Larson, 1984). Being with others and being in communication is in itself a very important leisure activity for young people.[2] Through these interactions, they receive social support, offer feedback on new skills, give advice and comfort and provide security just by being 'there' for friends. Through such *apparently* meaningless conversations, social bonds are negotiated and strengthened.

The importance of 'special' friends is stressed again and again when young people discuss the role of friendship and support. Interpersonal communication seems vital in their leisure lives:

> I talk mostly with Anna, we can be talking more than an hour about nothing, really, and that is what makes it so enjoyable, I would think.
> (SWF 14)

> I should not forget my great friends. They make life worth living, and it is because of them that I have very few problems . . .
> (SCM 15)

> I am feeling very fine. What's really important is friends. And regarding friends, I am not in any need. I have not only a few of them . . . I have a best friend, but I cannot be so often with her, she lives 25 kilometres away . . .
> (SWF 13)

> I have quite a lot of friends and we can talk about everything and that makes me feel very secure . . .
> (SCF 15)

When friends cannot meet face-to-face the telephone is much in use to enable the talking to continue, particularly in rural areas (Hendry *et al.*, 1998). This means of communication is obviously not new; however, it has gained even greater importance more recently with the arrival of mobile phones, enabling young people to communicate at virtually every hour of the day, wherever they are. By being able to send text messages, young people can even communicate secretly in places otherwise not suitable for private communication, such as under the classroom desk, in toilet cubicles or at home under the duvet. Furthermore, the creation of new linguistic practices for technologies such as text messaging allow new ways of communicating to which adults are not always able to easily gain access.

Computer activities provide another relatively 'adult-free zone,' because often many parents are not as computer literate as their children, and so may not always be able to monitor a young person's communication in online environments such as chatrooms, email, instant messaging, online games and so on. To some extent, the use of computers and gaming technology has 'demoted' leisure reading, although computers still lag behind television, CDs and radio (see, for example, Beentjes *et al.*, 1999).

Concerned by this development, adults often speculate about possible dangers emerging from a device over which they have little control. A Canadian study (D'Amours & Robitaille, 2002) showed that nearly half the parents interviewed indicated that they did not feel sufficiently skilled to supervise their children's activities on the internet because they did not use it as actively as their children. Asked by these researchers what they primarily did on the internet, young people said they searched for information (78%), exchanged emails (72%), listened to or downloaded music (70%), participated in chat rooms (66%) and played games online (56%). Compared to that, only 47 percent of the adults questioned used the internet for emails, and only 15 percent participated in chat rooms. Interestingly, in this Canadian study, young women used the net as much as boys, albeit for slightly different activities. Girls preferred email exchanges, whereas boys played online games (a gendered division that seems to mirror real-world differences). Arnett et al. (1995) view these cultural trends as new and important sources of socialization for young people, because to a large extent they select their own materials and programs.

Is extensive internet use preventing, substituting or complementing real life communication for teenagers? Research up to now has had few answers to that question. It seems that the lower young peoples' level of attachment to close friends is, and the fewer pro-social attitudes they express, the higher is their involvement with the internet (Mesch, 2001). However, that does not answer the question of whether the internet might be a convenient tool for shy people to try out social skills from a safe 'distance,' covered by anonymity and maybe an assumed identity, or if it prevents these individuals from going out into the real world and risking the challenges of face-to-face relationships. Nevertheless, some young people use the net to establish contacts initially: Wolak et al. (2002) showed that 14 percent of the teenagers they interviewed reported having formed close online relationships, often with same-aged peers and across gender lines. Most of these electronic links led to off-line contacts such as phone calls and meetings. Contrary to media stories, less than half a percent of these contacts were classified as being 'sexual in any way' [see chapter 11 [of the original publication]—for more discussion on these issues].

Quite often, computer activities are not only directed at communicating, but also engaged in as collaborative ventures. Young people meet together to play computer games, or to engage in online chats as a group:

> The main part of my leisure time I spend with X, one of my friends. We 'punish' his computer until the processor gets hot and the soundcard gives up. We also use X's house as a meeting place for me, X, Y and Zn, the famous PZ-gang.
>
> (SWM 15)

Since communication in many forms is an integral part of young people's leisure time activities, it offers both challenges and risks. Communication with friends is not unproblematic and involves many social skills that have to be acquired, practiced and tried out for effect. For this, leisure offers many opportunities to experiment, observe role models and rehearse skills, and to enact and try out future adult roles.

Leisure for communication

Personal choice, peer encounters, parental supervision, adult mentors, the commercial world and legal restrictions create the various leisure settings and contexts that young people seek out as they move from early adolescence toward adulthood. Yet these transitional patterns, following focal theory, are somewhat predictable.

Organized leisure

According to the leisure focal model described earlier, the first phase, running from childhood to the early adolescent years, involves young people associating with a range of adult-led organizations and activities and is concerned with conformity to adults and the observation and practice of 'appropriate' behavior in the presence of adults.

Adults play an important role in young people's leisure participation. Sports clubs, hobby groups, choirs and orchestras, youth clubs and uniformed organizations all tend to be arranged for young people by adults, and are often closely supervised by adults. Young people's involvement in such adult-sponsored situations, though nominally voluntary, may not be genuinely self-chosen, and may confront young people with the dilemma of choosing to participate in a setting which if anything perpetuates adult dominance in their lives, perhaps in exchange for the training of well-regarded skills and the advantages of acquired social status. Demonstrating the interests of early adolescence, one boy said,

> In winter one can go on slalom and cross country skis, skates, snowboard. During holidays and on weekends, there are always buses to the skiing area. I am interested in skating and hockey. We have a small sports hall. There we play indoor hockey, football, volleyball, basket, table tennis and so on . . .
> (SWM 14)

Many studies have shown a high involvement of school-age youngsters in fairly regular physical activity and sport. In Flammer *et al.*'s (1999) study, sport was the third most popular leisure activity during adolescence, after watching television/listening to music and meeting friends. However, there are age and sex/gender differences (Hendry *et al.* 1993; Kremer *et al.*, 1997). Put simply, younger male adolescents are the most likely group to be sports participants.

> Normally, when we come home from school, we'll be doing golfing, and straight after that we'll have a football tournament or something, football matches. . . We have training on Tuesdays, Thursdays and Sundays . . .
> (SCM 14)

Young women in all age groups are considerably less involved than young men (Hendry *et al.*, 2002; Mason, 1995). Future leisure participation patterns may, however, reveal fewer gender biases, and this is already emerging in countries where social equality between the sexes is more evident, such as Scandinavia (e.g., Wold & Hendry, 1998).

By what young people tell us themselves, it would seem that overall, in early adolescence many of them are not too dissatisfied with what is available for their leisure activities because the challenges they are offered in terms of activity skills, interactions with adult coaches and communication with peers in a secure environment more or less match their available psychosocial resources. But, with the onset of puberty, and as they move toward mid-adolescence, things seem to change.

As young people grow toward the mid-teens they become more critical, questioning and skeptical of adult-led organizations. They recognize that power and decision making in youth organizations lies with adults, though the adult leaders claim that they involve young people in decision making and offer truly collaborative participation (e.g., Love & Hendry, 1994). Furthermore, young people at this point feel more confident in communicating with peers in the organized and supervised setting of a leisure-time club.

When asked by Mahoney (1997) and by Hendry *et al.* (1993) the most important reason for dropping out, young people cited 'lack of interest' as the most important reason, together with the fact that other social activities had assumed more importance in their lives. This idea of conflicting social interests is mirrored in the comments of young people themselves. So what do mid-adolescents have to say about organized leisure, alternative leisure options, and their peer relationships? Now that they are more secure in their social skills, and would like to try them out in the peer group, an apparent rejection of adult organizations takes place, with social learning in the company of peers, 'hanging around' in the street, shopping malls or in the park, or at 'sleep-over' parties. In all cases, adults are not present except perhaps as peripheral, background figures.

> Well, just because I used to be quite athletic like I did a lot of running and stuff. I suppose it was when I started going out a lot I stopped.
> (SCM 17)

We found that views about youth clubs were particularly critical and negative, as the following quotations show:

> Youth club: Yeah there is but it's rubbish. They don't do anything. I used to go to it, it's all the popular ones and they're all in it and they just sit there and speak and it's just boring. You can play snooker but the boys always get there before you. There's a bit upstairs but you are not allowed to go up there anymore because they wrecked the joint. So it's just not worth it.
> (SWF 14)

> To be there is like being at home, constantly supervised by parents.
> (SCF 16)

Casual leisure

Having dropped out of organized leisure options, teenagers attempt to move into what they see as adult leisure settings, but they are seldom allowed to participate. Legal and practical restrictions such as pub and club laws, parental demands, prohibitive entry fees and the police all prevent young people from taking part in most aspects of adult leisure. Among the causes given for young people's frustration are lack of accessible contexts and the social sanctions prohibiting their use of such settings. There even exists a competition for 'space' (such as the local park, or shopping arcades) between young people and adults, which leads to entry restrictions and curfews (Hendry et al., 2002). So, not quite voluntarily, young people move to the phase of 'casual leisure,' described in Hendry's leisure focal model.

During this phase, one of the most often stated complaints young people have is that there is 'absolutely nothing to do.' In a cross-cultural study of young rural people, we and our colleagues found that up to 60 percent of rural young people indicated that 'nothing to do' was a serious problem in the area where they live, young women being significantly more critical than young men (see Hendry et al., 2002). 'Leisure boredom' seems to be a very prominent feature of teenagers' perceptions of rural living (e.g., Bone et al., 1993, rural Queensland; Jones, 1992, rural Tasmania), though it emerges as an issue in urban areas too (Caldwell et al., 1992; Shaw et al., 1996, Canada):

> The one thing that is correct in the picture of society is the lack of something to do. I am not in the age yet to be worried about unemployment and hang around during the weeks, no it's weekends that are the problem. What should one do on free days, evenings, nights? One cannot go to sleep at eleven. ELEVEN on a Friday night! No, one has to go out, but where to?
>
> (SWF 16)

> We have to continue to walk up and down the road. This society is not made for those of us between 14 and 18, sad but true. One looks into the youth club, circles the village, and if one is lucky, one is picked up by a car. Bloody shit is all I can say. If you want to have fun, you have to drink till you drop. But that's not good neither.
>
> (SWF 15)

> I think about all these weekends that have been spent doing absolutely nothing. The only thing that can save me from fading away totally is sports . . . What is there to do? The weekends all have the same pattern. Go down to the youth club, talk some shit, go up and down the main road. Is it that what life is about? I understand exactly why more and more get drunk during weekends.
>
> (SWF 15)

Interestingly, this complaint did not necessarily correlate with the actual amount of time young people spent in pursuits nor with the number of different leisure activities young people were engaged in. Hendry et al. (2002) suggested that it might not be the quantity, but the quality, of the activities that create feelings of boredom. What is on offer is no longer a sufficient challenge:

> When I was younger, I always knew what to do, and I could always be with my younger siblings. But when I grew older, all my interests vanished, and nowadays, there is nothing to do.
>
> (SWF 14)

> If one looks for entertainment, one has to look for a long time. The only thing that catches my interest is the lure of fish . . . There is not a lot to do in winter, unless one is either snowboarding or horse-crazy of course. If anyone is like me, they have to sit at home and twiddle their thumbs. If it gets boring, one can change direction for a change! OK, I am exaggerating a bit, one can do a lot here if one has the right interests, whatever they might be.
>
> (SWM 14)

Shaw *et al.* (1996) concluded that frequent experiences of boredom were not simply a matter of too little to do, but were associated in a more complex way with a young person's relationship with the wider community. Naturally, young people want to have time on their own to experiment with new roles, want to be trusted to do things away from protective, controlling adults. This leads to a struggle with parents and teachers, who see unsupervised time as synonymous with unprotected time (e.g., Caldwell *et al.*, 1999; Hendry & Kloep, 2002).

> And there is a hotel-pub for those over 18. And a pizza-restaurant, there we can't even use the bathroom after 22.00 hours.
>
> (SWF 14)

> It is awful to be young, because one doesn't have any money and one can't get into places, just because there is nothing for young people . . .
>
> (SWF 14)

The hypothesis presented here is that young people in many cases are not challenged enough. Overprotected by parents, teachers, youth leaders and the law, they are not given enough opportunity to try out their skills or to generate their own challenges; consequently they seize every opportunity to do so—only to find out that they often do not have the capabilities or resources to create meaningful leisure for themselves. Some retreat into passivity and boredom, whereas others overestimate their skills and engage in 'risky' behaviors as soon as they can escape from adult protection. Belonging to a generation that grew up being organized and entertained by adults since early childhood, young people might lack the skills necessary for organizing and entertaining themselves. As a consequence of earlier poor training in self-management, young people admit that they cannot organize their own leisure time, when they search for alternatives to adult-led offers.

In the meantime, many provisional locations serve as settings for the leisure pursuits of younger teenagers, such as supermarkets, urban shopping malls, amusement arcades, street corners, parks, bus stops or fast-food restaurants

(Fisher, 1995; Giddens, 1991). Thus, young people are a common sight around many public places in the community. The possible effects of societal and cultural change in the last two decades may also impinge on patterns of leisure transition. It is possible to speculate, for instance, that involvement in casual leisure on the street corner has been replaced more and more by settings like cafés, pizzerias and fast-food restaurants as social meeting places.

Friends fill an obvious gap in providing guidelines for developing new social skills when organized leisure activities are abandoned. They provide young people with new sources of security in facing new challenges, such as romantic encounters [see chapter 8, original publication]. During mid-adolescence, dating, as an important leisure pursuit, begins to complement activities with friends, and romantic partners become a crucial source of social support at this time—and a source for acquiring new communication skills:

> In leisure time, when we are with friends, we most often talk about boys . . . That is among the best things to do. Or else we go to a disco . . . preferably a disco down town, where one has a real chance to meet guys who are nice and sweet, and who do not sit in a corner with the gang, discussing how ugly and sexy the girls are and what big tits they have . . .
>
> (SWF 15)

> But there are also peak moments in my life. The days I spend kissing and cuddling with my girl friend A. She is the best thing that's happened to me for a long time . . . and I have one of the world's nicest and sexiest birds.
>
> (SWM 15)

Unlike other aspects of social learning, young people receive very little help from family or school, and sometimes not even from peers, in the acquisition of romantic strategies and sexual techniques (e.g., Shucksmith & Hendry, 1998). As we ourselves have written (see Kloep & Hendry, 1999) such relational 'competencies' are seldom discussed, and only covered inappropriately in pornographic material accessed on the internet and in romanticized women's magazines, which offer a limited view of sexuality (Kaplan & Cole, 2003).

From their comments it becomes clear that both sexes in their teens start out with somewhat negative views of each other's romantic qualities:

> And all the boys of your age just sit in front of the TV and they're all boring and uninteresting. They're all sheep farmer's sons or football fanatics who don't care about girls. I think the ones you get on with are the ones that come up on holiday and stuff like that. They're nice. There are about 5 really nice good-looking ones but every single girl in the school is after them. It's a cat-fight who is going to get off with them at the next dance. And it turns out to be nobody. Because they are off with someone from the next village!
>
> (SCF 15)

100 *Young people talking*

> We played football and went to the dance. I pulled an ugly dog. I pulled a dog. I went to the dance and had a few drinks. I got off with her on the bus on the way home. I fell asleep on top of her and Tim stabbed me with a fag and Sally slapped me. I think that was what happened to me. I can't remember. Ugly girls. There's not that many tidy birds at all. There's only about 6 in the whole school, if that. Even if there are no good looking girls you still get off with them at dances . . .
>
> (SCM 15)

These quotes show how young heterosexual people hide their underlying anxieties and lack of romancing techniques behind a tough attitude and a 'sour grapes' reaction. Like other skills, the abilities needed to relate romantically to others have to be practiced. This is where the leisure sphere becomes highly significant and important. Many young people follow leisure activities not for the intrinsic value of the pursuits themselves but as contexts for making and meeting friends and beginning romantic attachments. Some commercial leisure venues are especially designed to enhance ambience, which enables romantic exploration (Alapack, 1991; 1999). However, any setting from pubs, clubs and cinema back rows to sports clubs, swimming pools and ski slopes will do:

> The best thing about snowboarding is that I can go with Jonas, Stefan and Andreas, who are the tastiest boys in school. . . .
>
> (SWF 14)

Commercial leisure

Once young people have learned some skills for relating to friends and romantic partners, and have reached an age when they are allowed to, they join the world of adult commercial leisure. Indeed, some teenagers simply and quickly skip casual activities and join commercial leisure contexts directly:

> I was friends with someone for a while and I think we went wandering around for one night and I got so bored. I thought 'No. It's so cold and rainy. It's cold'. And you see people sitting there all cold and wet but they still sit there. And you think why! It's the same, cruising round in cars. It's absolutely pointless. They go round the square, again and again. You might not be saying that when you've passed your test. Oh I hate it, I hate it. I think it is so boring. My sister does it and she goes round and round. It's all right a couple of times if you just want to see who is out and about, if you want to speak to someone. But there's folk that come onto the street 9 to 10 and they're still going round at 2 o'clock when the pubs close, and they've gone round and round. *We seem to have skipped the whole hanging around the streets bit and gone straight into pubs*. I just couldn't hang around.
>
> (SCF 17)

In the commercial leisure context, new challenges await them: communicating with adults, and being accepted and respected as adults themselves. Therein lies perhaps the main attraction of venues like pubs, restaurants and 'adult-only' activities: they are symbolic for showing the world that one has achieved the transition to adulthood. This leads to another function of leisure, its symbolic value to the world at large.[3]

Leisure as communication

Apart from being an opportunity to entertain oneself, to socialize with friends and to learn new skills, leisure pursuits are also aspects of self-image—expressing one's identity and lifestyle. By choosing certain activities, by wearing the 'right' gear and using the 'right' language, one can communicate to the world what kind of person one wants to be perceived as being. A mobile phone is not only a technology for interpersonal communication but it is also a fashion statement— its style, color, attached gadgets and price communicate quickly to the wider world what kind of person the owner is (or aspires to be). For that reason, many leisure activities are associated with a certain type of fashion, with distinctive behaviors and other symbols to mark the owner as a *skater*, a *surfer*, a *rebel*, a *fashion freak* or an *outsider*, to name but a few. We can all very quickly come up with our own stereotypic mental picture of a *punk*, a *goth*, a *soccer supporter* or a *lager lout*.

Further, when young people gather in public places, they invariably see other groups as somehow 'different' in style of dress and behavior, and, at times, perhaps threatening to give rise to 'trouble.' The attempt to establish and maintain a local 'identity' creates powerful rivalry among different adolescent crowds, and 'territory' is important to the creation of clear-cut—if varied—community 'identities.' Hendry, Kloep and Wood (2002) found that other groups were typically seen as either 'cool' or 'bad' or 'sad,' whereas friendship groups regarded themselves as 'normal' in their dress, interests and activities. This suggests that young people try to establish their identity through group belonging, thus compensating for the security lost when they left adult-led organizations. At the same time, this creates strong 'in-group/out-group' feelings and the creation of 'negative identities.'

> It's about the townies and the country boys. It's the ones from X and Y, and we don't want them. The boys from Z are supposed to be big and strong, and they always come and start fights, just because they're in the town. The boys from V normally get involved as well. It's a bit pointless, it just ends up happening.
>
> (SCM 15)

> There's an adventure playground in the park and everyone used to go there when it opened but it's all 18-year-olds and all that and they've graffitied all over it and all that and they just go and drink and smoke and all that. That's where they sit and all that, they don't let anybody else on it. The police are

always doon ['down'] there and all that. It's not safe to go down there at night in case like they attack you or anything. They just sit on the swings and drink and all that. If you just look, glance at them they'll do you!

(SCM 15)

The choice of leisure activity, and its accompanying symbols, is not only a signal to other peers about what kind of person one is. It is also a signal that the young person is ceasing to be a child and wants to be accepted in the adult world. This means abandoning 'childish' activities and distancing oneself from the past:

I used to be a Brownie but I'm not in anything now. I played the clarinet until a little while ago but I got sick of it.

(SCF 17)

In some cases, rebelling against adult-initiated leisure activities makes this point:

And the other half of my life is concentrated around slalom. Dad thinks it is really cool, but I don't. I have told him that I want to quit next year, but he seems not to understand. But next year I will quit forever . . .

(SWF 15)

In their narratives, young people point out, that they now see through adult manipulation and vicarious achievement motivation, and distance themselves from it:

I learned a lot during these years. Amongst other things, that it is not always the children who compete. I saw many parents who were more engaged than their children. These are those who were not successful themselves in any sports, and who want success through their children.

(SWF 16)

The void that is created by rejecting adult-led organized leisure creates certain problems for young people, who may lack the skills and the opportunities to organize their own leisure. Yet, this situation also provides them with an opportunity to communicate their resentment against being excluded from adult leisure venues, and puts responsibility for this situation onto adult society: 'Nothing to do' in leisure as an expression of rebellion:

A 'little' mistake that I cannot accept is that 99 percent of the youth fund's money goes to that fucking youth sport . . . OK, there is one percent left. That percentage goes in its totality to our YoUTh cLUb, which is as weird as I spell it. I am there myself now and then. That youth club has the motto: 'If you want to have fun, do it yourself'. That is nice, ok, if there were anything there to have fun with . . .

(SWM 15)

In this context, young people like to put the blame for their own risk-taking on adults, because they do not provide them with appropriate leisure activities (seldom stating what exactly these activities could be):

> I think that you adults and other persons should fix something for us youngsters to do at weekends. That would be better than us 'hanging around' in the streets and drinking ourselves 'senseless' and poisoned by alcohol as many of us do . . . But the community doesn't care a fig and invests in a lot of useless things.
>
> (SWF 14)

In later adolescence most of the social skills learned to date are carried out for their acceptance by grown-ups. Older adolescents want to try out adult behaviors, often within the commercial leisure sphere, as a way of testing whether they can be accepted as a 'real' adult, knowing only too well that adults would regard them as too young to do these things, and would prevent them if they could (e.g., the challenge of getting into a pub and to be served an alcoholic drink rather than to enjoy the actual drinking of it). In this way, young people observe, rehearse, and perform the skills and behaviors they perceive to be necessary for adult status. The need to feel both independent and secure may be the vital reason why older adolescents move toward commercial leisure provision. Because they suffer fewer legal and social restrictions, they can initiate their own developmental challenges. The factors leading young people toward an involvement in commercial leisure (pubs, clubs, discos, commercial squash or health clubs, window shopping, and even foreign travel) have to do with the desire to be seen as having an independent adult-like leisure role.

Hence, in the light of media advertising in Western societies, which are typically more affluent, the desire to access commercial contexts—in the company of peers—may have accelerated down the age-scale. Even in pre-adolescence, so-called 'tweenagers' want to be like teenagers, copy their behavior and attempt to be regarded as older than they actually are, with all the attendant social and psychological risks that may present themselves, and because older adolescents as 'emerging adults' want to protect their social domain, they don't want to be associated with younger teenagers. So they 'police the boundaries' in certain ways to make sure of exclusion from their territory by keeping the 'kids' out:

> Like discos. We'd love discos just for us, without like the druggies or the cruisers. Just like for us. But that's the problem . . . there is not a lot of folk like us here. There's a lot that's younger, but we don't want them.
>
> (SCMs 15/16)

For example, Sharp and Lowe (1989) have suggested that young people's drinking is a part of the socialization process from child to adult and a symbolic practice related to their seeking social acceptance in adult society. Thus it is important to be sensitive to the subtext in what young people are trying to tell us about their drinking. In rural areas in Scotland, Sweden and Norway, for example, we found that young people reported that one of their main reasons for drinking was to be seen to be 'adult' and to be accepted into adult venues (Kloep et al., 2001). Hence, there is supporting evidence for the finding that, among other reasons for drinking and smoking, it is the wish to gain adult status as soon as possible, at least symbolically, which leads many youngsters toward drink (e.g., Pavis et al., 1997).

This desire for acceptance into adult society seems to lie behind much of young people's behavior that adults disapprove of, not fully realizing that it is actually imitative behavior, and, as young people perceive it, a wish to be socialized 'conventionally.' These are some of the symbols of adult society, well advertised through the mass media, which attract many young people to a process of emulating their older, adult role models and in meeting the challenge of the transitions to adult status.

Furthermore, even apparently risky activities such as underage drinking may contain elements of challenge, offering the potential of growth. Pape and Hammer (1996), for instance, suggest that young male abstainers, and men who were latecomers to drinking, show indications of a delayed entry into adult roles, and a reluctance to adopt adult role-behaviors. Thus, according to the authors, perhaps getting involved in drinking for the first time in mid-adolescence can be an ingredient within the normal developmental process of young people in Western societies.

Some concluding comments: Linking theoretical frameworks

In this chapter we have seen how important communication is to relationships throughout adolescence. Furthermore, we have argued that leisure activities and communication are intimately intertwined in the lives of young people as they progress through various relational transitions across adolescence. From the analyses of our qualitative data—from the ideas teenagers have given us—we have suggested three interrelated strands between leisure and communication.

Communication as leisure. Communicating can be a vital part of leisure time—just talking, relating, and being with each other are important relational aspects of leisure time. Yet, after a while, for a relationship to be sustained and strengthened, it needs the participants' engagement in activities that can be talked about, planned, participated in and reminisced about, together. Thus, communication and leisure become two sides of the same coin. Young people have told us how important these leisure times of apparently casual conversation are, when aspirations are shared, outings discussed, problems tackled, social skills and fashion styles rehearsed, sports events or tactics tried out, romantic strategies planned and so on.

Leisure for communication. This leads us to a second association between 'talkin', doin' and bein' with friends.' In leisure time and in leisure settings there are opportunities to actually acquire communication skills, negotiate social roles, and learn about rules, rule violation, time management, teamwork, leadership, conflict resolution and other interpersonal competencies. This is not unique to adolescence; for example, on becoming an adult, one has to learn new, additional communication skills—intergenerational communication with younger and older people at home, at work and in leisure, and interethnic communication in a multicultural society. However, adolescence is an important phase of the lifespan in which to begin learning and rehearsing these skills and competencies. The young people we have interviewed indicate that such an array of cultural and other communication abilities enable them to reflect on their identity development, acquire the ability to both 'fit in' with the crowd and yet retain a sense of self. Overall, they perceive such social and communicative 'navigations' as necessary to their mental health (e.g., Hendry & Reid, 2000).

Leisure as communication. Thirdly, we have outlined leisure as symbolic communication in social settings in which young persons can 'use' their appearance, hairstyle, makeup, clothes, language and fashion style to display a social identity, a sub-cultural allegiance or individualism. This can include identifying with a particular fashion style, 'being a sports fan,' demonstrating group membership of a local crowd such as being a 'goth' or a 'punk' and declaring 'separateness' from other groups (see Hendry, Kloep & Wood, 2002; Thurlow, 2001). Additionally, Maffesoli (1996) has stated that both adults and young people can 'dip into,' or sample, a range of varied groupings which meet regularly, even weekly, but all can possess different values and behaviors. Thus, contemporary (Western) society encourages individuals to display multiple identities and varied, if transient, allegiances to different social groups, which may cut across age, gender, class and ethnic boundaries [also see chapter 1, original publication]. For instance, we can imagine the varying 'identity displays' of dress and behaviors that a company director may provide at a formal dinner, at the tennis club, and with their partner on a casual outing to the pub: at all times the intention is to communicate to the world (and to the people with whom one is interacting) what leisure mode and context and what mood one is in. Thus, we should not be too surprised that teenagers use these symbolic and communicative identity displays of different kinds on different occasions as a means of trying out different identities. This phase Erikson (1968) described as being a psychosocial 'moratorium' in which the young person is given the opportunity by adult society to experiment with and rehearse social roles, develop a clear-cut identity and delay major life decisions.

These three leisure-communication styles we have described in this chapter are enacted in concert with the *focal* shifts in relationships (Coleman, 1978) and leisure types (Hendry *et al.*, 1996) apparent in young people's transitions to adulthood. We believe also that these focal transitions can be explained by what we have called a *Lifespan Model of Developmental Challenge* (Hendry & Kloep, 2002), which looks at developmental shifts from a challenge/risk perspective whereby people search for a balance between security, boredom and stagnation on the one hand, and challenge, anxiety and development on the other. Translated into the world of leisure, this means that young people try to find challenges in leisure contexts that match or just slightly exceed their leisure and communication skills. They choose leisure contexts that provide a 'goodness of fit' with their increasing communication resources and abandon those that do not offer any new challenges. They also choose friends and communication partners appropriate to their leisure interests. With increasing capabilities and experiences in communication and in the leisure 'sphere,' the nature of relationships and leisure interests will shift, as the leisure focal theory indicates: early adolescents engage in adult-led organized activities which provide them with developing 'status' skills and enough security to begin to try out the new skills of relating to peers. Once young people feel secure in mastering these relational skills, organized adult-dominated activities may become boring and adult-dominated from their perspective. Since peers now reaffirm identities, it is more challenging to 'try out' certain social roles and new skills informally in the peer group. Finally, these social skills are tested out for their acceptance in the adult world.

What the developmental challenges of adolescence are, and what resources are available to young people, of course, varies greatly with social class, gender/ sexuality, ethnicity, nationality and so on. For instance, in the poorer countries young people face a completely different set of challenges and risks, and have to draw on different resources. Nevertheless, the mechanism of development—the interaction of challenges, resources and risks—are the same whatever the cultural context. Acquiring social skills in various contexts is a formidable developmental task, which may have to exist hand-in-hand with other cultural challenges such as exams or finding employment. We should not be surprised that some young people need help in acquiring such skills to progress successfully across the teenage years. In talking with young people, it seems that, consistent with our Lifespan Model of Developmental Challenge, they consider their leisure time in early adolescence to be a rich source of development and challenge. However, as they move into mid-adolescence young people often report that they are less satisfied with what is 'on offer.' There are insufficient challenges to test out their newly developing skills, and some young people slide into passivity and boredom. Others overreact and resort to risky acts and situations, where challenges exceed young people's resources, and into settings in which they take chances, do not reflect on goals and consequences, and do not assess risks effectively (see Parker et al., 1998).

Leisure can act as a regulatory device in times of too many or too few challenges: if there are too few challenges in the young person's life, then leisure can be a 'life sphere' for the opportunity to face more challenges; and if there are too many tasks to meet in the young person's life, then leisure challenges can be reduced. Hence, leisure is a life sector for seeking out challenges and learning opportunities in times of little challenge from other sources—it is a self-administered antidote for boredom, and a context for fulfilling developmental tasks. It is important therefore for young people to acquire the ability to assess accurately the 'goodness of fit' between their resources and developmental leisure tasks, which varies not only between individuals, but also, depending on context, within the same individual. The array of interactive psychosocial factors involved suggests the importance of examining processes and mechanisms, as Rutter (1996) and we ourselves (Kloep & Hendry, 1999) among others have proposed. It is necessary for researchers to try to find out more about these interactive mechanisms in order to understand variations in leisure patterns and what they actually 'mean' for young people in acquiring the social and communicative skills for growing up in a rapidly changing and highly technological society. Such studies demand that the young person's perspective and the adolescent voice need to be given much more significance in future research.

Note

In quoting our young participants' voices here, we have indicated a little biographical information in terms of nationality (SC = Scottish, SW = Swedish), sex (M = Male, F = Female) and age.

References

Alapack, R. J. (1991). Adolescent first kiss. *The Humanistic Psychologist*, 19(1), 48–67.
Alapack, R. J. (1999). Jealousy in first love: Unwitting disclosure. In A. C. Richards & T. Schumrum (eds), *Invitations to Dialogue: The Legacy of Sidney M. Jourard* (pp. 91–106). New York: Kendall/Hunt.
Arnett, J. J., Larson, R. & Offer, D. (1995). Beyond effects: Adolescents as active media users. *Journal of Youth and Adolescence*, 25(5), 511–518.
Beentjes, H. J., d'Haenens, W. J., van der Voort, T. H. A. & Koolstra, C. M. (1999). Dutch and Flemish children and adolescents as users of interactive media. *Communications*, 24, 145–166.
Bone, R., Cheers, B. & Hil, R. (1993). Paradise lost—young people's experience of rural life in the Whitsunday Shire. *Rural Society*, 3, 1–7.
Caldwell, L. L., Darling, N., Payne, L. L. & Dowdy, B. (1999). 'Why are you bored?' An examination of psychological and social control causes of boredom among adolescents. *Journal of Leisure Research*, 31, 103–121.
Caldwell, L. L., Smith, E. A. & Weissinger, E. (1992). The relationship of leisure activities and perceived health of college students. *Leisure and Society*, 15, 545–556.
Coleman, J. C. (1978). Current contradictions in adolescent theory. *Journal of Youth and Adolescence*, 7, 1–11.
Csikszentmihalyi, M. & Larson, R. (1984). *Being Adolescent: Conflict and Growth in the Teenage Years*. New York: Basic Books.
D'Amours, L. & Robitaille, P-A. (2002). 99% of Quebec teens use the internet! *CE-FRIO*, Available (29 November 2004) online at: <http.//www.cefrio.qc.ca/English/Communiques/commun_6.cfm>
Erikson, E. H. (1968). *Identity: Youth and Crisis*, London: Faber and Faber.
Fisher, S. (1995). The amusement arcade as a social space for adolescents. *Journal of Adolescence*, 18, 71–80.
Flammer, A., Alsaker, F. D. & Noack, P. (1999). Time use by adolescents in an international perspective. I: The case of leisure activities. In F. D. Alsaker & A. Flammer (eds), *The Adolescent Experience. European and American Adolescents in the 1990s* (pp. 33–60). Mahwah: Lawrence Erlbaum.
Giddens, A. (1991). *Modernity and Self identity: Self and Society in the Late Modern Age*. Oxford: Polity.

Goossens, L. & Marcoen, A. (1999). Relationships during adolescence: Constructive versus negative themes and relational dissatisfaction. *Journal of Adolescence*, 22, 49–64.

Hendry, L. B., Glendinning, A., Reid, M. & Wood, S. (1998). *Lifestyles, health and health concerns of rural youth: 1996–1998*. Edinburgh: Report to Department of Health, Scottish Office.

Hendry, L. B., Glendinning, A. & Shucksmith, J. (1996). Adolescent focal theories: age trends in developmental transitions. *Journal of Adolescence*, 19, 307–320.

Hendry, L. B. & Kloep, M. (2002). *Life-span Development: Resources, Challenges and Risks*. London: Thomson Learning.

Hendry, L. B., Kloep, M., Glendinning, A., Ingebrigtsen, J. E., Espnes, G. A. & Wood, S. (2002). Leisure transitions: A rural perspective. *Journal of Leisure Studies*, 21, 1–14.

Hendry, L. B., Kloep, M. & Wood, S. (2002). Young people talking about adolescent rural crowds and social settings. *Journal of Youth Studies*, 5, 357–374.

Hendry, L. B. & Reid, M. (2000). Social relationships and health: The meaning of social 'connectedness' and how it relates to health concerns for rural Scottish adolescents. *Journal of Adolescence*, 23(6), 705–719.

Hendry, L. B., Shucksmith, J. S., Love, J. & Glendinning, A. (1993). *Young People's Leisure and Lifestyles*. London: Routledge.

Jones, G. W. (1992). Rural girls and cars: The phenomena of 'blockies'. *Rural Society*, 2, 4–7.

Kaplan, E. B. & Cole, L. (2003). 'I want to read stuff on boys': White, Latina and black girls reading *Seventeen* magazine and encountering adolescence. *Adolescence*, 38, 141–154.

Kloep, M. (1999). Love is all you need? Focusing on adolescents' life concerns from an ecological point of view. *Journal of Adolescence*, 22, 49–63.

Kloep, M. & Hendry, L. (1999). Challenges, risks and coping. In D. Messer and S. Millar (eds), *Exploring Developmental Psychology* (pp. 400–416). London: Arnold.

Kloep, M. (1998). *Att vara ung i Jämtland: Tonåringar berättar om sitt liv*. Österåsen: Uddeholt.

Kloep, M., Hendry, L. B., Glendinning, A., Ingebrigtsen, J. E. & Espnes, G. A. (2003). Peripheral visions? A cross cultural study of rural youth's views on migration. *Children's Geographies*, 1, 105–123.

Kloep, M., Hendry, L. B., Ingebrigtsen, J. E., Glendinning, A. & Espnes, G. A. (2001). Young people in 'drinking societies': Norwegian, Scottish and Swedish adolescents' perceptions of alcohol use. *Health Education Research*, 16(3), 279–291.

Kremer, J., Trew, K. & Ogle, S. (1997). *Young Peoples' Involvement in Sport*. London: Routledge.

Kroger, J. (1985). Relationships during adolescence: A cross-national comparison of New Zealand and United States teenagers. *Journal of Youth and Adolescence*, 8, 47–56.

Love, J. & Hendry, L. B. (1994). Youth workers and youth participants: Two perspectives of youth work? *Youth and Policy*, 46, 43–55.

Maffesoli, M. (1996). *The Time of the Tribes*. London: Sage.

Mahoney, A. M. (1997). Age and sport participation. In J. Kremer, K. Trew & S. Ogle (eds). *Young People's Involvement in Sport* (pp. 98–113). London: Routledge.

Mason, V. (1995). *Young People and Sport in England, 1994*. London: The Sports Council.

Mesch, G. S. (2001). Social relationships and internet use among adolescents in Israel. *Social Science Quarterly*, 82(2), 329.

Miles, S. (2000). *Youth Lifestyles in a Changing World*. Buckingham: Open University Press.
Pape, H. & Hammer, T. (1996). Sober adolescence—Predictor of psychosocial maladjustment in young adulthood? *Scandinavian Journal of Psychology*, 37(4), 362–377.
Parker, H., Aldridge, J. & Measham, F. (1998). *Illegal Leisure*. London: Routledge.
Pavis, S., Cunningham-Burley, S. & Amos, A. (1997). Alcohol consumption and young people. *Health Education Research*, 12, 311–322.
Rutter, M. (1996). Psychological adversity: Risk, resilience and recovery. In L. Verhofstadt-Deneve, I. Kienhorst & C. Braet (eds), *Conflict and Development in Adolescence* (pp. 21–34). Leiden: DSWO Press.
Sharp, D. & Lowe, G (1989). Adolescents and alcohol—a review of the recent British research. *Journal of Adolescence*, 12, 295–307.
Shaw, S. M., Caldwell, L. L. & Kleiber, D. A. (1996). Boredom, stress and social control in the daily activities of adolescents. *Journal of Leisure Research*, 28, 274–292.
Shucksmith, J. & Hendry, L. B. (1998). *Health Issues and Young People*. London: Routledge.
Thurlow, C. (2001). The usual suspects? A comparative investigation of crowds and social-type labelling among young British teenagers. *Journal of Youth Studies*, 4(3), 319–334.
Wolak, J., Mitchell, K. J. & Finkelhor, D. (2002). Close online relationships in a national sample of adolescents. *Adolescence*, 37, 441–456.
Wold, B. & Hendry, L. B. (1998). Social and environmental factors associated with physical activities in youth. In S. Biddle, J. Sallis & N. Cavill (eds), *Young People and Physical Activity* (pp. 119–132). London: Health Education Authority.

7   Adolescents speaking out about health

The book this extract is taken from has a cover picture of a young person injecting with a syringe though the book is actually about adolescents' positive views on health – A fine example of adult society's demonising images of adolescence!

Furthermore, most research and policy agendas relating to young people's health are dominated by 'adultist' concerns despite the fact that many adolescent issues are influenced by wider societal and global factors. Differently, this book, based on qualitative research, set adult agendas aside and explored young people's own views about their health, health behaviours and lifestyles. In this extract we sum up what young people have told us and present a general analysis of findings as a series of themes together with some interpreted approaches for enabling and empowering young people, rather than misrepresenting them.

CONCLUSIONS
'I'm not going to do anything stupid!'

J.S. Shucksmith and L.B. Hendry

Introduction

In this final chapter [of the original publication] we want to review what young people have told us, by outlining a number of broad themes which emerged from our discussions with mid-adolescents and by considering and interpreting those themes a little more deeply. We conclude the chapter and the book by reviewing why it is critical for young people to be given a voice and why this poses challenges for many who work with young people on a range of issues including health. Can we listen to young people and believe them when they tell us that they won't do anything stupid . . .?

Young people's perceptions of their health needs

First, and most obviously, health is not seen by young people as a major life concern in the same way as adults perceive their health status. Adults' personal concerns relate to feelings of general well-being and the maintenance of good health and are influenced by various sociocultural influences across the life course (Backett and Davison, 1992). Young people's concerns tend to be short-term and to relate to the 'here-and-now'. Therefore young people's perceptions are centred, for example, on their personal and physical appearance, diet and the maintenance of a slim physique, decisions around drinking, smoking and drug use. When we look at issues with regard to sexual relationships and practices and risk-taking, these also figured significantly in young people's discussions with us.

Many of these perceived concerns of mid-adolescence are apparently reflections of wider cultural images. Desirable stereotypes and ideal body types produced in the mass media and the fashion and film scenes are filtered through magazines via glamour and/or pop culture role models, and these impinge on young people. These concerns are reinforced by peer pressures around pop and fashion subcultures. The impact of this on young people, despite their general current good state of health, results in 'distorted' views of their physique and appearance and also produces unrealistic ideas about the function of diet and exercise in relation to health, fitness and good appearance. Crash diets and sudden bouts of exercising are the manifestations of their attempts to approximate to these desirable cultural images. Hence there may be some value in considering health behaviours within a broader view of lifestyle development. Young people are either not knowledgeable about good diet and exercise practices or else wil-fully ignore them. Cultural images set the scene for poor dieting and exercise behaviours. The possible danger here, expressed in recent media stories, is that such practices may be linked to hunger suppression by the use of drugs, bouts of high activity levels in dancing and at raves, or 'binge' syndromes linked to anorexia or bulimia. Health educators too, in confusing leanness with fitness or wellness, are perhaps guilty of perpetuating these broad influences on young people's attitude to eating.

Community factors

The strong association between different styles of leisure pursuits and young people's health practices was notable in a number of the contexts in which this study was carried out. In some urban settings, the freedom given to young people to wander in a variety of built environments and contexts creates settings allowing experimentation with various types of unhealthy practices without parental checks and balances being readily available. In suburban and rural areas leisure activities were more carefully monitored by parents, with young people 'steered' more towards adult-run clubs and organisations or being driven by parents to sports and community facilities. Such freedom on the one hand, and constraining factors on the other, creates considerable difference in the lifestyle patterns, in attitudes to health and in health practices of different types of young people.

The patterns of community based leisure pursuits mentioned to us by young people reflected embedded social class values and the different transitional pathways for those mid-adolescents who intended to progress to higher education or who attempted to join early the 'world of work', and projected a life-view of early marriage and family responsibilities. Thus, for the latter (mainly urban working-class) group, early relational and sexual encounters were seen as necessary preliminaries to being able to merge into the local sub-cultural scene as an adult. Equally, their involvement with smoking and drinking was consistent with the values and norms of the adult communities in which they were growing up.

Parental influences

With regard to parental influences on health, these were perceived to be multi-faceted in that parents could be perceived as positive role models, that is, young people were impressed by parental health practices and copied these and integrated them into their own developing lifestyles. Alternatively, parents could be perceived as negative role models, that is, young people were repelled by parental behaviours and quite deliberately chose alternative behaviour patterns. Finally, parents were often perceived by young people as selective advice givers, that is, parental views on major health issues were not necessarily seen as particular issues for the adolescent.

These patterns of parental influence on health behaviours are further complicated by the fact that parental advice on health is both gendered and structured by social class. Put crudely, and generally, middle-class parents seem to use affection as an emotional bait, giving clear indications that certain behaviours were not approved of. Further, they encouraged deferred gratification in health behaviours, reflecting embedded social class values. Working-class parents on the other hand appeared often to veto young people's actions and behaviour by fairly aggressive and confrontational strategies. Their attempts at harm minimisation were conducted by focusing on key aspects of their own perceived major health risks.

On the other hand, the approach of working-class parents might be seen as being more *realistic* in enabling socialisation into the accepted adult cultural practices of such communities by teaching young people *over time* to acquire the necessary social skills in drinking and smoking 'sensibly'.

Peers and friends

Coleman and Hendry (1990) have stressed the important need in mid-adolescence for peer acceptance, and comments about peer pressure were particularly noticeable in young people's attitudes and behaviours as expressed to us. But 'peer pressure' was also used to explain inappropriate, unhealthy activities. So in a sense the wider peer network within which young people spend their day-to-day existence can act as a 'health hazard' in creating unfavourable norms by both providing incorrect, or indeed false information and by producing inaccurate expectations about behaviour at this particular stage of adolescence. However, it was clear from their comments that many young people do go through an experimental stage, perhaps in response to peer expectations and pressure, which passes as they mature and become more confident in their independence and self-agency. Such expectations and pressures can create a period of uncertainty and 'risk' for young people, before they develop the social skills, self-knowledge and self-competence to withstand (to some extent) group norms, to pass through group 'initiation' stages, to find an accepted place in the peer network, and to develop a realistic knowledge about the behaviours and claims of others.

By contrast closer friendship groups appeared to develop by choice and by preference of characteristics and collaborative activities, and in a sense allowed the young person a reaffirmation of chosen identity in mid-adolescence. They further enabled young people to perceive, understand and accept the values of their chosen groupings. This in turn allowed them to be fairly critical, and even scathing, of the fashion styles, health behaviours, and general social conduct of other groups. Here was clear evidence in 'in-group'/'out-group' perceptions which further strengthened and affirmed lifestyle and identity choices. Social reinforcement around a clustering of behaviours and attitudes allowed greater cohesion and selection of friends by preference and by commonalties of hobby interests, dress, leisure interests, attitudes to school, pop music, allegiances, and so on.

Gender and friendships

With regard to friendship, boys and girls in mid-adolescence relate to their companions within group settings in different ways. Girls appear to 'use' friends to develop social skills, rehearse social encounters, share feelings and give advice about social strategies and problems, whereas boys used the group for the sharing of experiences and activities, and to gain social status and reputation. For boys, little is exchanged among group members in terms of information or the sharing of feelings. Rather there is a great deal of exaggerated boasting, particularly in relation to sex, in order to gain group status and a position in the hierarchy. Indeed, our interviews showed that boys would not discuss intimate issues with other boys, but very often would go to discuss their more serious personal concerns with girls with whom they were friendly. With their friends girls show more tolerance to other groups and to other viewpoints than their own in relation to behaviour and health. Boys are fairly intolerant, and need, in a sense, to use this prejudice to prove their conformity and 'traditional' macho conventionality. This became abundantly clear in their attitudes towards homosexuality where in the main they were extremely homophobic.

Information on health matters

Since the sharing of information and feelings differed between friendship groups according to gender, another aspect of our interviewing showed that sources of information differed between the sexes. Girls were much more likely to gain accurate information from a vast array of teenage girls' and women's magazines. Boys tended to rely on pornography and on a 'word of mouth' peer system which on occasions led to an absorption of inaccurate information and the development of sexist stereotypes. The dangers inherent in such exchanges of misinformation are that exaggerated boasting and similar social 'messages' are used as strategies for gaining social status and 'saving face' amongst young men. These exchanges are also often accompanied by externalised aggressive behaviour, which can be a successful short-term strategy in peer group exchanges and it is thus reinforced, thereby encouraging similar strategies to be adopted in future social encounters. A 'double standard' social norm emerges in the sense that 'boasting' girls are seen by peers to violate norms of sexuality and gender. Misinformation often begins from the use of basic sexist stereotypes emerging from pornographic magazines, books and videos which boys often access in the absence of other more reliable local sources of information.

Both genders, however, were united in their views about schools as sources of information in health matters. School materials and the health curriculum and the ways that teachers presented health topics were considered to be inappropriate to their needs. A number of changes in the status of the subject and its presentation would seem to be a very necessary consideration for the future. Young people wanted more up-to-date information, more up-to-date videos and teaching materials and the opportunity to discuss realistically and relevantly the matters that concern them, rather than being given 'information' in a way which does not allow them to discuss in any great detail intimate matters. Schools are important given that they are the only social institution (beyond the family) that almost all young people pass through on their way to adulthood, but it seems to us that it is necessary to carry out a re-examination of the aims, objectives, procedures, processes and professional servicing of school-based health education. In this more attention should be given to young people's views – their need for discussion; their wishes regarding single-sex groupings; and their demands for accurate non-judgemental information, to be allowed to reach their own conclusions on issues, and to learn knowledge and skills appropriate and relevant to their day-to-day lives. The teachers' role in this process also begs consideration, with perhaps a greater need being expressed for teaching–learning collaborations to involve teachers, parents and pupils working together with a range of health and medical professionals from the local community.

Risks and challenges

When we examine the relationship between the influence of the peer group and self-agency of the young, we come to consider a number of aspects related to decision-making in the health sphere. As we mentioned earlier, experimentation in various domains is characteristic of mid-adolescence but what emerges in terms of self-agency is the idea of 'rites of passage'. Young people seem by and large to learn from what on the surface may appear to be an unhappy or negative experience. In resolving not to repeat such an experience in the same manner, they nevertheless gain a reputation within the peer group for having undertaken the actual process of resolving a crisis. Rutter and Smith (1995) have talked about such experiences as 'steeling' activities which enable resilience and the development of coping mechanisms for future use to develop in adolescence. This ability to make choices for the self despite possible peer group pressures reflects both the learning of positive social skills from possibly negative experiences and the development of maturity and independence in decision-making and behaviour. For instance, young people's views on sex and marriage showed an understanding that these relationships require a maturity of outlook, sound judgement, and time for relationships to mature. However, middle-class young people were more likely in general to perceive the values of deferring gratification within relationships, whereas working-class adolescents were generally more likely to report that they perceived sexual encounters as fairly inevitable and unromantic fumbling experiences that possibly led to early pregnancy and marriage. Nevertheless, it must be stated that an aspiration towards early marriage was not expressed by *any* of the mid-adolescent girls we talked with.

A number of issues seem relevant here. First, experimentation is an important process in gaining independence and responsibility for self-action. It is a step on the way to becoming more mature and adult-like and in learning to make choices and come to decisions. Second, as Coleman and Hendry (1990) have outlined, adults often give adolescents conflicting messages, different sets of expectations about both mature independence and childlike obedience in their behaviour. Hence young people struggle to gain independence and self-agency in a society riddled with many inconsistencies, few social 'signposts' to maturity, and major anomalies regarding rights and citizenship status (Jones and Wallace, 1992).

Thus, third, with regard to risk and risky health behaviours, adults can become very concerned – and over-anxious – on behalf of their adolescent offspring when 'catastrophes' occur. However, as Gore and Eckenrode (1994) stated, no issue is just one event! For example, a divorce can alter family relationships, change material circumstances, introduce 'strangers' into the family circle, create withdrawal and depression in one child, give another freedom from tensions and conflict and provide yet another with opportunities and challenges to become the new 'bread-winner'. Gore and Eckenrode suggest, therefore, that any event in a young person's life can be a challenge or a near immovable obstacle to further psycho-social development. The important elements of success or failure, according to Gore and Eckenrode are: the young person's competencies in perception, planning, decision-making, learning capacities and interpersonal skills that can be brought to bear on the issue, together with the prioritisation of key aspects of the tasks involved, and the appearance or absence of other concurrently stressful events. Their analysis of risk contexts and processes of skills and resilience development are useful extensions of Coleman's (1979) original focal theory of coping behaviours and 'overlap' of psycho-social difficulties in adolescence.

Lifestyles and health

The Young People's Leisure and Lifestyle Project (Hendry *et al.*, 1993b) showed various adolescent life trajectories which were fairly firmly embedded within social class boundaries. It was suggested, therefore, that in general terms, by mid-adolescence health behaviours and health concerns are essential component parts of a more holistic pattern of social class based lifestyles. In terms of Bronfenbrenner's ideas (1979) about individual development within socio-cultural settings, this would be where wider cultural norms filter down via community expectations and sub-cultural values to be translated into lifestyle developments by the individual's social behaviour and social learning in a variety of local contexts and social institutions. In turn, these lead to decision-making choices as various life events occur.

An alien race?

In a recent paper given at a conference on urban childhood Ulvik (1997) quotes the words of a Swedish folk singer, Olle Adolfson, from his song 'The Mysterious People':

> Children are a people, and they live in a distant land.

In this depiction children are perceived as a strange tribe, hardly understandable to adults. It highlights a view that has gained currency, namely that it is pointless to assume simply that children are little adults. It has become accepted that children's perceptions, attitudes and patterns of reasoning are often distinct and very different. Sometimes the realisation of the very different ways in which young people construe and make sense of their lives has encouraged adults to identify children as a race apart, creatures from a parallel planet. There have been many good accounts in recent years of the ways in which we construct and reconstruct childhood (James and Prout, 1990). The cultural images which we use to describe children and childhood are important, as they give direction and shape to the attempts which we make to understand children's and young people's worlds. The changing cultural images of the child constitute what Wertsch (1991) has called 'cultural tools' shaping how children are seen by adults as well as by themselves.

It is clear that until very recently the way in which children were viewed by adults emphasised their powerlessness, their weakness, dependency and incompetence. Franklin (1995: 9) comments:

> Definitions of a 'child' and 'childhood' entail more than a specification of an age of majority; they articulate society's values and attitudes towards children. They are typically disdaining and ageist.

The most popular recent discourses around childhood and youth would seem to move us towards a different conception of young people. Academics, policy makers and practitioners have all seemed keen to participate (in theory at least) in a new formulation which concerns the necessity to implement children's rights and to see each child as an individual, and there have been myriad calls for adults to start listening to 'children's voices', so that young people's perspectives can be used in planning interventions and programmes. The study from which this book results is just such a piece. Any such attempt must be applauded, because, as Lansdown comments:

> Children's views are still, for a substantial proportion of the adult population, often treated as ill-informed, irrational, irresponsible, amusing or cute. It is much more unusual for them to be given serious recognition, and then primarily when their views coincide with those of adults.
>
> (1996: 75)

We must not be fooled into thinking that this is a simple agenda, however. Simple vox-pop journalistic recordings of young voices are insufficient. There is not one *single* children's voice, a fact that we have attempted to demonstrate in this study. Young people's age, gender, social class, ethnicity and life experience all combine to give them as varied a set of 'voices' as would be expressed by the adult community.

Then, too, there is the fact that young people do not exist in childish worlds of their own, untouched by the constructions and discourses of the adult world with which they interact. As Bruner and Haste (1987) point out, meaning is constructed and negotiated in the way they live the child–adult interaction in their everyday lives. These interactions are discursive practices – ones where meaning is produced and constantly negotiated (Davies and Harre, 1990).

The third difficulty with which this new paradigm confronts us is that of how we respond to the identification of young people's perspectives. There have been warnings from many that it is insufficient for adults to listen to young people's voices and then to try to frame rights on their behalf (Waiton, 1995). Instead there is a call for responses which are empowering for young people themselves, leading them towards full participative citizenship. This raises immediate concerns for many observers. Just how competent are children and young people to take on these sorts of roles? Is this not just a way of abdicating our role as responsible adults or parents, and one that we will live to regret as we watch our young people possibly stumble and falter as they try to reinvent the wheel for themselves?

Descriptions of young people's transition to adulthood in the last few years have seen an increasing emphasis on the concept of citizenship as a desirable end goal of that maturational process (Jones and Wallace, 1992). Central to the notion of becoming a citizen is the idea that one's childhood and teenage years see a progressive gain in the development of various competencies, giving one also rights of self-determination and rightful access to a range of opportunity and institutional and welfare aid. In much of what has been written this transition is shorthanded, using terms such as 'empowerment'.

Empowerment

We might pause here briefly to consider the concept of empowerment as it is currently construed in popular rhetoric and in the professional rhetoric of the caring services. We should also examine the way in which empowerment is now interpreted (in a new and non-reflexive sense) as a professional task of those working with young people in various welfare settings. So recent is this shift in popular perspective on the professional role of those working with young people that there has been little opportunity to evaluate the implications for the recipients of 'empowering practice'.

Research literature would seem to indicate that 'empowerment involves a more complicated set of processes than its invocation as a moral imperative implies' (Baistow, 1994: 35). Adams defines empowerment as 'the process by which individuals, groups and/or communities become able to take control of their circumstances and achieve their goals, thereby being able to work toward maximising the quality of their lives' (1990: 43). Such a definition captures the essential individualism of modern rhetoric. It is power over self rather than power over other individuals which is desirable. Control of self is emphasised and seen as good in itself.

A number of conflicting themes appear in the literature on empowerment. While the language used in identifying candidates for empowerment is often overtly political (Barr, 1995), for instance, the solutions suggested are often overwhelmingly psychological in tone (Stevenson and Parsloe, 1993). Moreover, the connections between individual empowerment and community or collective empowerment are implied but poorly explained.

Empowerment (rather like children's rights) is increasingly being seen as something done by professionals to people in need. Thus candidates for the empowerment activities of professionals might be the clients of health promoters, social workers, health visitors, youth workers and so on. They may also be consumers who should be able to exercise choice or rights. Such a formulation fits in with the agenda both of the new right with its free-market analysis as well as that of the liberal left with its needs-based consumerist analysis. Such articulations of the ideas around empowerment share common themes – solutions are seen as being ground level, bottom-up, localised, designed to increase user choice, participation and, critically, personal control.

We might ask how empowerment has come to have this new meaning, to have become something which is 'done unto' people by others in professional positions. Some have seen it as a reaction to the extent to which ordinary life has been colonised by professionals. Empowerment becomes a way of defining clients anew as consumers and of wresting some of the power away from professionals who were seen as having established an over-bureaucratic stranglehold on the organs of the welfare state. It is ironic, therefore, that 'far from being left roleless, or less powerful, by the process of empowerment, professionals are increasingly being seen as central to it in a number of ways which extend rather than reduce their involvement and interventions in the everyday life of citizens' (Baistow, 1994: 39).

These kinds of changes in the professional roles of workers in health and welfare agencies would seem to imply the need to acquire a whole different set of professional skills and know-how, and, on the part of the recipients, a new framework of relationships with workers. Despite much evidence in the professional literature urging the new paradigm, there is little material to date explaining how the desired outcomes might be achieved in practice or any indication of how these actions might make a difference in the lives of those candidates for empowerment.

This latter point has been explored a little by Beresford and Croft (1993), by Lord and McKillop Farlow (1990), and by Love and Hendry (1994), but they are almost alone in being concerned with the views of putative empowerment candidates. There is a dearth of research on user's experiences and views of empowerment. We simply do not know whether users desire empowerment or, if they do, whether their ideas about the nature of this are at odds with those of professionals. Our ignorance on this point is ironic in the context of the rhetoric about empowerment.

Given this ignorance there is a further danger that professional empowerment discourses will take the form of ones amenable to institutional organisation and evaluation, and that they will ignore the lessons from naturally occurring instances of mentoring and empowerment. Empirical studies tend to show that such instances occur in a voluntary setting, and are influenced by a level of empowerment beyond the individual psychology, that is, at a group or community level where experience has become collectivised and participative. Kieffer's (1984) model emphasises, for instance, that the empowerment process consists of several phases, the first of which he entitles 'entry'. Kieffer insists that the process of empowerment starts in a recognition by the individual of some challenge to his/her integrity – a threat to individual or familial self-interest. Kieffer maintains that the common daily experience of injustice or powerlessness is insufficient to trigger entry into the empowerment cycle. Similarly he feels that these initial reactions are never fostered by consciousness-raising, intellectual analysis or merely educative interventions. If this is true it poses interesting dilemmas for those working with young people within the new paradigm. Kieffer does, however, identify the central role of a mentor as a key link in the chain of a sustaining empowerment experience.

In a recent study Philip and Hendry (1997a) reflect on the fact that the most empowering examples of mentoring encountered by them in their research involved a much higher degree of reciprocity than is commonly found in worker–client relationships. Mentoring was seen to be a trigger for many young people to look for support elsewhere. Issues or problems once voiced to a supportive adult or same-near-age peer had become something that could be talked about, and young people were then happier to be referred on to another agency or individual for specialist advice or longer-term intervention. This project (Philip and Hendry, 1997b) provided evidence that mentoring gave young people some of the resilience or 'steeling mechanisms' that Rutter and Smith (1995) allude to in their work.

Concluding remarks

The study described in this book set out to explore young people's own feelings about their own health needs. Listening and responding to those voices will involve health workers themselves in developing different strategies towards the user groups of these services. Are those working with young people able to develop styles of operating which deliver true empowerment, or are notions of empowerment being slowly built into professional practice within an ironic new paradigm which does little to really connect with the health issues and problems young people have to surmount?

Such questions are critical in the lives of vulnerable young people. How can health educators and health promoters use these ideas to help young people through the transition points of their childhood and young adulthood?

We started this chapter by allowing one mid-adolescent to claim a degree of self-agency and the skills and abilities to behave sensibly in ways that are health-enhancing. We conclude this book by giving our support to the general principles behind the young person's 'message' to us. If health education is successfully to meet the needs of our young people, it is important that it is designed to encourage proactive behaviour in adolescents. Health educators can do this by providing non-judgemental knowledge, learning opportunities, and personal and social support networks. This would mean that young people make their own informed choices and decisions, and would be able to say, like our young interviewee: 'I won't do anything stupid.' And the reason why adolescents could say this would be because adult society has become sufficiently 'open' and collaborative with youth to enable them to have a future as genuine participants and to be considered, for the present, as learning partners with a voice in health concerns and social matters.

References

Adams, R. (1990) *Self-Help, Social Work and Empowerment*, London: Macmillan.
Backett, K. and Davison, C. (1992) 'Rational or reasonable? Perceptions of health at different stages of life', *Health Education Journal*, 51, 2: 55–59.
Baistow, K. (1994) 'Liberation and regulation? Some paradoxes of empowerment', *Critical Social Policy*, 42, 14: 34–46.
Barr, M. (1995) 'Empowering communities: beyond fashionable rhetoric? Some reflections on the Scottish experience', *Community Development Journal*, 30, 2: 121–132.
Beresford, P. and Croft, S. (1993) *Citizen Involvement – A Practical Guide for Change*, London: Macmillan.
Bronfenbrenner, U. (1979) *The Ecology of Human Development*, Cambridge, Mass.: Harvard University Press.
Bruner, J. and Haste, H. (1987) *Making Sense. The Child's Construction of the World*, London: Methuen.
Coleman, J. C. (ed.) (1979) *The School Years*, London: Methuen.
Coleman, J. C. and Hendry, L. B. (1990) *The Nature of Adolescence*, 2nd edn, London: Routledge.
Davies, M. and Harre, R. (1990) 'Positioning: the discursive production of selves', *Journal of the Theory of Social Behaviour*, 20, 1: 20–33.
Franklin, B. (ed.) (1995) *The Handbook of Children's Rights*, London: Routledge.
Gore, S. and Eckenrode, J. (1994) 'Context and process in research on risk and resilience', in R. J. Haggerty, L. R. Sherrod, N. Garmezy and M. Rutter (eds) *Stress, Risk, and Resilience in Children and Adolescents: Processes, Mechanisms, and Interventions*, New York: Cambridge University Press.
Hendry, L. B., Shucksmith, J., Love, J. G., and Glendinning, A. (1993b) *Young People's Leisure and Lifestyles*, London: Routledge.

James, A. and Prout, A. (eds) (1990) *Constructing and Reconstructing Childhood: Contemporary Issues in the Sociological Study of Childhood*, London: Falmer Press.

Jones, G. and Wallace, C. (1992) *Youth, Family and Citizenship*, Milton Keynes: Open University Press.

Kieffer, C. H. (1984) 'Citizen empowerment: a developmental perspective on prevention in human services'. Special issue – *Studies in Empowerment: Steps Towards Understanding and Action*, 3, 2–3: 9–36.

Lansdown, G. (1996) 'Respecting the rights of children to be heard', in G. Pugh (ed.) *Contemporary Issues in the Early Years*, London: Paul Chapman.

Lord, C. and McKillop Farlow, M. (1990) 'A study of personal empowerment: implications for health promotion', *Health Promotion, Health and Welfare, Canada*, 29, 2: 1–8.

Love, J. and Hendry, L. B. (1994) 'Youth workers and young participants: two perspectives of youth work', *Youth and Policy* (Special issue, *New Directions in Youth Work*), 46: 43–55.

Philip, K. and Hendry, L. B. (1997a) 'Young people and mentoring: towards a typology', *Journal of Adolescence*, 19: 43–62.

Philip, K. and Hendry, L. B. (1997b) *Young People, Mentoring and Youth Work*, Report to the Johann Jakobs Foundation, Zurich.

Rutter, M. and Smith, D. (1995) *Psychosocial Disorders in Young People: Time Trends and Their Causes*, London: Wiley.

Stevenson, O. and Parsloe, P. (1993) *Community Care and Empowerment*, York: Joseph Rowntree Foundation.

Ulvik, O. S. (1997) 'Discourses of childhood – perspectives of children committed to care by the child welfare'. Paper given at Urban Childhood Conference, Trondheim, Norway, June 1997.

Waiton, S. (1995) 'When children's rights are wrong', *Scottish Child*, December 1994/January 1995: 14–16.

Wertsch, J. (1991) *Voices of the Mind. A Sociocultural Approach to Mediated Action*, London: Harvester/Wheatsheaf.

8 Challenges, risks and coping in adolescence

What is seen as a risk by most people may, for example, be simply thrilling to a downhill skier. Similarly, parental concerns about risks may be 'at odds' with an adolescent's views of the excitements of risk-taking activities. Thus, the various kinds of developmental challenges young people engage with in their life transitions allow a range of motivational factors to be experienced, as seen through their eyes, and again, as in the previous extract, offer a different perspective from the 'usual' view of risks in adolescence as being problems against which adult society needs to guard. It may well be that risk-taking in adolescence is an important developmental rehearsal of skills and competences needed in adult life. This idea of neutrality fits well with my positive, non-judgemental view of adolescent development, where risk-taking need not always be seen as a negative way of considering their transitions towards maturity. This extract is the second of two chapters – the first dismissed the 'storm and stress' view of adolescence and, rather, discussed the developmental tasks young people face, as well as the resources available to them to achieve these tasks, in their transitions to maturity. Here we draw attention to the way that challenges and risks can have different meanings dependent on perspective. What is considered as a challenge or a risk may change from individual to individual and whether the view is from the individual's perspective or 'from the outside'. A further complication is that sometimes when a task is seen as 'objectively' difficult and likely to obstruct the individual's development it can actually and existentially result in gain in personal growth for the individual concerned. Then the chapter offers a framework for developing learning processes and experiences based on the concepts of: 'Responsibility', 'Reflection', and 'Relationships' – The new three R's?

CHALLENGES, RISKS AND COPING IN ADOLESCENCE

Marion Kloep and Leo B. Hendry

Introduction

At the beginning of this chapter, we will discuss concerns that are created for young people such as matching up to cultural images of attractiveness, family relations, school and romantic love, then proceed to look at problems young people might create for themselves – risk-taking behaviours such as alcohol use or delinquent activities. Finally, we will outline a theoretical model of how the development of meta-awareness skills may be a powerful coping device, while admitting that research has not yet fully uncovered the processes and mechanisms involved. Thus, this chapter does not present a detailed review of research on adolescence. Rather, taken together the ideas in both this and the previous chapter [of the original publication] can create a reasonable framework for integrating information and findings about adolescent development and so enhance our understanding of this transitional period of the lifespan.

Normative events and non-normative shifts

In the previous chapter [of the original publication], we examined the variety of 'tasks' adolescents have to deal with. Apart from 'normative' events that most adolescents encounter, some also experience 'non-normative shifts' which are problems that arise from the social environment, from unsuccessful coping (Rutter, 1996a) or from special life events such as a death in the family. Although all adolescents have to cope with the psychosocial challenges associated with their maturing body, new relationships with parents and peers, with school and the transitions towards employment, a growing number encounter additional problems like family disruption, economic deprivation or social or cultural changes. Sometimes, a normative shift can turn into a non-normative one, if it is dealt with unsuccessfully, or if there are other circumstances that cause a normal development 'task' to become more difficult. If the onset of puberty, for example, occurs too early or too late (compared to age-norms), or if conflicts with parents cannot be resolved, these basic 'normative shifts' can turn into 'non-normative' ones for particular adolescents.

Risks or challenges?

Normative and non-normative shifts that young people are likely to encounter can turn out to be either challenges or risks, depending on their psychosocial properties. In order to find out what makes specific events or circumstances into a challenge or a risk we need to differentiate between risk indicators and risk mechanisms (Rutter, 1996a). Rather than simplistically assigning certain events like family break-up as a risk, we should try to understand what mechanisms are involved which turn these events into problematic contexts for some, whereas the same events leave other adolescents unharmed or may even lead to personal growth.

Having briefly described the different functions of developmental challenge and risk, we want to illustrate this with a few examples in relation to psychosocial functions in young people's lives.

Some examples of risk and challenge

Aspects from the social environment

CULTURAL BODY IMAGES

Amongst others, Davies and Furnham (1986) have shown that the average adolescent is not only sensitive to, but also critical of their changing physical self. Because of gender and sexual development young people are inevitably confronted, perhaps for the first time, with cultural standards of beauty in evaluating their own 'body image'. Direct influences may come, for instance, via media images or by the reactions of others, as we can illustrate with some quotes from a qualitative study by Shucksmith and Hendry (1998):

> 'You look in these magazines and you see all these super models. You don't see any that are 22 stone! They're all about seven stone.'
>
> (Girl, age 15)

> 'O God, where did all this fat come from. It never used to be there or I never noticed it. I used to be able to eat lots of sweets and the only thing that grew were my feet.'
>
> (Girl, age 15)

That this may lead to a non-normative shift is seen by the fact that concerns about weight and body shape are frequently associated with dieting practices and sometimes by serious eating disorder. In the Mayfly study (Balding, 1986), over half of the girls and 20 per cent of the boys had tried to exert control over their weight, whereas Coleman and Hendry (1990) described how young people may be especially vulnerable to teasing and exclusion if they are perceived by peers as either over- or underweight. Fear of such teasing can itself lead to feelings of self loathing and isolation (Shucksmith and Hendry, 1998) and thus implies a clear risk for further development.

Realizing that you lack the physical attractiveness to make friends *just* by being good-looking can become a challenge leading to the development of alternative skills to gain peer acceptance. Being helpful, having listening skills, having a sense of humour or possessing 'entertainment' skills like playing an instrument, or being good at highly regarded sports, are all accomplishments that can outweigh physical attractiveness (Hendry et al., 1993).

FAMILY LIFE AND TRADITIONAL VALUES

Turning to family life, we have seen that adolescence is a time for renegotiating roles. If done skilfully on both sides, this will lead to heightened autonomy and the development of many necessary life-skills like managing one's own economy, personal hygiene, short- and long-term planning and a continuing warm relationship with parents. Done in an unskilled way, this can result in less effective solutions and may lead to further problems – running away, marrying or becoming pregnant early, joining a religious cult, drug abuse or self-harm and suicide attempts.

Another factor that can disturb parent–adolescent relationships is the 'non-normative shifts' that affect family-life. Examples of this are economic hardship, which can weaken the marital bond and, as a consequence, distort parental styles (Silbereisen et al., 1990), or sudden value changes in society after political unrest (e.g. Kloep and Hendry, 1997), or in some traditional south-European countries, media-influence (Georgas, 1991; Deliyannis-Kouimtzi and Ziogou, 1995). Young people, in particular girls, who readily adapt to new Western ways, find themselves in conflict with their parents and the older generation over traditional values (Pais, 1995). In families with a supportive climate, parent–adolescent discussions can be an opportunity for the development of social and intellectual skills, whereas in families where conflicts are numerous, an additional issue can be disastrous.

Similarly, a non-normative shift like parental divorce can have positive or negative implications for a young person, depending how the separation is conducted. Research has shown that children of a 'happy' divorce are better adjusted than children of unhappy marriages (Hetherington, 1989). If there is conflict between the parents and particularly if adolescents are involved in the conflicts, they are likely to suffer (Kloep et al., 1995). Further, the young person's coping style seems to make a difference: avoidance of dealing with their parent's divorce either cognitively or behaviourally or even blaming themselves for the incident seems to be related with poorer functioning (Emery and Forehand, 1996).

On the other hand, divorce can give youths the opportunity to assume a responsible role in the family, helping them to 'grow up faster'. Hetherington (1989) concluded:

> 'Depending on the characteristics of the child, available resources, subsequent life experiences and especially interpersonal relationships, children in the long run may be survivors, losers, or winners of their parents' divorce or remarriage.'

When young people leave their parents' home, many of them continue to live locally, often deriving help from an extended kin network (Harris, 1993). It is those who do not enjoy this family support who are at risk, for example, of becoming homeless. The pervasive influence of unemployment has created a shifting population of homeless people who inhabit the 'cardboard cities' of many European towns. Voluntary organizations estimate that 200,000 young people experience homelessness each year in Great Britain alone (Killeen, 1992). This last example shows how a 'non-normative shift' like the liberalisation of 'market forces' has an enormous impact on the life of young people – though varied for different adolescents [Hendry, 1987].

The omnipresence of multinational companies, consumerism and the ascent of service industries enable individuals to access the global marketplace to create and sustain a variety of lifestyles – if they have available financial resources. As Büchner et al. (1995, p. 57) concluded:

> '... apart from those 'winners' of modernisation who are able to integrate modern life style features into their everyday lives, there are also quite a number of children who must be regarded as 'losers' of modernisation. Such children do not have the necessary material or personal resources at their disposal nor do they have adequate support networks to live modern individualised lives. Rather they are at risk, both socio-economically (for example, new poverty) and personally (for example, deviant, psychosomatic syndrome)'.

Not only large sections of working class youth in affluent nations, but also the majority of young people in former socialist countries find themselves so trapped: Cashmore (1984) called this the 'luxury gap'.

This situation constitutes a risk rather than a challenge for most young people. There are only a limited number of strategies at their disposal which may be approved of by adult society. So, a small number make their way by succeeding in a sports- or arts-career, by obtaining outstanding academic qualifications or, as in the case of many poorer countries, by emigrating. Others are left to adopt potentially damaging strategies: turning to delinquency, rioting, drugs or becoming totally apathetic.

ROMANCE AND SEXUALITY

Young people's awakening sexuality creates possibilities of both challenge and risk. If first sexual experiences are positive ones, this can provide a basis for learning the new skills of intimate relationship (such as respect, intuition, negotiation and 'give and take', conflict prevention and resolution, developing a positive relationship to one's own body and specific sexual skills). These can provide a firm foundation for future interpersonal understanding. Even the pain of ending a love-relationship can be an important learning experience for coping with loss or for helping to make a future better choice. Yet, having sex with the 'wrong' partner and/or under the wrong circumstances can be such a traumatic experience that it may lead to difficulties in establishing and maintaining future romantic, or even friendly, relationships (Martin, 1996). Such an experience was summed up by a 15-year-old young woman who said:

> 'Then I went on holiday and I had sex with this guy and it was a total mistake and then I came back and I wished I hadn't done it. There's nothing special to it. There's nothing to look forward to . . .'
>
> (Shucksmith and Hendry, 1998)

Hendry et al. (1991) have shown that power and intimacy are two dimensions around which young people need guidance and help to understand the ways in which romantic and sexual relationships are negotiated. In particular, the dangers of learning a masculine role which separates sexual practices from emotional feelings cannot be overstated. For young men, the threat of loss of a precarious masculine identity makes them reluctant to engage emotionally with sexual partners or to acknowledge their needs. The importance of assertiveness in young women's refusal of unwanted sexual advances has to be pointed out because rational models of decision-making can be affected by a number of interpersonal and social factors. Hendry et al. (1991) found that amongst their sample of young women, being seen to carry condoms, to be assertive about their own sexual needs or to be defined as sexually active would be interpreted as a loss of reputation as being 'respectable' and make them vulnerable in other areas of their lives. The creating and sustaining of an acceptable sexual reputation is clearly highly gendered. Moreover, this reputation will have a significant impact on attitudes and beliefs in other social contexts and activities (Wight, 1992).

All the foregoing relates to heterosexual activity. Kent-Baguley (1990) noted that not surprisingly the majority of young lesbians and gays feel marginalized, isolated and unhappy at school and are often feeling obliged to pretend to participate in 'queer bashing' talk to avoid self-revelation: gender orientation carries with it particular risks and challenges.

In this section, we have looked at normative and non-normative shifts in adolescence and given some examples of influences from interpersonal relations, from primary groups like the family and from wider society which turn transitional 'tasks' into challenges or risks – or normative shifts into non-normative ones.

Behavioural aspects

Such examples from the social environment lead us to problems adolescents might build up for themselves by engaging in behaviours that might be a risk for their health or their psychosocial development.

Defining risk-taking

At this stage, it is important to stress the distinction between problems from the social environment and actions taken by the adolescent (i.e. behavioural aspects). With regard to behavioural aspects we mean activities which are normally referred to in the literature as adolescent risk-taking. The concept of risk-taking is ill defined. Is it part of the psychological make up of youth – a thrill seeking stage in the developmental transition – or a necessary step to the acquisition of adult skills and self-esteem? Or is it a consequence of a societal or cultural urge by adults to marginalize youth because in their transitions from controllable child to controlled adult they are seen as troublesome and a threat to the stability of the community?

Before we even try to answer such questions, we need a clearer definition of what is meant by risk-taking. Hendry and Kloep (1996) offered the following three categories of risk-taking behaviour:

First, there are *thrill-seeking behaviours*. These are exciting or sensation-seeking behaviours which arouse and test the limits of one's capacities. Such behaviours can be observed in children as well as in adolescents and adults. Children, though, lack resources such as money or non-supervised time to engage in these behaviours. Most adults, on the other hand, know their limits reasonably well after years of experimentation and do not need to engage in so much risk-taking behaviour, beyond meeting new challenges. What distinguishes adolescent thrill-seeking behaviour is a combination of:

- *Frequency* – they engage in these activities more often than adults to test themselves and learn.
- *Resources* – they have more access than children to money and time.
- As a result of limited experience, they *lack judgement* of their own capacities and the extent of risk they are undertaking.

Next, there are *audience-controlled risk-taking behaviours*. In order to be accepted, to find place in a peer group and to establish a social position, people have to demonstrate certain qualities and abilities. Thus, it is obvious that most risky behaviours need an audience. This may be the reason why adults do not engage so often in demonstrative risk-taking: they have symbolic means of displaying their status in titles, expensive clothes or sports cars.

There is a special sub-category of audience-controlled risk-taking behaviour that young people engage in with the intention of impressing or provoking other people. These 'other people' can be peers, parents or adult authority figures. Adults restrict many adolescent behaviours and activities and defying norms is for many adolescents a step in the development of independence. Eager to break adults' dominance by refusing to obey their commands and prohibitions, adolescents may not always be able to discriminate which rules were made to suppress them and which were in their best interests. This can lead to risk-taking (i.e. *norm-breaking*) behaviours, reinforced by adults' negative reactions.

Third, there are risk-taking behaviours which are *irresponsible behaviours*. These are not performed because of the risk they imply, but in spite of it, in order to achieve other desired goals. Such irresponsible behaviours demonstrate the inability of individuals to see long-term consequences, or, if these are apparent, to be unwilling to abstain from them because of perceived short-term advantages. Examples of such behaviours are smoking and drinking, abstaining from exercise, or engaging in unprotected sex. It is obvious that behaviours such as getting drunk or failing to use condoms are not attractive because of the risks they imply, but are pursued for other reasons that are temporarily more important than these consequences. As Arnett (1998) has suggested, cultures must accept a trade-off in socialization between promoting individualism and self-expression on the one hand and in promoting social order on the other. Societies such as ours pay the price for promoting individualism and achievement by having higher rates of adolescent risk-taking in response to adult culture.

Alcohol and other drugs

Hendry et al. (1993) showed that five per cent of 13–14-year-old Scots and nearly 50 per cent of 17–18-year-olds were frequent drinkers (once a week or more often), and Kloep (1998) found similar figures in Swedish rural youth (nine per cent of 13–14-year-olds and 45 per cent of 17–18-year-olds had been drunk at least once during the last four weeks). Looking at drug use: 15 per cent of young people in Stockholm (Barnombudsmannen, 1995), 18.5 per cent of English youth (Coleman, 1997), and 4 per cent of Swedish rural youth (Kloep, 1998) admit that they have tried Marihuana at least once. As Hurrelmann and Losel (1990) have suggested, personal behaviours in adolescence can contribute to morbidity and mortality: smoking, drinking, using illegal drugs, precocious and unprotected sexual activity, little involvement in sports and exercise, delinquent activities 'indicate that the image of healthy adolescence is inaccurate'. Gofton (1990) examined the practices of young drinkers in the North of England, and found that their aim with drinking was principally 'to get out of it' at the weekend and to lose control. Courtship, or the search for 'talent' and sex were important possible outcomes for both young men and women, and discourses of spontaneity and 'getting carried away' were drawn on to excuse risky behaviours. The search for a 'high' and for 'magical' transformations from the reality of the ordinary work-a-day world was highly prized.

Assessing patterns of illicit drug use among youth is notoriously difficult, due to illegality and the low numbers seeking treatment from drug agencies. Traditional assumptions derive from beliefs that young people are manipulated by a range of factors – peer pressure, insecurity, the desire to be different, and so on. More recently, researchers have suggested that this perspective is overly simplistic and unhelpful in teasing out the dimensions of drug misuse (Coggans *et al.*, 1993). Often this has been matched with explanations given by young drug users who do not see themselves as weak or manipulated but rather actively involved and purposeful in their assessment of the risks, costs and benefits of particular substances. For some young people the desire for 'flow', for a transformation of reality, for going beyond the day-to-day grind, or for belonging to a leisure subculture may be important and may be compared to some adults' rationalisations for use of alcohol. As in many contexts, the risks created by society for young drug users by criminalising them may be far beyond the risks of drug usage itself (e.g. Christie and Bruun, 1985).

The degree to which the adolescent's contact with alcohol and other drugs is a risk or challenge depends on which functions they fulfil for the individual, to what degree the young person is able to derive similar experiences by less harmful means, and by the young person's variety of skills around which they can make reasoned choices in leading a 'balanced' life. Where alternative behaviours

130   *Challenges, risks and coping in adolescence*

are not possible and drugs are perceived as the only means of reaching desired gratification, they will be a serious risk factor, especially when the adolescent lacks self-control skills.

Given the necessary self-control and a wide range of behavioural alternatives (to create excitement in one's life and to gain the respect of one's friends), the possibilities of over-indulgence may be lessened. Then an occasional bottle of beer or wine, for example, is just another step in learning 'sensible' drinking and adding some pleasure to one's life. Yet:

> Among the young people we met, the non-drinker is the deviant and talk about sensible drinking is openly ridiculed. ... (Young people) tend to dismiss any possible health risks because they 'bounce back' so quickly and without any apparent ill-effects.
>
> (Coffield, 1992: 2)

As Berndt (1998) has suggested, adolescents are influenced by their friends' attitudes and behaviours, but adolescents can also influence their friends: over time this mutual influence increases similarities.

What is being suggested in this section is that both legal and illegal drugs are used by young people (and adults) as transformation. Additionally, for adolescents, they can be symbolic (e.g. looking 'cool' or 'grown up'). As with other behaviours, the circumstances of learning to drink present young people with a risk or challenge within cultures where adult drinking is approved.

Delinquent behaviour

Delinquent behaviour is regarded by many as the most prominent form of adolescent risk-taking (Farrington, 1995a,b). The majority of those convicted for car-theft, vandalism, shoplifting, theft and burglary are young men between 14 and 17 years. Yet, the media picture of the dangerous, criminal teenager is exaggerated and may be a sign of perceived hostility by adults towards adolescents (Davis, 1990). Together with the fact that it is not *many* young men who commit *some* crimes, but relatively *few* young men who commit *many* crimes (e.g. Farrington and West, 1993), this begins to suggest that juvenile delinquency may be less of a problem than is perceived by most adults.

To these views should be added a perspective that crime and delinquency in our society are in some measure the cost of certain kinds of social development. It has been argued that the predominant ethic of our society is acquisitiveness and desire for success. The values underlying juvenile delinquency may be far less deviant than commonly assumed. A number of theorists have emphasized the role of identity processes in determining delinquent behaviour (e.g. Emler and Reicher, 1995). The desire to identify with a peer group requires adherence to particular types of behaviour even when anti-social actions may result. Thus, delinquency can have different functions for different adolescents: for some, it may be socially controlled in helping them to attain status in the peer-group or to enable them to challenge adult society, for others it may be the thrill of sensation-seeking or a means of survival in a society stressing individual achievement and gain.

Sports

One activity which *is* socially approved and can provide self control, sensation-seeking and peer approval, yet is seldom regarded as true risk-taking behaviour, is sports participation. Yet it is a useful example of how almost any activity can be viewed as a challenge or a risk, depending on the psychosocial circumstances. If sport is experienced as the only way of gaining peer acceptance and/or adult approval, the adolescent may invest too much time and effort, to the neglect of other achievements like scholastic endeavour, or 'success' may be enhanced by cheating and illegal means, creating a 'hidden curriculum' in sports (e.g. Hendry, 1992). If sport is the *only* way of experiencing 'thrill', the young person may take higher risks, influenced by the 'negative' elements inherent in many sport activities: high skill demands, parental pressure, 'insensitive' coaches or physical education teachers focusing only on talented athletes (Hendry, 1992).

As Hendry et al. (1993) have noted, organized sports and physical activities are not particularly attractive to certain adolescent groups (e.g. young women) nor at certain times during adolescence (e.g. leaving school). Yet casual fun-oriented sports can be popular, especially with young women, when there is more focus on sociability, enjoyment and competence rather than on competition. Longer term goals related to cardiovascular health do not seem to be a potent impetus to participation. 'Competing' leisure and social interests and the influence of mass media in projecting 'desirable' adult role models may direct young people away from sports despite their initial positive attitudes.

Risk-taking behaviours in adolescence serve a variety of developmental functions which seem to be related to seeking 'escape', identification or 'fitting in' with peers and with seeking adult status. Within this we have outlined that different functions of risk-taking can be thrill-seeking, audience-controlled or irresponsible behaviours. Outwardly similar behaviours can be totally different functionally, while seemingly different behaviours can serve the same psychological purpose.

Developing meta-skills

Throughout this chapter we have argued that one of the most important factors that turns risks into challenges and vice versa, is the competency level of young persons themselves. If they have a variety of skills with which to tackle psychosocial tasks, the danger of engaging in certain potentially risky behaviours such as unprotective sex, joy riding, excessive dieting diminishes. If the young person has self-management and self-control skills, they can cope with occasional 'irresponsible' acts and if the young person has experiences in successful problem-solving, new tasks will more likely be seen as a challenge rather than a risk. Thus, one thing adults could do to help young people's transitions to adulthood, would be to encourage and enable them to develop an appropriate repertoire of psychosocial life skills. This repertoire might encompass *basic living skills* for societies such as ours, like computing, reading, writing, personal economy, understanding directions and time-tables, domestic capacities and *interpersonal social skills*. Adolescents should also acquire a wide range of skills to ensure a satisfying *leisure-time and occupational life*. Fürntratt and Möller (1982) proposed the main goal of education as the creation of 'homo excercens': the acting person, rather than 'homo sapiens', the (passively) knowing person.

Clausen (1991) emphasized that a 'socialization for competence' should enhance knowledge, abilities and controls: knowing something about one's own intellectual abilities, social skills, about available options and how to maximize or expand them, with the ability to make accurate assessments of the actions and reactions of others. Most importantly, one should be able to apply these 'competences' to everyday living. What skills should these be? Some clues might be given by our earlier discussions of normative changes: assertiveness, negotiating, giving and taking feedback, listening, discussing, legitimate protesting, coping with injustice, hobby skills, educational skills, sexual skills and so on.

Yet, the key question in all this is: how can we empower youth to prepare for 'non-normative shifts', for all the unpredictable problems they may meet throughout life? As with learning strategies in schools (Nisbet and Shucksmith, 1984) we cannot teach every life skill. So we propose that we teach 'learning to learn' strategies, meta-skills which enable young people to learn whatever they need by organizing their learning themselves (e.g. Hendry, 1993; Kloep, 1984).

The new 3 R's?

If we can support and encourage learning processes and experiences which enhance self-esteem and self-efficacy, we may avoid the complex, fragmented transitions from youth to adulthood which are heavily influenced by systematic social inequalities. Hendry (1993), for instance, proposed a new emphasis in education – a new 3R's for pupils to learn: Responsibility, Reflection and Relationships. Here we elaborate on this model (*see* Fig 8.1).

Responsibility essentially means an enhancement of the young person's self-agency. As shown in Fig 8.1, these qualities demand the employment of 'meta-awareness': the ability to see a contingency between self-initiated behaviour and the consequences it produces. This ability is mainly acquired by successful experiences, by actually seeing that one's actions lead to the desired outcome. But it can also be trained by mental trial-and-error exercises.

Reflection implies the cognitive skills that allow the transfer of knowledge or behaviours from the context in which they were first learned to new or problematic situations. This involves the abilities of discrimination (i.e. seeing the differences between two contexts) and generalization (i.e. seeing the similarities between two contexts), notions that are related to the Piagetian concepts of accommodation and assimilation. Usually, pupils are not taught to take responsibility for monitoring the way or the contexts in which skills can be used. Thus adolescents

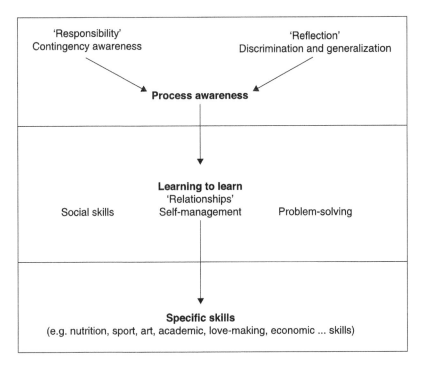

Figure 8.1 Meta-skills as the basis of development, the 'three R's'.

have trouble applying them again in new situations on their own initiative. Nisbet and Shucksmith (1984) suggested a hierarchical (classroom) learning model which distinguishes task-oriented, *highly specific skills* from *learning strategies*. Strategies represent super-ordinate skills, generalized procedures or sequences of activities such as self-monitoring, reviewing and self-evaluating. Many of these strategies are meta-cognitive in character, that is they involve individuals in being aware of their own preferred learning and thinking styles, orientations to learning contexts and awareness of alternative strategies, thus placing them in a position of choice within a framework of 'learning to learn'. In our model, 'Responsibility' and 'Reflection' can thus be regarded as 'process-awareness' skills, or, as Fürntratt and Möller (1982) described them, as skills 'that support task-solution'.

'Relationships' in the original 3 R's-model Hendry (1993) referred to the competent youngster having an understanding of, and skills needed for, successful social relationships: thus it is the *application* of meta-skills to the broad social context of inter-personal encounters that is important in learning with, from and about others. We agree with Gardner's (1984) broad definition of intelligence as a set of 'appropriate skills' related to exploring and solving problems, not only in the cognitive domain, but also in psychomotor, artistic, musical, leisure and social spheres and in other aspects of life. Therefore, as fig 8.1 shows, we should add to

social skills other 'learning to learn' strategies, like self-management (skills such as planning, time-management, setting objectives, self-reinforcement) and the skills of general problem-solving (e.g. operationalization of goals, information-seeking, decision-making).

Then, these meta-skills, with a high degree of process-awareness, should enhance the acquisition of more *specific skills* (*see* fig 8.1) needed for everyday life, in leisure and working-life, and provide young people with an arsenal of tools to meet whatever challenges and risks they are likely to find on their way to becoming an adult – and beyond.

Chapter summary

Within this [and the previous chapter of the original publication], we have proposed that adolescents' psychosocial 'tasks' can be categorized at three levels: 'maturational shifts', 'normative shifts' and 'non-normative shifts', and that these 'tasks' present adolescents with both challenges and concomitant risks.

To some extent we can enable young people to acquire appropriate skills to successfully work through 'tasks' at the first two levels, since the onset of these is fairly predictable and sequential. However, 'non-normative shifts' are more problematic especially with rapidly changing 'globalized', technologically oriented societies which influence and are influenced by individuals within them.

We have argued that meta-skills can best enable adolescents to 'fit in' to the culture in which they are growing up. This also requires the use of meta-awareness (*see* Fig 8.1) in understanding the social parameters of a particular culture, so that the individual adolescent knows when they 'drift' across value-boundaries into alternative – and perhaps illegal – ways of life. Additionally, they can empower adolescents to become more proactive in their own development and be potential 'societal agents for change'.

Opportunities need to be found for the development of an *individual* identity, the creation of *personal* social meanings and the acquisition of *self* – competency. These permit the flexibility and resilience necessary to cope with the more unpredictable 'non-normative shifts', cultural changes or social 'dislocations' in life.

Although we cannot predict future 'paradigm shifts' with any certainty, the development of meta-skills puts the individual in a stronger position to face challenges by having a range of choices from which to select a range of generalizable competences.

It has to be said that at present developmental psychologists have not begun to consider in any detail what these meta-skills, mechanisms and processes are which enhance (or hinder) young peoples' ability to meet challenges and risks. It is this area to which researchers should now turn their attention (*see also* Rutter, 1996b).

Thus adolescence differs from earlier years both in the nature of challenges (and risks) encountered and in the capacity of the young person to respond effectively to these. Adolescence is a particular phase of life stimulating and requiring adult-like patterns of coping behaviours in relation to various tasks, in creating opportunities to 'try out' strategies and to experiment in relatively supported contexts and hopefully in giving young persons the skills with which they can confidently start their journey through adult life.

References

Arnett, J. 1998. The young and the reckless. In Messer, D., Dockrell, J. (eds) *Developmental psychology: a reader*. London: Arnold.
Balding, J. 1986. The Mayfly study. (HEA) University of Exeter. School of Education.
Barnombudsmannen 1995. *Upp till . . . 18*. Halmstad: Statistiska Centralbyrån.
Berndt, T. J. (1998) Friendship and friends' influence in adolescence. In Messer, D., Dockrell, J. (eds.) *Developmental psychology: A reader*. Arnold: London.
Büchner, P., du Bois-Reymond, M., Krüger, H.-H. 1995. Growing up in three European regions. In Chisholm, L., Büchner, P., Krüger, H.-H., du Bois-Reymond, M. (eds) *Growing up in Europe*. Berlin: Walter de Gruyter.
Cashmore, E.E. 1984. *No future*. London: Heinemann.
Christie, N. and Bruun, K. 1985. *Den gode fienden*. Stockholm: Rabén and Sjögren.
Clausen, J.S. 1991. Adolescent competence and the shaping of the life course. *American Journal of Sociology* 96, 805–42.
Coffield, F. 1992. Young people and illicit drugs. Northern Regional Health Authority and Durham University.
Coggans, N., Shewan, D., Henderson, M., Davies, J. D., O'Hagan, F. J. 1993 National evaluation of drug education in Scotland. (SOED) Edinburgh.
Coleman, J. 1997. *Key data on adolescence*. Routledge: London.
Coleman, J.C., Hendry, L.B. 1990. *The nature of adolescence*. (second edition). London: Routledge.
Davies, E., Furnham, A. 1986. Body satisfaction in adolescent girls. *British Journal of Medical Psychology* 59, 279–88.
Davis, J. 1990. Youth and the condition of Britain. London: The Athlone Press.
Deliyannis-Kouimtzi, K., Ziogou, R. 1995. Gendered youth transitions in Northern Greece. In Chisholm, L., Büchner, P., Krüger, H.-H., du Bois-Reymond, M. (eds) *Growing up in Europe*. Berlin: Walter de Gruyter, 209–19.
Emery, R.E., Forehand, R. 1996. Parental divorce and children's well-being. In: Haggerty, R.J., Sherrod, L.R., Garmezy, N., Rutter, M. (eds) *Stress, risk and resilience in children and adolescents*. Cambridge: Cambridge University Press, 64–99.
Emler, N., Reicher, S. 1995. *Adolescence and delinquency*. London: Blackwell.
Farrington, D.P. 1995a. The Twelfth Jack Tizard Memorial Lecture: The development of offending and antisocial behaviour from childhood: Key findings from the Cambridge Study in delinquent development. *Journal of Child Psychology and Psychiatry* 36, 929–64.
Farrington, D.P. 1995b. The challenge of teenage antisocial behaviour. In: Rutter, M. (ed.) *Psychosocial disturbances in young people*. Cambridge: Cambridge University Press.
Farrington, D.P., West, D.J. 1993. Criminal, penal and life histories of chronic offenders. *Criminal Behaviour and Mental Health* 3, 492–523.
Fürntratt, E., Möller, C. 1982. *Lernprinzip Erfolg*. Frankfurt: Peter Lang.
Georgas, J. 1991. Intrafamily acculturation of values in Greece. *Journal of Cross-Cultural Psychology* 22, 445–457.

136 Challenges, risks and coping in adolescence

Gofton, L. 1990. On the town: drink and the 'new lawlessness'. *Youth and Policy*, 29, 33–9.

Harris, C. 1993. *The family and the industrial society*. London: Allen & Unwin.

Hendry, L.B. 1987. Young people. In Fineman, S. (ed.) *Unemployment*. London: Tavistock, 195–218.

Hendry, L.B. 1992. Sports and leisure. In Coleman J.C., Warren-Adamson, C. (eds) *Youth policy in the 1990's*. London: Routledge, 62–87.

Hendry, L.B. 1993. Learning the new three Rs? *Aberdeen University Review* **189**, 33–51.

Hendry, L.B., Kloep, M. 1996. Adolescent risk-taking. Paper presented at the EARA Conference, Liège.

Hendry, L.B., Shucksmith, J., Love, J.G., Glendinning, A. 1993. *Young people's leisure and lifestyles*. London: Routledge.

Hendry, L.B., Shucksmith, J., Philip, K., Jones, I. 1991. *Working with young people on drugs and HIV in Grampian region*. Grampian Health Board and Aberdeen University.

Hetherington, E.M. 1989. Coping with family transitions: winners, losers and survivors. *Child Development* **60**, 1–14.

Hurrelmann, K., Losel, F. 1990. *Health hazards in adolescence*. DeGruyter: Berlin.

Kent-Baguley, P. 1990. Sexuality and youth work practice. In: Jeffs, T., Smith, M. (eds) *Young people, inequality and youth work*, London: Macmillan.

Killeen, L. 1992. Leaving home, housing and income. In Coleman, J.C., Warren-Adamson, C. (eds) *Young people in the 1990s*. London: Routledge, 189–202.

Kloep, M. 1984. Bildung als Lebensbefähigung. *Die Deutsche Schule* 6, 487–93.

Kloep, M. 1998. *Att vara ung i Jämtland*. Österåsen: Uddeholt.

Kloep, M., Hendry, L.B. 1997. 'In three years we'll be just like Sweden!' *Young* **5**, 2–19.

Kleop, M., Olsson, S., Olofsson, A. 1995. 'Your mother doesn't love me anymore . . .' Paper presented at International Conference on Conflict and Development in Adolescence, Gent.

Martin, K.A. 1996. *Puberty, sexuality and the self*. London: Routledge.

Nisbet, J., Shucksmith, J. 1984. *Learning strategies*. London: Routledge & Kegan Paul.

Pais, J.M. 1995. Growing up on the EU periphery: Portugal. In: Chisholm, L., Büchner, P., Krüger, H.-H., du Bois-Reymond, M. (eds) *Growing up in Europe*. Berlin: Walter de Gruyter, 195–208.

Rutter, M. 1996a. Psychosocial adversity. In Verhofstadt-Denève, L., Kienhorst, I., Braet, C. (eds) *Conflict and development in adolescence*. Leiden: DSWO Press, 21–34.

Rutter, M. 1996b. Stress research. In: Haggerty, R.J., Sherrod, L.R., Garmezy, N., Rutter, M. (eds) *Stress, risk and resilience in children and adolescents*. Cambridge: Cambridge University Press, 354–85.

Shucksmith, J., Hendry, L.B. 1998. *Health issues and young people*. London: Routledge.

Silbereisen, R.K., Walper, S., Albrecht, H.T. 1990. Family income loss and economic hardship. *New Directions in Child Development* **46**, 27–47.

Wight, D. 1992. Impediments to safer heterosexual sex: a review of research with young people. *AIDSCARE* **4**, 1, 11–25.*Figure 8.1* Meta-skills as the basis of development, the 'three R's'.

9 Young people's unemployment lifestyles

One challenge facing adolescents and young adults in present-day society is to find a job. When young people are leaving school and view the labour market to assess their personal work opportunities, it is clear a range of choices emerge, dependent on a variety of geographic, social, contextual and psychological factors. Some 'school-leavers' will be anxious, some will avoid decision-making for the moment, some will reflect on their current and future situations and some will find effective coping strategies. The following article, written some years ago, seems poignantly relevant to the current situation in Western societies. It presents a range of young people's responses to job-seeking and may open up policy and practice ideas where a 'goodness of fit' is attempted between the individual teenager and the world of work and unemployment. This is also a good example of how one life-event can affect individuals differently to the degree that it can be seen positively as well as negatively. This article explores young people's meanings of, and responses to, the state of being unemployed. Schools do not seem to be considered as institutions that prepare young people for an unemployed lifestyle. Again, what becomes evident is that responses to being unemployed are varied and coping mechanisms come into play to enable some adolescents to deal successfully with the experience and even thrive on it.

Another situation facing young people in modern society is making decisions about social and geographic mobility and the processes involved leading up to the actual moments of decision about leaving or staying in one's local community. This may be particularly true in rural areas. In a three-nation research we could demonstrate that a variety of psychosocial and environmental forces interact with the young person's personal desires in leading up to the actual decision-making process (see, e.g., Kloep et al., 2003).

UNEMPLOYMENT, SCHOOL AND LEISURE

An adolescent study

L. B. Hendry, M. Raymond and C. Stewart

This study attempts to provide some insight into the experience of unemployment from the perspective of young people themselves. The school's role in preparing young people for society is considered, and a prospective view of post-school life by pupils in their final year of compulsory schooling is examined. Results indicated that while schools continue to place a stress on vocational preparation, pupils did not appear to believe they had been given an adequate understanding of work and unemployment. Further, there was little continuation of school-based leisure activities into post-school life.

Introduction

The Scottish Council for Community Education (1981) recently stated:

> It is suggested the many young people already living will never have paid employment of the traditional kind. It is irrefutable that very many people will find themselves with vastly increased amounts of what has been regarded in the past as 'leisure'. . . .

The present study therefore sets out to examine some young people's experiences of unemployment. By comparing the views of employed and unemployed teenagers, differences in their respective lifestyles and leisure patterns are considered. The study also speculates about the school's role in preparing adolescents for society.

While work may be central in giving structure to an individual's life (Kelvin, 1981a), it is also a key element in local value systems. Braun (1977), Dennehy and Sullivan (1977), Hill (1978) and Pahl (1978) have all agreed that the unemployed feel a sense of guilt about spending their days in idleness. In Pahl's study, school-leavers were aware that in reality they might be forced to deviate from the expected progression that school is followed by work.

The relationship between schooling and occupation and the demands associated with an employee's role have been continually stressed in works on education (Nisbet, 1957; Entwistle, 1970). Equally important, secondary school education has been seen by many pupils, teachers and parents as being primarily a preparation for work (Morton-Williams and Finch, 1968; Lindsay, 1969; Hendry, 1978, 1983). As in government vocational training schemes, this emphasis helps to reinforce assumptions about the centrality of work to the human life plan, and by implication increases the individual's social and psychological dependence on it.

Yet the studies of Weir and Nolan (1977), Willis (1977), Corrigan (1978) and Ashton and Maguire (1980) suggest the possible conceptualization of the labour market in dualistic terms by adolescents and that many young people are pleased at the prospect of putting their schooldays behind them. Thus, on closer examination we find a profound ambivalence exhibited by adolescents towards work. Carter (1971) has previously argued that many adolescents are not particularly interested in a future job or jobs but rather in 'the status and perquisities of a young worker'.

In our society, leisure has been normally structured and given meaning by its relation to working time. Parker (1983), for example, sees leisure as a time of freedom bounded by the constraints of work and non-work commitments. Thus, in approaching the problem of youth unemployment, and in particular how this affects adolescent leisure patterns, we are faced paradoxically with both a surfeit and a dearth of relevant evidence. Adolescent leisure has been investigated by studies such as Jephcott (1967), Emmett (1971), Leigh (1971), Scarlett (1975), Eggleston (1976), Fogelman (1976) and Hendry (1978, 1981), which have helped to build up a fairly detailed picture of the free-time interests and leisure preoccupations of teenagers, while Murdock and Phelps (1973), Patrick (1973), Corrigan (1978), Brake (1980) and Kitwood (1980) among others have enhanced our understanding of the values and attitudes which lie behind a variety of teenage leisure activities both organized and casual.

By contrast, the social and psychological aspects of youth unemployment have received less research attention. The studies of Hill (1977, 1978) and discussion papers by Jahoda (1979) and Frazer (1980) have only touched on the particular problems of unemployed teenagers. Analytical work by Hayes and Nutman (1981) gives similarly superficial attention to the plight of the school-leaver. Nevertheless, what little evidence there is suggests that young people without jobs tend to be those with fewest academic qualifications, and they tend to come from families of manual workers in which other members are also unemployed (Holland, 1978; Raffe, 1983).

Kelvin (1981b) has suggested that the term 'unemployed' will become an accepted term of reference for young people's self-perceptions and for their position in society; at present, however, as Kitwood (1980) stated:

> When a boy or girl personally accepts the label 'unemployed' the subjective environment changes; it becomes a state of inactivity and lassitude, where personal powers cannot be adequately used or expressed.

What are the implications for adolescents' leisure pursuits? Studies which deal specifically with youth unemployment (Phillips, 1973; Pettman and Fyfe, 1977; Murray, 1978; Casson, 1979) do not set out to analyse in any detail the lifestyles and leisure patterns of the young people concerned. A recent paper by Roberts *et al.* (1982) does attempt some examination of the lifestyle of unemployed adolescents, but pays little specific attention to their leisure patterns. Indeed, as Smith and Simpkins (1980) made clear, there is little descriptive or theoretical work on the relationship between leisure and unemployment.

Gurney and Taylor (1981) have pointed out that there is a need for a diversification of research approaches to unemployment, and it seemed appropriate in the present study to select a variety of perspectives on youth unemployment. The investigation is, therefore, concerned with the effects of potential unemployment on the attitudes and perceptions of young people in their final year of compulsory schooling, and juxtaposes their views with the impressions of aspects of post-school life — work, unemployment and leisure — as described by a group of employed and a group of unemployed adolescents.

Methodology

Sample

In an attempt to look in some detail at the links between unemployment and leisure, an investigation of employed and unemployed adolescents aged 16–18 years and school pupils aged 15–16 years was carried out. The research strategy was designed on the premise that to concentrate on unemployed school-leavers would simply present a distorted picture of the reality of unemployment and would fail to investigate its wide-ranging influences. The basic design was therefore a three-cornered one incorporating pupils in their final year of compulsory schooling and employed and unemployed school-leavers. The sample size was 338 boys and girls divided into three subgroups:

1   Unemployed school-leavers ($n = 72$).
2   Employed school-leavers ($n = 33$).
3   School pupils ($n = 233$).

Research strategies

Interviews with unemployed adolescents took place in the local office of the Department of Health and Social Security (DHSS), the local careers office and a local authority centre which offered day-time facilities for unemployed adolescents. Subjects were sampled in the DHSS office and the careers office by the counter staff inviting every second client at a particular counter to take part in the interview. At the local authority 'drop-in' centre youth workers were asked to select subjects in a similar manner. In both contexts few adolescents refused to take part in the interviews.

In order to obtain a reasonable cross-section of employed adolescents, two local textile firms were randomly selected from a list of occupations requiring few formal entry qualifications. In addition, respondents with more academic qualifications were selected from day-release students attending two local technical colleges. The staff in both the textile firms and in the colleges were asked to choose subjects from an alphabetical name list by inviting every fourth person in the age range 16–18 years to take part in the interview so as to provide as representative a sample of employed adolescents as possible.

The interviews were devised to allow a compromise between questions which would provide statistically valid material and more open-ended questions which would give a fuller account of the individual opinions and interpretations of the youngsters. A draft schedule was piloted at the local authority 'drop-in' centre.

The two versions of the interview schedule, that used with employed adolescents and that used with the unemployed, were deliberately kept as similar as possible. The schedule fell into five groups of questions:

1 Personal history.
2 School.
3 Leisure activities and attitudes.
4 Attitudes to unemployment and work.
5 Future aspirations.

The interviews depended on the accuracy of recall. However, unstructured observations of a small number ($n = 12$) of unemployed adolescents in a variety of settings (Job Centre, street corner, community centre, sports club) tended to confirm the behavioural patterns they had described. (It is acknowledged that some settings were easier to observe than others, and that certain settings were impossible to observe.) Both groups of adolescents responded thoughtfully to the questions, and the unemployed adolescents in particular seemed glad of the opportunity to explain their situation.

The six schools which took part in the study were selected because they were either designated 'community schools' or schools which had a reputation for having close links with their local communities. School staff were asked to administer self-explanatory questionnaires to mixed-ability fourth-year form classes. By complying with these requests, the schools ensured that the sample was representative of the year grouping.

The pupils' questionnaire was devised from the interview schedule and concentrated on two general areas of interest: a general picture of pupils' leisure activities and a more general investigation of their attitudes towards work, leisure and unemployment. Piloting was accomplished at one of the local comprehensive schools. The questions fell into three main groups:

1 Personal factual data.
2 Present leisure activities.
3 Attitudes to work and leisure in the future.

Results

Pupils

1. The current prospect of reduced employment opportunities had not curbed pupils' enthusiasm for leaving school. Boys particularly (90%) were looking forward to leaving.

2. Interest in a job or a career was high, with 144 pupils aspiring to full-time employment on leaving school. For boys, the most popular career choices were skilled manual occupations ($n = 56$), while managerial jobs ($n = 7$), the emergency services ($n = 5$) and the armed forces ($n = 4$) were also mentioned. Girls showed an interest in clerical ($n = 27$), skilled ($n = 17$) and managerial ($n = 17$) jobs.

3. To assess their interest in working life further, pupils were asked to rate the importance of 'having a job you enjoy' along with nine other aspects of adolescent life such as pop music, dress and fashion or family life. [These items were selected

from the Morton-Williams and Finch (1968) study.] An enjoyable job was seen as being 'very important' by 97 boys and 113 girls. By comparison, the next most popular item 'having a good time', was 'very important' for 47 boys and 34 girls.

4. The attraction of work was not seen in purely vocational terms. When asked why they wanted to leave school, 94 pupils mentioned the social and financial independence of working life, another 48 mentioned the intrinsic interest of a job or career itself, while 49 pupils stated that their hostility to school was their reason for wanting to leave.

5. A total of 200 pupils (out of 233) indicated that the possibility of becoming unemployed was a source of worry. The difficulties of finding work had been widely discussed in school, but only seven pupils specifically mentioned that classroom discussions had centred on the problems and experiences of life on the dole. Pupils had a realistic view of the difficulties involved in finding a job, with only 44 subjects believing they could find employment as soon as they left school.

6. Pupils appeared to be satisfied with their present leisure, and 77 boys and 66 girls took part in extra-curricular school activities. Roughly half the sub-sample were regular visitors to youth clubs, while 'hanging about' with friends, watching television and visiting friends' houses were the most popular casual leisure activities with both boys and girls.

7. The 97 pupils who believed that their leisure would change on leaving school had a clear conception of how their leisure would adapt in post-school life. Many of these pupils stated in an 'open-ended' question that their future leisure would become more 'adult', using facilities like discotheques and public bars rather than youth clubs.

Employed and unemployed adolescents

1. Employed adolescents ($n = 23$) who took a hostile or apathetic retrospective view of school stated that their education had been of little value as a preparation for work. None of the unemployed, not even the minority who took a positive retrospective view of school, stated that their education had prepared them adequately for unemployment.

2. Only 15 employed adolescents (all in skilled occupations) said that they found their work enjoyable. Although only nine workers had had any experience of unemployment, all but three of the sub-sample said they were worried by the prospect of being out of work. When asked about their future, 18 adolescents answered that they would be in the same job no matter how unpleasant they found it.

3. There was little continuation of extra-curricular school activities into post-school life by those adolescents who had taken part in school activities (less than 40%), although unemployed adolescents (75%) tended to maintain their attendance at youth clubs more than employed teenagers (less than 50%).

4. For employed adolescents weekend leisure revolved around going out. Twenty-three youngsters said they made regular weekend use of commercial leisure facilities like bars, clubs and discos, and 17 youngsters said they 'went down the town' on Saturdays either to shop or 'hang about' with friends. On

midweek evenings watching television and visiting friends were the most popular activities.

5. Virtually all the employed interviewees talked about their leisure in relation to their work. The majority saw leisure in terms of escape from work. Nine teenagers, employed in more demanding occupations, saw leisure as a complementary source of satisfaction to their work.

6. Unemployed adolescents did not use commercial leisure provision on a regular basis because of financial constraints and spent considerable time at home.

The experience of unemployment

1. Ten unemployed boys said that they preferred unemployment to having a job, while the rest of the sub-sample ($n = 62$) showed a strong preference for work. Ten girls and 10 boys out of the 62 wishing to work expressed an interest in returning to school, primarily to increase qualifications. The majority of adolescents ($n = 62$) saw unemployment as an unpleasant and unsatisfactory period of their lives. They described the experience as boring, soul-destroying and frustrating. This type of interview response was named by the researchers as 'an ordeal' (see Fig. 9.1). Ten boys dissented, seeing positive aspects in being unemployed. Although they admitted the experience could be boring at times, five boys said that unemployment offered freedom from the constraints of work, not unlike a school holiday. This type of response was named by the researchers as 'vacational' (Fig. 9.1). The other five boys interpreted their period of unemployment as a useful 'breathing space', giving the opportunity to formulate and consider career plans, named as 'vocational' by researchers (Fig. 9.1).

2. Irrespective of which of these three broad attitudes to unemployment was held by adolescents, the amount of self-structure and organization which was imposed on free-time varied considerably from subject to subject (Fig. 9.1). These built-up pictures of typically structured days of unemployed adolescents were derived from interview responses to questions about how mornings, afternoons, evenings and weekends were spent and should be seen to represent strong tendencies rather than carefully constructed time-based statistics.

3. Analysis of adolescents' descriptions of day-time activity from the interview data produced an array of lifestyles outlined on a continuum ranging between fairly rigidly structured and completely unstructured time (Fig. 9.1). Along this continuum, several consistently different and discrete styles of response to free-time were constructed by the researchers and grouped into identifiable lifestyles. Some of these styles are briefly described below:

Domestic servants. These girls ($n = 13$) found that their free-time was taken up almost completely by domestic responsibilities. The household and childcare tasks imposed on them put as many constraints on their time as a full-time job.

Ritual job hunters. While many adolescents made use of the Job Centre and careers offices, a few (boys $n = 4$; girls $n = 1$) used the process of job hunting

144 *Young people's unemployment lifestyles*

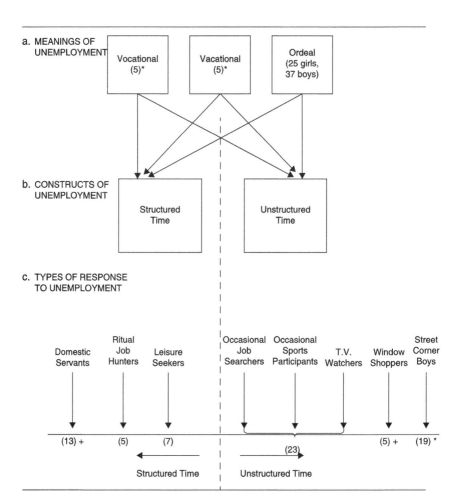

Figure 9.1 Meanings of and responses to unemployment. ( ) denotes *n* values; + denotes female only groups; * denotes male only groups.

(visits to employers, Job Centre and careers office) with a regularity and routine which imposed a clear structure on their free-time.

Leisure seekers. A number of adolescents (boys *n* = 6; girls *n* = 1) used hobbies, sports and unofficial 'work' (helping with home-decorating, working on motor bikes etc.) as a strategy to structure their free-time.

Shoppers. Rather than just 'hanging about', some girls (*n* = 5) went through the motions of shopping (or window shopping) often in the company of friends.

Street corner boys. Like the girl 'shoppers', these boys (*n* = 19) spent their time in social, but completely unstructured and casual, peer groupings. The popularity of 'hanging about' was partly due to the tensions which many respondents said developed between adolescents and their parents. More than half also stated that they were aware that the result of wandering about with friends created opportunities for getting involved in delinquent acts.

Discussion

What do the present findings tell us about the experience of youth unemployment? Two important trends emerge: first, that unemployment extends its influence beyond those adolescents out of work; and secondly, that the question of how to cope with unstructured free-time emerges as a major problem faced by unemployed adolescents.

Influence of unemployment on adolescents

The pervasive influence of unemployment, reaching beyond those adolescents actually out of work, was clearly noticeable in our data. From our study of adolescents in one city it was apparent that pupils about to enter the job market were fully aware of the problems of finding a job, and the school's emphasis on this aspect of unemployment stressed the importance of work in the eyes of pupils. Their reaction to the immediate future was realistic: they were aware of the problems which might lie ahead in the job market, but there was no indication that the fear of unemployment had destroyed their confidence. However, their knowledge of the experiences of unemployment did not appear to have come from the classroom. Very few pupils stated that there had been any discussion of life on the dole or how to cope with large amounts of free-time. The role of schools in the adolescents' transition to society is crucial. Without lessening the emphasis on qualifications and work (Raffe, 1983), perhaps schools need to offer pupils greater insight into the processes and patterns of living in modern society (Ashton and Maguire, 1980). Obvious examples, such as youth training schemes, job sharing, continuing education and a changed emphasis within leisure education programmes (Hargreaves, 1982) can be cited in this connection.

Pupils tended to view future day-to-day living and leisure patterns in terms of the opportunities that only a job could provide. They envisaged a shift away from sports, hobbies and youth clubs towards new, more sophisticated 'adult' leisure interests. Seen together with their enthusiasm for a working life, their view of the future seemed to amount to a 'package deal' where both work and increasingly sophisticated forms of leisure would create facets of an adult lifestyle. This view of work and leisure in post-school life offering status and independence is, in their eyes, necessarily dependent on finding a job.

Similarly, unemployment had an indirect but powerful effect on working adolescents, creating feelings of insecurity about their jobs and forcing them to remain in jobs that some admitted to finding unpleasant and unsatisfying. Simon (1978) has pointed out that enthusiasm for working life tends to evaporate quickly on leaving

146 *Young people's unemployment lifestyles*

school. This was reflected in the cynical attitude to work expressed by the employed school-leavers in our study. There was little intrinsic satisfaction in working: work was only acceptable as a source of money, as a chance to be with friends and as an alternative to the boredom of unemployment. Additionally, most of the employed group interviewed saw the value of leisure in terms of escape or relaxation from work (Parker, 1983), and they tended to make more use of commercial leisure activities, while the unemployed adolescents made more use of cheaper entertainments like youth clubs and 'hanging about'. Unemployed adolescents felt that they were being excluded from the more 'adult' leisure of their employed contemporaries.

Yet in no sense did the unemployed seem to blame themselves for their situation or to be conscious of having low status in the eyes of society. As Kelvin (1981b) has suggested, unemployment is becoming an acceptable aspect of young people's self-perceptions and self-identity as more and more adolescents fail to find a niche in the job market when they leave school. Nevertheless, the results of the present study suggest that unemployment creates a structureless confused time-state for many adolescents within which leisure, with all its concomitant social opportunities, vanishes. It is important to ask, therefore, what use do unemployed adolescents make of their free-time? How does unemployment affect their behaviour, attitudes or sense of social identity? Are there characteristics common to unemployed adolescents analogous to the pattern of values and outlook shared by most employed teenagers?

Unemployed lifestyles

We have suggested that three broad, yet distinct, descriptions can be noted in adolescents' expressions of the experience of unemployment. These descriptions indicate possible variations which may exist in the way young people regard unemployment; being unemployed does not have the same meaning for each adolescent. Within the sample, unemployment, as interpreted by the researchers, was viewed as being 'vocational', 'vacational' or 'an ordeal' (Fig. 9.1).

Unemployment was interpreted as 'an ordeal' – and this was the major perception – if the adolescent saw it as time which should be spent at work. Further rejected job applications, lack of day-to-day structure and continuing boredom had led in many cases to a feeling of apathy which affected any enthusiasm for tackling problems.

When the adolescent perceived unemployment as a long-term 'career' or in terms of a temporary escape from the constraints of work, then the experience seemed to be given a more positive meaning. By seeing the experience as a 'holiday' from the constraints of work, a few adolescents had given their period of unemployment some meaning.

Others tried to treat unemployment as much like work as possible. The formalities and obligations of 'signing on' and looking for work took on a disproportionate importance as a way of structuring time and giving the experience some kind of direction and meaning.

In the same way as it was possible to identify different 'meanings' of unemployment, it was also possible to identify a variety of responses to the problem of free-time among the adolescents in the sub-sample. The variations in lifestyle, therefore, can perhaps best be identified on a continuum of fairly consistent living patterns ranging between relatively rigidly structured time to completely unstructured time. While this analysis is essentially exploratory, it is a first step towards an understanding of youth unemployment which takes account of how individual differences shape the nature and form of the experience in a variety of broadly recognizable ways.

Additionally, unemployment appears to have hidden consequences in reinforcing rather traditional sex roles, with some girls imposing a structure on their day by turning to domestic chores and becoming the family's unpaid servant girl, while several boys used the rituals of 'signing on' and 'job hunting' to recreate the single-sex street corner groupings so noticeable in the 1930s (Jahoda et al., 1933). It is worth noting in this context that about one-quarter of the unemployed teenage boys mentioned that unemployment leads to boredom, and this in turn leads to thoughts of exciting and possibly delinquent activities. Concern about delinquent behaviour has also been outlined by Murray (1978). The question of sex differences is important in that the decline of work should not mean that women find themselves constrained by domestic roles while the possible development of alternative lifestyles is available only to men.

Clearly, these variations in lifestyle need to be considered within a broader social context, and further investigations would require to take account of a number of important social factors. For instance, within the present study adolescents frequently mentioned parental attitudes in relation to unemployment. They suggested that family ethos could range from one of being supportive to one of being oppressive. It might prove illuminating to interview parents with a view to establishing an understanding of the processes and family interactions which produce either support or put pressures on the unemployed adolescent. These interviews might also attempt to investigate the origins of tensions which unemployed adolescents themselves can create within the family.

Further, the economic and employment histories of various regions of the country are different, and a comparative study might reveal a variety of attitudes towards work and unemployment as a reflection of community values. It can be hypothesized that in areas with traditionally higher levels of unemployment there would be less 'stigma' attached to being unemployed; that family attitudes might be less hostile to the plight of the adolescent; and that in schools teachers' attitudes and curricular approaches would be more positively directed to the particular local circumstances of immediate post-school life.

The major impact of unemployment on adolescents, however, may be its social and psychological effects on the transition to adulthood. Being unable to find work appears to thwart adolescents' expectations of post-school patterns of work and leisure, and the frustrations experienced by young people in the loss of a work–leisure 'package deal' may make growing up more difficult for those who cannot find a job.

References

Ashton, D. N. and Maguire, M. J. (1980) The functions of academic and non-academic criteria in employers' selection strategies, *British Journal of Guidance and Counselling* **8**, 146–57.
Brake, M. (1980) *The Sociology of Youth Culture in Youth Sub-Cultures*, Routledge and Kegan Paul, London.
Braun, F. (1977) Youth unemployment in West Germany: the psycho-social aspect, in *Youth Unemployment in Great Britain and the Federal Republic of Germany* (edited by B. O. Pettman and J. Fyfe), MCB, Bradford.
Carter, M. (1971) *Home, School and Work*, Pergamon, London.
Casson, M. (1979) *Youth Unemployment*, Macmillan, London.
Corrigan, P. (1978) *Schooling the Smash Street Kids*, Macmillan, London.
Dennehy, C. and Sullivan, J. (1977) Poverty and unemployment in Liverpool, in *The Conscript Army: a Study of Britain's Unemployed* (edited by F. Field), Routledge and Kegan Paul, London.
Eggleston, J. (1976) *Adolescence and Community*, Arnold, London.
Emmett, I. (1971) *Youth and Leisure in an Urban Sprawl*, Manchester University Press, Manchester.
Entwistle, H. (1970) *Education, Work and Leisure*, Routledge and Kegan Paul, London.
Fogelman, K. (1976) *Britain's Sixteen Year Olds*, National Children's Bureau, London.
Frazer, C. (1980) The social psychology of unemployment, in *Psychology Survey No. 3*, (edited by M. A. Jeeves), Allen & Unwin, London.
Gurney, R. and Taylor, K. (1981) Research on unemployment: defects, neglects and prospects, *Bulletin of the British Psychological Society* **34**, 349–52.
Hargreaves, D. H. (1982) *The Challenge for the Comprehensive School*, Routledge and Kegan Paul, London.
Hayes, J. and Nutman, P. (1981) *Understanding the Unemployed*, Tavistock, London.
Hendry, L. B. (1978) *School Sport and Leisure*, Lepus, London.
Hendry, L. B. (1981) *Adolescents and Leisure*, Sports Council/SSRC, London.
Hendry, L. B. (1983) *Growing Up and Going Out*, Aberdeen University Press, Aberdeen.
Hill, J. (1977) *The Social and Psychological Impact of Unemployment: a Pilot Study*, Tavistock Institute, London.
Hill, J. (1978) The psychological impact of unemployment, *New Society* 19 January.
Holland, G. (1978) MSC: securing a future for young people, *Coombe Lodge Report* **2**, 4.
Jahoda, M. (1979) The impact of unemployment in the 1930s and the 1970s, *Bulletin of the British Psychological Society* **32**, 309–14.
Jahoda, M., Lazarsfield, P. F. and Zeisel, H. (1933) *Marienthal: the Sociography of an Unemployed Community*, Tavistock, London.
Jephcott, P. (1967) *Time of One's Own: Leisure and Young People*, Oliver and Boyd, Edinburgh.
Kelvin, P. (1981a) Work as a source of identity: the implications of unemployment, *British Journal of Guidance and Counselling* **9**, 2–11.
Kelvin, P. (1981b) Social psychology 2001: the social psychological bases and implications of structural unemployment, in *The Development of Social Psychology* (edited by R. Gilmour and S. Duck), Academic Press, London.
Kitwood, J. (1980) *Disclosures to a Stranger*, Routledge and Kegan Paul, London.
Leigh, J. (1971) *Young People and Leisure*, Routledge and Kegan Paul, London.
Lindsay, C. (1969) *School and Community*, Pergamon, London.

Morton-Williams, R. and Finch, S. (1968) *Enquiry 1: Young School Leavers*, HMSO, London.
Murdock, G. and Phelps, G. (1973) *Mass Media and the Secondary School*, Macmillan, London.
Murray, C. (1978) *Youth Unemployment: a Social-psychological Study of Disadvantaged 16–18 Year Olds*, NFER, Slough.
Nisbet, S. (1957) *Purpose in the Curriculum*, University Press, London.
Pahl, R. E. (1978) Living without a job: how school leavers see the future, *New Society* 2 November.
Parker, S. (1983) *Leisure and Work*, Allen & Unwin, London.
Patrick, J. (1973) *A Glasgow Gang Observed*, Methuen, London.
Pettman, B. O. and Fyfe, J. (ed.) (1977) *Youth Unemployment in Great Britain and the Federal Republic of Germany*, MCB, Bradford.
Phillips, D. (1973) Young and unemployed in a northern city, in *Men and Work in Modern Britain* (edited by D. Weir), Fontana, Glasgow.
Raffe, D. (1983) Youth unemployment in Scotland since 1977, *Scottish Educational Review* **15**, 16–27.
Roberts, K., Duggan, J. and Noble, M. (1982) Out of school in high unemployment areas: an empirical investigation, *British Journal of Guidance and Counselling* **10**, 1–11.
Scarlett, C. L. (1975) *Euroscot: the New European Generation*, Conference of Voluntary Youth Organizations, Edinburgh.
Scottish Council for Community Education (1981) *Community School in Scotland*, SCCE, New St Andrews House, Edinburgh.
Simon, M. (1978) Young people's attitudes to work, in *Youth in Contemporary Society* (edited by C. Murray), NFER, Slough.
Smith, M. A. and Simpkins, A. F. (1980) *Unemployment and Leisure: a Review and Some Proposals for Research*, Salford University Press, Salford.
Weir, D. and Nolan, F. (1977) *Glad to be Out?* SCER, Edinburgh.
Willis, P. (1977) *Learning to Labour*, Saxon House, Farnborough.

10 Young people in modern society

Sometimes it is fun to be provocative and challenge others to respond to one's ideas and offer different viewpoints. The role adults play in young people's socialization is vital to their development as future citizens. So, how do adults in Western societies enable adolescents to make 'successful' transitions to adulthood? This extract is a polemic, though based on empirical finding, in order to coax academics, professionals and policy-makers to re-consider the issue of adolescents' societal roles, and, for example, to re-consider their approaches to working with, and planning policies for young people's development.

'OVER-PROTECTION, OVER-PROTECTION, OVER-PROTECTION!' YOUNG PEOPLE IN MODERN BRITAIN

Marion Kloep and Leo B. Hendry

There is no doubt that institutionalisation represents a mechanism for adapting children to norms and rules of modern technological society; but by doing so it is an effective way of colonising children's time. Besides their protective and caretaking qualities, institutions can also deprive children of alternative options for using their own time. As Büchner commented:

Taking possession of social space thus ensues under the protective accompaniment and control of adults ... Road and traffic conditions force urban children away from playing in the street with the result that independent and unsupervised opportunities for social contacts are less available. Children's street world, formed relatively independently and composed of children from a variety of backgrounds and age groups, is increasingly replaced by integration into various peer-group social sets, often chosen and supervised by parents for particular purposes and activities.

(Büchner, 1990, p.79)

In modern societies, with their expanding synthetic and technological environments, children move less freely and have fewer opportunities to learn to experience and manipulate their 'natural' environment. They are increasingly confined to play-groups, clubs and commercial settings, designed by adults to protect young people from the environment. For example, the number of children killed in road accidents in Britain has declined dramatically over the past 30 years, at the same time as the number of children allowed to move around freely in the environment (visiting leisure parks or crossing roads alone) has decreased at the same rate. Qvortrup (2000) concluded that the price for reducing the number of children killed on the roads was partly paid by the children themselves, and added:

> *The car is seen by (male) adults as the ultimate epitome of freedom, while for children it almost literally means curfew.*
>
> (Qvortrup, 2000, p.92)

Zinnecker (1990) called this 'manufacturing of the environment', augmenting the 'Verhäuslichung' of young people in modern societies. Growing artificiality in Western societies creates situations where, increasingly, 'contrived' games substitute for real-life experiences. Children feed their plastic dolls and play 'mother-father-child' or experience family life by manipulating virtual personalities on a computer screen, while their age-mates in other societies actually take care of their younger siblings or help their parents in the fields. Adventure holiday centres and theme parks are attempts to substitute for real rivers to swim in, natural forests to explore, and fresh sea breezes to breathe. All adventures and challenges of unplanned, self-organised, explorative kinds on the part of children are carefully arranged and designed by adults to ensure that no-one is hurt, and so many get easily bored!

With adolescence, one of the most often stated complaints young people have about their 'unprotected' time, is that there is 'absolutely nothing to do'. Interestingly, this does not correlate with the actual amount of time spent on 'free' activities, nor with the number of different activities young people participate in. Hendry *et al.* (2002a) suggested that it might not be the quantity, but the quality of activities that create feelings of boredom. What is on offer has become too 'childish' and too 'adult-supervised' to be of interest, and there is no *real* challenge to the adolescent's perceived abilities. Sometimes adults give young adolescents the possibility of arranging their own leisure time – and find themselves disappointed with the results. Few adolescents are willing to take the initiative, some abuse the trust conferred on them, some even, at times, destroying the facilities given to them. Young people are often aware of their inability to create their own leisure time. This should not be too surprising. To create a meaningful free time, a wide range of personal, social and organisational skills are needed, skills young people may not have had the possibility to develop during childhood, when everything had been organised for them. These skills they must learn by gradual practice – and the learning process should ideally begin as early as possible.

From a Canadian study, Shaw, Caldwell and Kleiber (1996) concluded that the frequent experiences of boredom were not simply a matter of too little to do, but were associated in a more complex way with adolescence and its relationship to wider culture. Adolescents who experienced high levels of both stress and boredom may be particularly resistant to, or feel alienated from, the dominant adult culture and its set of values. Caldwell *et al.* (1999) suggest that boredom might be a 'resistance' response to external control such as the influence of parents or other adults, and as such might even develop into a habitual response that becomes a routine aspect of adolescent culture.

Sports clubs, hobby groups, choirs and orchestras, youth clubs and uniformed organisations all tend to be arranged for children by adults, and are often closely supervised by adults. Adolescents' involvement in such adult-sponsored situations, though nominally voluntary, may not be genuinely self-chosen, and may confront young people with the dilemma of choosing to participate in a setting which if anything perpetuates adult dominance in the adolescent's life, perhaps in exchange for the training of well-regarded skills and the advantages of acquired social status.

While *organised* leisure offers possibilities to learn skills under adult guidance, casual leisure offers the opportunity to enact and try out future adult roles, to socialise with peers and rehearse different social skills without adult intervention (Hendry *et al.*, 1996, 2002b). However, how often can modern young people engage in truly casual leisure? For example, in a study by McMeeking and Purkayasta (1995), young people indicated that regardless of location, the key issue of non-organised leisure was a shared concern about their general inability to independently access 'free' time facilities. Among the causes of frustration was the lack of accessible 'spaces' as well as the social sanctions prohibiting the use of such spaces for unstructured activities that young people so enjoy in adolescence. This finding was repeated in a rural study carried out by Hendry *et al.* (1998) where young people felt they were excluded and even driven away by adult citizens (or the police) because their numbers were seen to create a public nuisance. Yet from the young people's perspective such gatherings were designed to let them socialise, plan the evening's activities or arrange to travel home in company.

Young people desire 'unprotected' settings for meeting friends, socialising and 'trying out' social skills and strategies away from the presence or influence of adults. Either they have to submit to close adult supervision as in youth clubs or organised leisure, or they are excluded from other venues and confined to the street corner, public parks or shopping malls. They do not feel welcome in adult society, which only leaves them the choice between over-protection and no protection at all! Feeling over-protected and unchallenged, they need to alleviate boredom by creating their own adventures. This may conflict with society's values, and even at times with the law – thus confirming the horror picture some adults have of 'teenage monsters'. Popular image is focussed on the young person as the perpetrator of violence: young people mugging old ladies, joy-riding in stolen cars, videoing slap-happy incidents, bullying younger peers either virtually or in the playground.

Young people in modern society 153

On the other hand, there are strong forces in society that pressurise young people towards conformity. This can take extreme forms of prosecuting parents, sending under-aged offenders to a kind of concentration camp (like the Boot Camps promoted by certain American TV shows), though Finkenauer (1982) found that they failed to deter delinquency and possibly actually provoked increased criminality. A growing number of European countries have introduced juvenile curfew laws, prohibiting young people under a certain age being unaccompanied in the streets during late evening. This has been done in spite of studies that show that the curfew laws in the US have no discernible effect on juvenile crime or juvenile victimisation (e.g. Reynolds, Seydlitz & Jenkins 2000).

The hypothesis presented here is that adolescents in many cases are not challenged enough. They feel prevented from social learning with peers, trying out new skills and gaining new experiences. Such an enforced limbo leaves them with feelings of boredom, which for some lead to resignation, and for others to rebellion. Overprotected by parents, teachers and the law, they are not given enough 'space' to try out their skills and to generate their own challenges. Because of that, they seize every opportunity to do so – only to find out that they often do not have the capabilities to create meaningful activities for themselves, because up to now adults have provided these for them. Some retreat into passivity and boredom, while others over-estimate their skills and engage in risky behaviours as soon as they can escape from adult protection. This in turn provokes adults to react with even more over-protection, or even punitively, provoked by young people's attempt 'to seize adult rights', which grown-ups see as a status offence. In many cases young people 'choose' to accept conformity and limit their developmental potential, which may have implications for later in their life course and for society generally (Hendry & Kloep, 2002). In other words: It might be (developmentally) risky not to take risks from time to time!

We want to argue that even apparently risky activities may contain elements of challenge, offering the potential for growth (see, for example, Pape & Hammer's, 1996, study on adolescent alcohol use). People take risks and weigh up the enjoyment and advantages of their various social and leisure activities against the dangers and pitfalls of such involvement. This 'cost-benefit risk' assessment is an elaborate psychosocial process and an important generalisable 'meta-skill', because testing the 'goodness of fit' between challenges and one's skills and resources leads to learning how to assess whether one can cope with life or not.

Young people are controlled and 'protected' by a variety of social institutions like schools and youth organisations during most of their day. Yet, paradoxically, in modern society children and youths have to engage in more and more areas of independent living, which demand individuality and skills to decide, to act proactively, and to demonstrate individual taste, for example, in spending money, in time-planning, selecting friends, and in fashion, leisure and media consumption. In such settings, however, they may be 'at risk' due to lack of experience and/or a lack of relevant skills. It is vital for young people to be empowered to learn the skills and competencies that may be necessary for a rapidly changing world where self-efficacy and independence are at a premium to meet developmental challenges. In order to display genuine self-agency, young people have to seek out periods and contexts of 'unprotected' time and to engage in a series of self-activated developmental experiences.

Nowadays young people are increasingly required to take the initiative in forming work and personal relationships, gaining educational credentials and employment experience, and planning for their future. Those who address these issues in a proactive way and with self-agency may be most likely to form a coherent sense of identity towards their subsequent life course (e.g. Schwartz, Côté & Arnett, 2005). On the other hand, an inability to shape identity is linked to heightened risks, insecurity, and stress (e.g. Arnett, 2006; Parker *et al.*, 1998). Arnett (2004) has shown that emerging adults need an increasingly extended period to commit to adult vocational and social roles. We suggest that this is a result of years of over-protection and dependency.

Somewhat provocatively, it is claimed here, that over-protected time can be as dangerous as unprotected time. By caring too much for organising and structuring children's time, adults destroy important learning opportunities. Self-agency is not a characteristic young people are given automatically on their 18th birthday, it is a set of self-efficacy skills that has to be acquired through experiential learning. This includes reflecting on one's own mistakes. Mistakes, provided they are not overly disastrous, can actually serve as 'steeling' experiences (Rutter, 1996), 'immunising' young people against the negative effects of future failure. The key to all this is that we should not prevent risk-taking in young people, but rather, assist them to take moderate risks and to assess these in relation to their growing capabilities from early in the life course. This would imply giving opportunities to children to try out different competencies, breaking down tasks into manageable challenges and allowing them occasionally to take minor risks – and even suffer small negative consequences from such risk-taking (e.g. Rutter, 1996).

As we have pointed out: risks are part of the developmental experimentation of all human beings. Whilst it is vital that young people learn a range of skills under the tutelage of various adults in their lives, it is equally important for their development to experience periods of 'Under-protection, Under-protection, Under-protection!'

References

Arnett, J. J. (2004) *Emerging adulthood: The winding road from late teens through the twenties*. Oxford: Oxford University Press

Arnett, J. J. (2006) Emerging adulthood in Europe: A response to Bynner. *Journal of Youth Studies, 9*, 11–123.

Büchner, P. (1990) Aufwachsen in den 80er Jahren, in H. H. Krüger and L. Chisholm (Eds) *Kindheit und Jugend im interkulturellen Vergleich*. Leske und Budrich, Opladen, pp 79–123.

Caldwell, L. L., Darling. N., Payne, L. L. and Dowdy, B. (1999) "Why are you bored?" An examination of psychological and social control causes of boredom among adolescents. *Journal of Leisure* Research, *31*, 103–121.

Finkenauer, J. O. (1982) *Scared Straight! and the panacea phenomenon*. Englewood Cliffs, NJ, Prentice-Hall.

Hendry, L. B. and Kloep, M. (2002) *Lifespan development: Challenges, resources and risks*. London: Thomson.

Hendry, L. B., Kloep, M., Glendinning, A., Ingebrigtsen, J. E., Espnes, G. A. and Wood, S. (2002a) Leisure transitions: A rural perspective. Journal of Leisure Studies, 21, 1–14

Hendry, L. B., Kloep, M. and Wood, S. (2002b) Young people talking about adolescent rural crowds and social settings. *Journal of Youth Studies*, 5, 357–374.

Hendry, L B., Shucksmith, J and Glendinning, A (1996) Adolescent focal theories: Age trends in developmental transitions, *Journal of Adolescence*, 19, 4, 307–320

Hendry, L, Glendinning, A, Reid, M. and Wood, S (1998) *Lifestyles, health and health concerns of rural youth: 1996–1998*. Report to Department of Health, Scottish Office, Edinburgh.

McMeeking, D. and Purkayastha, B. (1995) I can't have my mom running me everywhere: Adolescents, leisure and accessibility. *Journal of Leisure Research, 27*, 360–378

Pape, H. and Hammer, T. (1996) Sober adolescence – Predictor of psychosocial maladjustment in young adulthood? *Scandinavian Journal of Psychology, 37*, 4, 362–377.

Parker, H., Aldridge, J. and Measham, F. (1998) *Illegal leisure*. Routledge, London.

Qvortrup, J. (2000) Macroanalysis of childhood, in P. Christensen and A. James (Eds.) *Research with children: Perspectives and practices* (pp 77–97). London: Falmer Press

Reynolds, K. M., Seydlitz, A. and Jenkins, P. (2000) Do juvenile curfew laws work? A time-series analysis of the New Orleans Law. *Justice Quarterly, 17*, 205–230.

Rutter, M. (1996) Psychological adversity: risk, resilience and recovery. In L. Verhofstadt-Deneve, I. Kienhorst, and C. Braet (Eds.) *Conflict and Development in Adolescence* (pp. 21–34) Leiden: DSWO Press.

Schwartz, S. J., Côté, J. E. and Arnett, J. J. (2005) Identity and agency in emerging adulthood. *Youth and Society, 37*, 201–229.

Shaw, S. M., Caldwell, L. L., and Kleiber, D. A. (1996) Boredom, stress and social control in the daily activities of adolescents. *Journal of Leisure Research 28*, 274–292

Zinnecker, J. (1990) Vom Strassenkind zum verhäuslichten Kind. Kindheitsgeschichte im Prozess der Zivilisation, in I. Behnke (Ed.) *Stadtgesellschaft und Kindheit im Prozess der Zivilisation* (pp. 142–162). Opladen: Leske und Budrich.

AUTHORS' RESPONSE TO PEER COMMENTARY

Marion Kloep & Leo B. Hendry

Finding a balance?

Discussing the discussants

In attempting to write a short but provocative article on over-protection it is pleasing to find in the main that valued colleagues agreed with our comments. Of course, we were very sensitive to the criticism that in a short article it is not possible to look at all the nuances and individual differences in young people's responses to their various relationships with adult society. Thus, we are thankful to our commentators for picking up and developing certain themes we were not able to develop as fully as we would have liked.

In particular, we liked Caldwell's idea of differentiating between necessary-protection, unnecessary-protection and over-protection, and Schoon for drawing attention to the fact that the world is still full of risks, particularly the cascading constraints of disadvantages associated with poverty. Of course, it was not these kinds of risks we were particularly thinking about. On the contrary, we believe, in an ideal world, children should not need to be protected from risks created by adult society: Rather, adult society should not create these in the first place! We agree totally that governments should put more effort into eliminating these risks emerging from poverty and inequality instead of, for example, writing EU regulations forbidding the building of south-facing metallic slides in children's playgrounds in case they could burn their little bottoms on the many hot summer days we experience in the UK! Already in the early 1970s, Sutton-Smith and Heron (1971) complained that society created the children's leisure environment in playgrounds by 'caging them in' and then expecting them to engage in 'free, expressive play'.

We also liked Wareham's comment that previous generations of young people were more involved with the productive adult activities of their parents, which helped them to learn real life skills. We have pointed out earlier (Hendry & Kloep, 2002) that there is more value in supervising one's own siblings than playing with electronic dolls – a point made long ago by pedagogues such as Celestine Freinet.

More importantly, however, Wareham misunderstood our key point about unsupervised time: We do not advocate more free time *per se* – rather we recommend, as do Caldwell and Christie, that children need to acquire the skills of self-organising their free time; and this is crucial in today's culture as there are many more leisure opportunities in modern Western societies than for previous generations. Further, we do not want these learning contexts to happen in 'still artificial and supervised' situations. One example, to make the point clearer, would be of a 5-year-old who wants to set the table for a meal. Instead of preventing him/her from doing this, the parent can allow the child to carry out the task – but be around to comfort and encourage the child, and be available to help clean up if the milk is spilled!

Adults should be available on request, but not be imposing or intrusive. It should be a mentoring rich environment, or as Schoon calls it a 'buddy system'. Some years ago Philip and Hendry (1996) offered a typology of mentoring styles, which ranged from adult mentors, through youth work team mentoring to peers and neighbours as mentors. The major principles were shown to be that the young person selected who their mentor was to be (older friends and friends' parents could fulfil the role) when support or guidance was needed, the mentoring process was initiated by the young person, and that they retained a degree of control of the process in terms of how often they met, what the agenda was and when the relationship could revert to being a friendship or could end. Of course, we have to add the caveat that not all young people find a mentor when they need one and that is an issue to which we should give some future attention.

Christie drew attention to the potential risks for young peoples' social development in an over-protected, over-organised world. Research in Norwegian nursery schools has shown that the constant intervention of adult staff in children's disagreements leads not only to an exacerbation of the conflicts, but also creates the situation whereby children miss the opportunity to learn adequate social conflict solving skills (Gravråkmo, 2000; Meisfjord, 2002).

Kirwan criticises us for not taking into account gender, class and ethnicity. We might not have made this clear in this short article, but all our theoretical arguments include individual variability to a very high degree. More than being aware of structural variables, our Lifespan Model of Developmental Challenge (Hendry & Kloep, 2002) recognises inter- and intra-individual differences, much in the same way that Caldwell described it: One youth in one setting is not the same as another youth in another setting – and even the same youth in the same situation may behave differently at various points in time. This also answers Wareham's question as to why all the people he knows seem to be well adapted. He is lucky to know the well adapted ones! Fortunately for British society they are in a majority, as Coleman and Hendry (1999) have shown, but the UNICEF (2007) report cited by our colleagues reveals that there are still far too many less fortunate ones. Furthermore, even the skills of the relatively well adapted ones could be improved. Studies on 'emerging adults' (e.g. Arnett, 2004) shows there is an increasing group of less proactive young adults, who have a poor self-image, lack of social and planning skills, are still considerably dependent on parents, have not settled on a career trajectory and are in an extended moratorium. This indicates a need for new thinking and new policy and practice solutions for those who work with young people to enable the acquisition of leisure time and self management skills.

We are aware that youth workers attempt to achieve this, as Kirwan emphasises. However, even youth workers do not necessarily succeed all the time. As one Swedish girl complained in one of our cross-cultural interview studies: *There is a youth-club there, but there is usually only five people around. To be there is like being at home, constantly supervised by parents* (cited in Hendry *et al.*, 2002). An extensive study of perceptions of youth work settings by Love and Hendry (1994) showed that whilst youth workers believed that they enabled young people to participate in organising activities, planning, decision making and negotiating democratically, young people themselves saw these contexts as adult dominated, autocratic and hierarchical. Some of these attempts to help adolescents by establishing meeting places even create negative outcomes: Frequent participation in youth centres has been linked to high rates of juvenile offending in Sweden (Mahoney *et al.*, 2001) and to social exclusion later in adulthood in Britain (Feinstein *et al.*, 2006). Clearly we haven't found the right balance yet, despite optimistic Governmental reports!

In our original paper, which was meant to provoke, and in the comments of our peer reviewers, which in general echo and extend our main thesis of over-protection potentially restricting adolescents' social and leisure involvement, and limiting their mastery of needed adult skills and roles, it appears a developmental issue is apparent – one that needs to be addressed by a range of professions in both formal and informal educational settings.

More than that, this exchange of ideas has raised a number of points worthy of further consideration and discussion in schools, youth clubs, sports organisations and between adolescents and adults, in order to help find a balance between activities where adults clearly lead and initiate learning opportunities for young people so that they can become integrated and effectively participating citizens, and those where young people can be self-initiating and proactive learners in order to develop their individuality and creativity in ways that assist in creating a multi-talented society.

References

Arnett, J.J. (2004). *Emerging adulthood: The winding road from late teens through the twenties*. Oxford: Oxford University Press.

Coleman, J.C. & Hendry, L.B. (1999). *The nature of adolescence* (3rd ed.). London: Routledge.

Feinstein, L., Bynner, J. & Duckworth, K. (2006). Young people's leisure contexts and their relation to adult outcomes. *Journal of Youth Studies, 9*, 305–327.

Gravråkmo, S. (2000). *Konflikt og aggresjon blant førskolebarn – en observasjonsstudie*. Unp. Hovedfagsoppgave, Psykologisk Institutt, NTNU.

Hendry, L.B. & Kloep, M. (2002). *Life-span development: Resources, challenges and risks*. London: Thomson Learning.

Hendry, L.B., Kloep, M., Glendinning, A., Ingebrigtsen, J.E., Espnes, G.A. & Wood, S. (2002). Leisure transitions: A rural perspective. *Journal of Leisure Studies, 21*, 1–14.

Love, J. & Hendry, L.B. (1994). Youth workers and youth participants: Two perspectives of youth work? *Youth and Policy, 46*, 43–55.

Mahoney, J.L., Stattin, H. & Magnusson, D. (2001). Youth recreation centre participation and criminal offending: A 20-year longitudinal study of Swedish boys. *Journal of Behavioral Development, 25*, 509–520.

Meisfjord, H.J. (2002). *Rettferdighet er å få det som man vill*. Unp. Hovedfagsoppgave, Psykologisk Institutt, NTNU.

Philip, K. & Hendry, L.B. (1996). Young people and mentoring – towards a typology. *Journal of Adolescence, 19*, 189–201.

11 Challenging the orthodoxy
What is 'emerging adulthood'?

Over previous decades Developmental Psychology's focus on the earlier phases of the life course has resulted in many publications suggesting that human beings reached a kind of developmental utopian state on becoming adult: This was, and is, blatantly untrue. The ideas encapsulated in my earlier writings dictated a shift in my thinking from simply considering 'developmental change' in adolescence towards a more comprehensive approach of studying lifespan change and an opportunity arose when I was challenged to debate the ideas behind 'emerging adulthood'.

It has been suggested in the literature that making transitions from adolescence towards adulthood has become more complicated for young people and that social forces mean that they are bereft of authoritative adult advice and lacking a social 'compass'. These suggestions have led certain theorists to propose that a new life-stage needs to be created and added to Erikson's eight stages. In 2007, Jeffrey Arnett challenged me to a public debate about transitions from adolescence to early adulthood at an international conference in Tucson, Arizona. This 'duel' roused considerable academic interest and ultimately resulted in 'friendly disagreements' within a joint publication (see Arnett et al., 2011).

The following extract is one of two articles previously written for Child Development Perspectives. From our viewpoint we disagreed that it is necessary to create a new age stage because age-based theories may describe, but cannot explain, human development. We further questioned whether emerging adulthood is necessarily a positive time for many young people and proposed that it could be problematic in Western societies. Finally, we suggested that, in concert with our lifespan model, the concept might be adapted to provide individual illustrations of certain developmental challenges within a hitherto neglected period of the lifespan.

We have always argued that the concept of 'stages' is not a valid or relevant way to take account of, and explain, the wide variety of developmental trajectories and transitional pathways that exist across the lifespan or to take account of sub-cultural and national variations. Additionally, from a developmental baseline of transitions from adolescence towards early adulthood, I gradually extended my research focus to consider the whole life course and in sections 12 and 13 I offer two examples of transitional processes, adjustments and adaptations from later in the lifespan. Theorists from Freud to Piaget to Erikson have discussed various stages of transition – and stage theories are still accepted by some social scientists today – though to my mind while they were useful in their day they became obsolete as new ideas stressed the importance of systemic processes. Nevertheless, they all agreed that some form of crisis obtained when change was occurring, and there is no doubt that changing a system evokes both uncertainty and instability for a time. To demonstrate such dynamism we consider, first, the differing responses of mid-life adults to their children's attempts to gain independence and, second, the perceived transitional adjustments of senior citizens to retirement.

CONCEPTUALIZING EMERGING ADULTHOOD

Inspecting the emperor's new clothes?

Leo B. Hendry and Marion Kloep

Academics worldwide have congratulated Arnett (2000, 2006) for focusing over the last decade or so on a previously under-researched phase of the life span. Societal and economic changes and shifts inspired him to ask what these forces meant to the transition from adolescence to adulthood. Arguably, this theory has been hailed by some as the most important theoretical contribution to developmental psychology in the past 10 years (Gibbons & Ashdown, 2006).

Nevertheless, in this article, we want to play the part of the little boy in Hans Christian Andersen's story who points out the Emperor's lack of clothes, because in our view, his ideas on this period of transition contain several limitations, which should be addressed if future research is to advance on firmer theoretical grounds. To examine these points, we concentrate on the following issues:

1   The configuration of adolescence, early adulthood, and adulthood.
2   Retrospect and prospect: Do we really need the term?
3   Is emerging adulthood experienced positively or negatively by most young people?
4   Is emerging adulthood good for society?

The configuration of emerging adulthood

Arnett (2004) is right in suggesting that the transition to adulthood has become increasingly prolonged as a result of economic changes, with many young people staying in education longer, marrying later, and having their first child later than in the past and that in present day society, it is difficult to determine when adolescence ends and adulthood begins. However, he is not the first to make this observation:

> The distinction between youth status and adult status is gradually blurring: Over the last fifteen years, the behavioural differences between youth and adults have drastically diminished. In a growing number of life spheres (sexuality, political behaviour, etc.) young people behave like adults or claim the same rights as adults.
>
> (Buchmann, 1989, p. 85)

What is new in Arnett's theory is the proposal of a new stage in human development, distinct from adolescence and adulthood, overlapping with both stages (Arnett, 2007; see Figure 11.1).

We do not agree with this model for several reasons. First, Arnett suggests that adulthood (however defined) is fully attained at a certain stage, though there is wide agreement among psychologists that development is domain specific and demonstrates plasticity (e.g., Baltes, 1987, 1997). Thus, not all areas of human functioning are affected to the same degree, in the same direction, or at the same time. Young people might reach adult status early in some domains, later in others, and in some aspects, never. Further, development is nonlinear and reversible (Baltes, 1987, 1997). Young people having reached adulthood according to their own perceptions and by societal markers may find themselves in circumstances where they have to "regress" both subjectively and objectively. For example, it is not uncommon that after cohabitation, some young people return to their familial house when the relationship breaks up, losing the feelings of independence associated with adult status. This can even happen temporarily when young (and not so young) people pursuing a career and feeling completely independent of their parents might in times of illness happily assume the role of cared-for child (Cohen, Kasen, Chen, Hartmark, & Gordon, 2003). The transition from adolescence to adulthood is not as smooth as Arnett proposes, being domain specific, variable, and reversible.

Second, given the few, if any, normative shifts in present-day life, the search for identity is a process of recurring moratoria and achievements extending over the entire life span (e.g., Hendry & Kloep, 2002). Fauske (1996) noted that if youth can no longer be interpreted as a bridge between childhood and adulthood as two stable statuses (as Arnett proposes), there is an alternative scenario, which is some kind of perpetual youth. Adults behave like young people, undergo cosmetic surgery, return to college, fall in love with new partners, start a different career, have exciting leisure pursuits, follow youth fashions, and even give birth in advanced biological age:

> Next time you visit the supermarket, you may encounter . . . newborn infants with their mothers who are aged fifteen and sixteen and newborn infants with mothers aged thirty-five to forty. You may encounter, in fact, grandparents in their early forties as well as parents in their sixties and seventies.
>
> (Fiske & Chiriboga, 1990, p. 286)

If there have to be stages to describe the human life course, the idea of emerging phases between them should be applied to the whole life course. In other

162 *Challenging the orthodoxy*

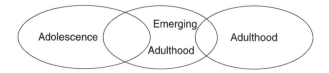

Figure 11.1 Arnett's conceptualization of emerging adulthood.

words, most of us are almost always in the state of being in between or emerging:

> Adult life, then, is a process—a process, we must emphasise, which need not involve a predetermined series of stages of growth. The stages or hurdles, which are placed in front of people and the barriers through which they have to pass (age-specific transitions) can be shifted around and even discarded.
> (Featherstone & Hepworth, 1991, p. 375)

In Figure 11.2, we illustrate our conceptualization of transitions (though the connections between phases should be in a continual state of dynamic fluctuation to indicate plasticity and reversibility).

Do we really need the term?

Arnett (2004) is right that in today's rapidly changing world, traditional developmental tasks such as gaining independence from parents, making personal living arrangements, orienting to a career, and developing new sets of relationships with parents, peers, romantic partners, and so on are differently ordered and present

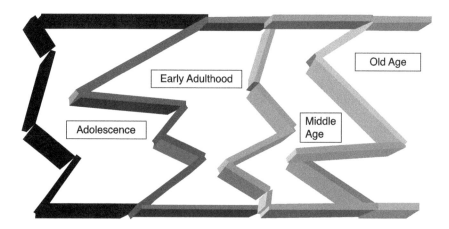

Figure 11.2 Hendry and Kloep's conceptualization of life transitions.

young people with significant challenges in gaining adult status. However, modern developmentalists have claimed that emerging adulthood is not a universal stage but depends on the cultural context in which young people develop and the social institutions they encounter (Bynner, 2005; Heinz & Marshall, 2003). Findings from studies of non-Western cultures and ethnic minorities suggest that generalizations about emerging adults do not capture the variations that exist within individuals and across cultures (Arnett, 2003; Cheah & Nelson, 2004; Nelson, Badger, & Wu, 2004). In many countries, young people, particularly women in rural areas, are granted no moratorium for identity exploration but glide quickly from childhood into adulthood. For example, in Turkey, the mean age for marriage is 21 years (Atak & Çok, 2007). Lloyd (2005) has stated that the largest generation of young people in history is now making the transition from childhood to adulthood, with 86% of this cohort, nearly 1.5 billion individuals, living in developing countries. Many of them do not experience adolescence, much less emerging adulthood!

The fact that socioeconomic conditions heavily influence the lifestyles and options of individuals in a given society is not new. Apart from Marx's well-known historic materialism, social scientists have repeatedly observed this, and Rindfuss, Swicegard, and Rosenfeld (1987) stated that the life course deviates from an idealized "normal" pattern from time to time because the shaping of early adulthood is conditioned by the historical context.

To give a few examples of varying transitional pathways to adulthood with an extended period of moratorium for some, centuries ago Jane Austen wrote about how many upper class youngsters never followed an occupation and remained dependent on their parents until they died. In the same historical period, many 12-year-old children left their families to join a ship's crew or go mining or serve as maids in wealthy households, whereas some women only became "independent" adults when they married. In the political sphere, Queen Mary of Scotland married the French Dauphin (aged 14) at age 15 and a year later became Queen of France.

Considering the points above, the theory of emerging adulthood is merely a description limited to a certain age cohort in certain societies at a certain historical time with particular socioeconomic conditions. This implies that the concept will almost certainly become outdated, given that Western societies are bound to change and new cohorts emerge with different developmental characteristics in different social contexts. New technologies have an impact on young peoples' socialization and learning. There are effects of the "war on terror" on family life, a changing work–leisure balance together with demographic shifts, and increasing migration, to name but a few possible societal trends into the future that will require new theories of development.

As such, Arnett's construct of emerging adulthood does not advance our knowledge and understanding of human development. On the contrary, by elevating it to the status of a theory, we are repeating an error psychology made decades ago when it regarded male behavior as the norm. We are now in danger of having a psychology of the affluent middle classes in Western societies, with other groups being seen as deviating from that norm.

This is not a problem of Arnett's theory alone. All age-bound stage theories, from Freud to Erikson, have been criticized for being ethnocentric and having social class and gender biases. There is a great diversity among people across the life span, and as Valsiner (1997) has said, whereas median trends are useful to observe, it is the error variance that is crucial to our understanding of human development. Age, like other structural variables such as gender, social class, or ethnicity, may predict, but do not explain, developmental phenomena. It is not age in itself that causes development; it is the experiences, and not necessarily associated with chronological age, that cause developmental change. Bynner (2005) proposed that there is a need to

> move away from a blanket categorisation of individuals in terms of stages bounded by chronological age towards a broader conception based on a range of trajectories or pathways.
>
> (p. 378)

In other words, how useful is it to create yet another age stage into existing theories that are neither universal nor explanatory? Rather, we need to investigate the processes and mechanisms of developmental change and abandon age stage theories altogether if we want to go beyond descriptions and seek explanations about development.

Is the experience of emerging adulthood a positive or negative one?

Relying on young people's own optimistic perspectives of the future, Arnett (2007) sees the period of emerging adulthood as mainly positive for the individual. Whether the experience of a prolonged moratorium is positive, however, depends to a large extent on what societal group they belong to and how they use this period of moratorium.

Castells (1998) observed that the contemporary contours of diffuse social, economic, and cultural conditions present new challenges because people must lead their lives without a road map. In Western societies, the signposts and symbols of approaching adulthood are inconsistent and difficult for the young person to understand and interpret. These complexities led Coles (1995) to compare adolescent transitions to a deadly serious game of snakes and ladders, where the main transitions are the ladders through which young people gradually move toward adult status. Although this may sound as if growing up in modern societies is risky, we often forget that many more young people survive childhood, adolescence, and emerging adulthood than in previous ages. It is true that young people are confronted with a range of challenges on their way to adulthood and that these challenges create anxieties. One of the significant contributions stage theorists have made to developmental psychology has been to pinpoint that without challenges, conflicts, and crises, there is no developmental change.

Thus, young people face a range of choices, challenges, and risks in relationships, schooling, higher education, and work (Coleman & Hendry, 1999). Although this may open up opportunities for some, there are fewer safety nets for others, with inequalities in the distribution of resources such as social class, ethnicity, gender, health, and education (Coleman & Schofield, 2005; Coles, 1995; Hendry, Kloep, & Olsson, 1998; MacDonald, 1997; Wyn & White, 1997):

> It can be misleading to present society as changing with all elements; in effect, "marching in step". We need to recognise that the traditional routes to adulthood, with far fewer signs of its emergent status, are still very much in place.
>
> (Bynner, 2005, p. 380)

Although it may be true that independence, possibilities, and choices are available for those who can access consumer markets, this may hold only for the young person who has an income or, better yet, supportive parents: Wealthy middle-class youths do have better options (e.g., Furlong & Cartmel, 1997).

Similar to Heinz's (2007) variety of pathways to occupational roles, we propose from our own research of 18- to 30-year-olds in Wales, who were either working or unemployed and not attending any school (Kloep & Hendry, 2007), at least three broad subgroups of young people in Western societies, each experiencing the period of emerging adulthood very differently. Of these, 74% stated that they considered themselves to be adult and only 13% felt "in-between" (whereas Arnett's, 2004, study found 60% feeling in-between).

One of the three groups identified was in extended moratorium, which was similar to Arnett's (2004, 2006) affluent, middle-class students. With parental support, they could afford a prolonged moratorium, live at home, seek new opportunities, delay in choosing a career, "have fun," and not be fully adult. Although this sounds a pleasant experience, the danger is that these young people would not develop adult skills and might experience "happy" developmental stagnation through over-protection (Hendry & Kloep, 2002). With regard to education, Levine (2005) argued that many young people in their mid-20s have not learned planning, organizational, decision-making, and interpersonal skills that are necessary for the transitions into working life. He believes that education leaves these young people unprepared to move into adulthood because they are both over-indulged and pressured by parents to excel in all life domains, leaving them uncommitted to deep, focused, and detailed learning. Relatively speaking, this group is forever emerging but never adult. The increasing number of young and middle-aged adults who cannot manage their credit card debts seems to point to a lack of life skills in the wider population.

A second subgroup found in the Wales sample was disadvantaged by their lack of resources, skills, and societal opportunities, though superficially they exhibited a somewhat similar lifestyle to the more affluent subgroup, living with parents and occasionally accepting temporary unskilled jobs. The difference here was that they were in this rut not through choice but through lack of opportunities. Rather than being in a state of emerging adulthood, they were more likely in a state of "prevented adulthood" and in "unhappy stagnation." Lack of affordable housing, education, and suitable jobs prevented them from gaining independence and self-reliance. Many noted that choices and possibilities were available *but not for them*, and this was unlikely to change in the near future. Members of this group not only lacked adult skills but also felt bitter and alienated from society. In drawing attention to the economic and social factors that keep some dependent until at least their mid-20s, Côté (2000) concluded that a significant number of young adults have transitional difficulties and greatest problems come to those with least economic, intellectual, and psychological resources.

Finally, there was a third, small subgroup that exhibited early maturity developed through "steeling experiences" (Rutter, 1996). These are life events that include parental illness or divorce, having to look after younger siblings or their own children, finding a responsible job, or being forced to become financially independent because their parents could not afford to support them (e.g., Evans, 2007). Growing up early added psychosocial resources and influenced their views of adult status. Barry and Nelson (2005) reported that those who perceived themselves to be adult had a better sense of their own identity, were less depressed, and engaged in fewer risk behaviors than those who saw themselves as in-between.

In general, internal markers of adulthood (taking responsibility for one's actions, making independent decisions, becoming financially independent, establishing equal relations with parents) appear to be of greater salience to young people than external markers (marriage, parenthood, beginning full-time work; Arnett, 2003, 2004; Barry & Nelson, 2005). Hence, there are several other developmental tasks than those traditionally seen as markers of adulthood. Experiencing and coping with different non-normative shifts can enhance maturity in exactly the same way as these normative shifts achieve: These experiences are causes, not consequences, of becoming adult.

In summary, the experience of emerging adulthood depends on whether a prolonged moratorium is the result of choice or constraints and whether it is used effectively to gain experiences. Some may acquire skills for adult living, whereas others idle their time away. Overall, it seems as if the long-term consequences are more beneficial to those who do not spend lengthy years in identity exploration.

Is emerging adulthood good for society?

What might be the societal effects of young people delaying their entry into adult roles? On this we can only speculate, though Arnett makes clear that he sees it as a positive experience for young people.

Large numbers of young adults not participating in the labor market and not being economically active in their first 30 years of life (as well as in their last) would cost Western societies dearly. Some emergent adults would fail to realize their full potential throughout life because they failed to acquire skills and qualifications needed for modern living. It will certainly place large financial and emotional burdens on middle-aged parents having to support their ever-emerging children at the same time as having to care for aging parents. The current increase in divorce and the decrease in fertility rates (e.g., Douglass, 2007) may also be a reflection of current trends in extended identity exploration. Further, emerging adults of today may not be particularly affluent parents, because they left both career and child bearing to their early 30s, and if many remain single parents, they will be unable to indulge their own children in a 30-year-long period of identity exploration. In other words, we predict that the current situation of emerging adulthood will regulate itself over time.

Already several European governments have reacted by increasing university fees, placing limits on time allowed to complete a degree course (United Kingdom and Germany), and establishing laws on cohabiting very similar to marriage laws (Ireland, United Kingdom, Sweden). These emerging adults, in extended moratorium, may also create opportunities for well-qualified non-Western immigrants within the labor markets of Western societies.

Concluding comments

In our view, Arnett's concept does not add to our understanding of human development. Instead of simply describing the effects of certain societal conditions on certain individuals belonging to a certain cohort, we should better understand and investigate the interactive processes and mechanisms (of which societal transformation is only one) that are involved in human development. Social scientists have already moved away from age-bound stage theories toward more systemic approaches. Significant in this have been Bronfenbrenner's (1979; Bronfenbrenner & Morris, 1998) interactive micro- to macrolevel theory; Elder's (1974, 1999) emphasis on both historical time and the timing of life events; Baltes' (1987, 1997) concepts of plasticity, multidirectionality, multifunctionality, and nonlinearity; Lerner's (1985, 1998) views on proactivity and self-agency; and Valsiner's (1997) explorations of systemic developmental changes. Understanding human development and life course transitions demands that we examine the interplay among many factors and forces, including structural factors, individual agency and experience, encounters with social institutions, and cultural imperatives. This is more complex than descriptions of age stages, which cannot embrace all facets of developmental changes. In other words, contemporary developmental scientists should consider human interaction within cultural, historical, and psychosocial shifts and the peculiarities of time and place and embrace dynamic, systemic, interactive models as a way of charting and understanding development across the adolescent–adult transition and, indeed, across the whole life span (e.g., Côté, 1996, 1997; Hendry & Kloep, 2002; Magnusson & Stattin, 1998).

Today, young people are increasingly required to take the initiative in forming work and personal relationships, gaining educational credentials and employment experience, and planning for their future. Those who actively address these issues with self-agency may be most likely to form a coherent sense of identity toward their subsequent life course (Schwartz, Côté, & Arnett, 2005). On the other hand, an inability to shape identity is linked to heightened risks, insecurity, and stress (e.g., Arnett, 2006; Parker, Aldridge, & Measham, 1998). Arnett's descriptions of a new age stage do not penetrate the layers of variations in transitional trajectories. A complementary perspective is necessary, and we would claim that a dynamic, systemic framework would suit.

To finally return to Hans Christian Andersen's story, it is fair to say that Arnett's ideas on emerging adulthood are not denuded of value. However, a new fashion designer is needed to clothe the emerging framework in the more sophisticated drapes of interactive processes and mechanisms if we are going to research and interpret the many variations within this transitional period accurately and sensitively.

References

Arnett, J. J. (2000). Emerging adulthood: A theory of development from the late teens through the twenties. *American Psychologist, 55,* 469–480.

Arnett, J. J. (2003). Conceptions of the transition to adulthood among emerging adults in American ethnic groups. *New Directions for Child and Adult Development, 100.* Retrieved April 20, 2007, from http//www.jeffreyarnett.com/articles/ARNETT_conceptions_ethnic_groups.pdf

Arnett, J. J. (2004). *Emerging adulthood: The winding road from late teens through the twenties.* Oxford, England: Oxford University Press.

Arnett, J. J. (2006). Emerging adulthood in Europe: A response to Bynner. *Journal of Youth Studies, 9,* 111–123.

Arnett, J. J. (2007, February 15–16). *Emerging adulthood: What is it and what is it good for?* Debate Third Emerging Adulthood Conference, Tucson, AZ.

Atak, H., & Cok, F. (2007, February 15–16) *Emerging adulthood and perceived adulthood in Turkey.* Symposium paper, Third Conference on Emerging Adulthood, Tucson, AZ.

Baltes, P. B. (1987). Theoretical propositions of lifespan developmental psychology: On the dynamics between growth and decline. *Developmental Psychology, 23,* 611–626.

Baltes, P. B. (1997). On the incomplete architecture of human ontogenesis: Selection, optimisation, and compensation as foundations of developmental theory. *American Psychologist, 52,* 366–381.

Barry, C. M., & Nelson, L. J. (2005). The role of religion in the transition to adulthood for young emerging adults. *Journal of Youth and Adolescence, 34,* 245–255.

Bronfenbrenner, U. (1979). *The ecology of human development: Experiments by nature and design.* Cambridge, MA: Harvard University Press.

Bronfenbrenner, U., & Morris, P. A. (1998). The ecology of the developmental process. In W. Damon & R. M. Lerner (Eds.), *Handbook of child psychology* (5th ed., Vol. 1, pp. 993–1028). New York: Wiley.

Buchmann, M. (1989). *The script of life in modern society.* Chicago: University of Chicago Press.

Bynner, J. (2005). Rethinking the youth phase of the life course: The case for emerging adulthood? *Journal of Youth Studies, 8,* 367–384.

Castells, M. (1998). *The end of the millennium.* Oxford, England: Blackwell.

Cheah, C. S. L., & Nelson, L. J. (2004). The role of acculturation in the emerging adulthood of aboriginal college students. *International Journal of Behavioural Development, 28,* 495–507.

Cohen, P., Kasen, S., Chen, H., Hartmark, C., & Gordon, K. (2003). Variations in patterns of developmental transitions in the emerging adulthood period. *Developmental Psychology, 39*, 657–669.

Coleman, J. C., & Hendry, L. B. (1999). *The nature of adolescence* (3rd ed.). London: Routledge.

Coleman, J. C., & Schofield, J. (2005). *Key data on adolescence* (5th ed.). Brighton, England: Trust for the Study of Adolescence.

Coles, B. (1995). *Youth and social policy: Youth, citizenship and young careers.* London: University College London Press.

Côté, J. E. (1996). Sociological perspectives on identity formation: The culture-identity link and cultural capital. *Journal of Adolescence, 19*, 417–428.

Côté, J. E. (1997). An empirical test of the identity capital model. *Journal of Adolescence, 20*, 577–598.

Côté, J. E. (2000). *Arrested adulthood: The changing nature of maturity and identity.* New York: University Press.

Douglass, C. B. (2007, February 15–16). *Where have all the babies gone? Low fertility and emerging adulthood in Europe.* Invited Keynote Address, Third Conference on Emerging Adulthood, Tucson, AZ.

Elder, G. H., Jr. (1974). *Children of the great depression: Social change in life experience.* Chicago: University of Chicago Press.

Elder, G. H., Jr. (1999). *Children of the great depression: Social change in life experience* (25th Anniversary Edition). Boulder, CO: Westview Press.

Evans, K. (2007, February 15–16). *Concepts of bounded agency in education, work and the personal lives of young adults.* Invited Symposium Paper, Third Emerging Adulthood Conference, Tucson, AZ.

Fauske, H. (1996). Changing youth: Transition to adulthood in Norway. *Young, 4*, 47–62.

Featherstone, M., & Hepworth, M. (1991). The mask of ageing and the post-modern life course. In M. Featherstone, M. Hepworth, & B. Turner (Eds.), *The body, social process and cultural theory* (pp. 371–389). London: Sage.

Fiske, M., & Chiriboga, D. (1990). *Change and continuity in adult life.* San Francisco: Jossey Bass.

Furlong, A., & Cartmel, F. (1997). *Young people and social change: Individualisation and risk in late modernity.* Buckingham, England: Open University Press.

Gibbons, J. L., & Ashdown, B. K. (2006). Emerging adulthood: The dawning of a new age. *American Psychological Association.* Retrieved February 20, 2007, from http//www.apa.org/books/4317092c.pdf

Heinz, W. R. (2007, February 15–16). Social pathways from youth to adulthood: The many faces of emerging adulthood. Invited Symposium Paper, Third Emerging Adulthood Conference, Tucson, AZ.

Heinz, W. R. and Marshall, V. W. (Eds.). (2003). *Social dynamics of the life course.* Somerset, England: Transaction.

Hendry, L. B., & Kloep, M. (2002) *Lifespan development: Resources, challenges and risks.* London: Thomson Learning.

Hendry, L. B., Kloep, M., & Olsson, S. (1998). Youth, lifestyles and society. *Childhood, 5*, 133–150.

Kloep, M., & Hendry, L. B. (2007). *Transitions to adulthood for young Welsh people not in education.* Manuscript in preparation.

Lerner, R. M. (1985). Adolescent maturational changes and psychosocial development: A dynamic interactional perspective. *Journal of Youth and Adolescence, 14*, 355–372.

Lerner, R. M. (1998). Theories of human development. In W. Damon & R. M. Lerner (Eds.), *Handbook of child psychology* (5th ed., Vol. 1, pp. 1–24). New York: Wiley.

Levine, M. (2005). *Ready or not, here life comes.* New York: Simon & Schuster.

Lloyd, C. B. (2005). Growing up global: The changing transitions to adulthood in developing countries. Washington, DC: National Academies Press.

MacDonald, R. (1997). Dangerous youth and the dangerous class. In R. MacDonald (Ed.), *Youth, the underclass and social exclusion* (pp. 1–25). London: Routledge.

Magnusson, D., & Stattin, H. (1998). Person-context interaction theories. In R. M. Lerner (Ed.), *Handbook of child psychology: Vol. 1. Theoretical models of human development* (5th ed., pp. 685–759). New York: Wiley.

Nelson, L. J., Badger, S., & Wu, B. (2004). The influence of culture in emerging adulthood: Perspectives of Chinese college students. *International Journal of Behavioural Development, 28,* 26–36.

Parker, H., Aldridge, J., & Measham, F. (1998). *Illegal leisure.* London: Routledge.

Rindfuss, R. R., Swicegard, G. C., & Rosenfeld, R. R. (1987). Disorder in the life course: How common and does it matter? *American Sociological Review, 52,* 785–801.

Rutter, M. (1996). Psychological adversity: Risk, resilience and recovery. In L. Verhofstadt-Deneve, I. Kienhorst, & C. Braet (Eds.), *Conflict and development in adolescence* (pp. 21–34). Leiden, The Netherlands: DSWO Press.

Schwartz, S. J., Côté, J. E., & Arnett, J. J. (2005). Identity and agency in emerging adulthood. *Youth and Society, 37,* 201–229.

Valsiner, J. (1997). *Culture and the development of children's action: A theory of human development* (2nd ed.). New York: Wiley.

Wyn, J., & White, R. (1997). *Rethinking youth.* London: Sage.

12 Parental views of emerging adults

We were interested to follow through ideas associated with transitions to adulthood and thus explored ways in which parents might contribute to delaying/enhancing independence in their adult children and looked at ways parents may have a powerful effect on their offspring's decision-making. It is interesting to note that not only were there a variety of parental responses to this family situation and its resolution, but also that in some instances parental strategies appeared to be aimed at keeping the individual at home rather than facilitating a move to independent living. Allied to this, there was evidence of family politics in operation in the sense that if the young person's plans for the future 'matched' those of the parent then all was well. However, if there was disagreement between parents and their children, then parents were emotionally upset and attempted quite powerfully to manipulate the young person to their way of thinking.

LETTING GO OR HOLDING ON? PARENTS' PERCEPTIONS OF THEIR RELATIONSHIPS WITH THEIR CHILDREN DURING EMERGING ADULTHOOD

Marion Kloep and Leo B. Hendry

Adopting an ecological perspective (e.g., Bronfenbrenner & Morris, 1998; Elder, 1998), the present paper sets out to explore the perceived experiences of mid-life parents of young people during the life period designated by Arnett (2004, 2006) as 'emerging adulthood'. Specifically, parents' perceptions of their relationships with their grown-up children and their striving for independence, together with their own coping with the process of this family transformation will be considered.

Bronfenbrenner and Morris' (1998) ecological theory demonstrated how the family as a micro-system exists within a wider societal level (the macro system) with both interacting and influencing the other. Hence, with the socio-economic and social changes in Western societies over the last few decades, the roles of parents and families have been transformed significantly. Arnett (2004, 2006) has described the age period from about 18 to 25 years as 'emerging adulthood', a time when young people do not take on full adult responsibilities and shy away from various relational and personal commitments, while exploring possible lifestyles. This requires the material and emotional support of parents, as to whether or not their near-adult children stay at home or move away to study at university. Nowadays prolonged education, rising house prices and youth unemployment make it more difficult – and less attractive – for young people to move out of the parental home and start a completely independent life when they reach young adulthood. All this has had a profound effect on family life and on relationships within the family.

While a number of issues regarding mid-life development have been previously written about and various topics examined by research, there are still gaps in what is known theoretically about the general elements and mechanisms that encompass this period in the lifespan. For instance, Lachman and James (1997) have highlighted the many different facets of adult development, including the various changes involving the self and others that middle-aged adults experience in the realms of work, family, and health and how these different experiences inter-relate. These interactions create individualistic transformations across mid-life into old-age.

In present-day society, this phase of the life course is not necessarily age-bound, and retirement is no longer an upper-boundary 'marker' into old-age. Rather it is a series of pathways or trajectories differentiated by historical, cultural, social, psychological forces, and factors (e.g., Lachman, 2001; Lachman & James, 1997). For instance, beyond the aspects of physical and physiological change such as a decline in physical prowess, reduced sexuality and fertility, and the onset of the menopause (e.g., Willis & Reid, 1999), various major developmental and social tasks face mid-life adults. Central amongst these are relationships and family ties (Lachman, 2001), As Ryff and Seltzer (1996) have noted the longest period of parenthood – when children grow into adolescence and young adulthood and parents themselves are not yet elderly – and the complex factors that influence the quality of the mid-life parenting is poorly understood, such as the rewards and costs of parenting, where women rather than men seem to be more accepting (Pudrovska, 2006). Since work is now central to self-and social identity, Carr (2005), for example, has shown how middle-aged men draw occupational, family life, and 'good provider' comparisons with their young adult sons with differential effects on their self-esteem depending on their 'cultural capital' or 'resources' (Hendry & Kloep, 2002) while mid-life women lament their own traditional role by comparisons with their adult daughters' careers (Carr, 2004). Yet, perhaps the most significant adjustment to be made is in the process of young adult children leaving home during the post-parenthood phase, namely mid-life (e.g., Dennerstein, Dudley, & Guthrie, 2002). Modern living has complicated this previously normative 'shift' because nowadays young people leave home later and often return to the parental house when their relationships do not work out well or when they cannot afford to live independently and this can have differential effects on the family ethos (e.g., Aquilino, 2005).

Additionally, there are cultural differences in expectations and traditions of young people leaving home and becoming independent. For example, Coleman and Brooks (2009) report that over 65% of men and 50% of women between the ages of 18 and 24 in Britain are still living in their family, and this is comparable with most of northern Europe, while in Italy and other southern European countries the majority of adult children stay at home till their early thirties. Yet little is known of the reasons for these cultural differences. It is clear that there is a paucity of detailed research into this 'turning-point' in family relationships and its perceived influences in mid-life development and change. How do parents view their children's leaving and returning? What are their feelings about this process?

Within the shifts at a societal level, the family unit (at the micro-level) has to adjust and adapt, influencing the roles and relationships of family members. For instance, whilst the postwar years brought about a change from authoritarian to authoritative parenting (e.g., Schnaiberg & Goldenberg, 1989), the trend has moved towards more permissive parenting (Hendry, Shucksmith, Love, & Glendinning, 1993; Shucksmith, Hendry, & Glendinning, 1995), with parents acting to some extent as their children's best friends (Mitchell, 2006). Research findings have shown that there are few conflicts between older adolescents and their parents nowadays (Kloep, 1999; Settersten, Furstenberg, & Rumbaut, 2005), partly due to the fact that struggles for control and power between parents and their offspring usually occur in childhood and middle adolescence (John & Alwyn, 2005). Later in life, parent–child conflicts are rare, even though they still exist (Wittman, Buhl, & Noack, 2000), and they occur less often around issues of autonomy, but stem more from the fact that parents and children are at discrepant points in their development (labelled 'developmental schism' by Fingerman, 1996).

Studies on parent–child interactions have been mainly focused on the early years, while investigations of familial relations in early adulthood have been somewhat neglected (e.g., Gitelson & McDermott, 2006) – a time described by Ryff and Seltzer (1996) as the least studied period of parenting practices. A few studies (e.g., Kins, Beyers, Soenens, & Vansteenkiste, 2009; Ryan, Deci, Grolnick, & La Guardia, 2006; Soenens, Vansteenkiste, Luyckx, & Goossens, 2006) have shown that autonomy-enhancing parental styles facilitate individuation in young people, and there are several studies investigating the various experiences of adolescents' and early adults' home-leaving in different settings and cultures (e.g., Mitchell, 2006). Residing at home with parents for too long seems to have a negative effect on young people's development, and it is reported to restrain their gaining of independence, adult status, and well-being (White, 2002), though this effect seems to be mediated by young people's degree of choice in their decision of whether or not to leave home (Kins *et al.*, 2009). However, while there are a number of studies about the effects of parenting styles and the process of separation on the well-being and adjustment of young people, there is a paucity of research investigating the effects of family transformations on parents.

From an ecological perspective, it could be expected that macro-social changes affecting the life trajectories of emerging adults should also have a profound effect on parents' lives. Elder's (1998) ideas on linked lives allow consideration of the possibility that familial transformations change the life course of parents, who in present-day Western societies not only assume parental responsibilities at a later point in life than earlier generations – the mean age of first birth to mothers in 1990 was 24.2 in the USA (Matthews & Hamilton, 2006), 27.3 in the UK, 26.6 in Germany and Ireland (Eurostat, 2006), and 26.7 in Canada (Statistics Canada, 2008) – but also retain their parental responsibilities for a longer period of the life course. The relatively few studies (e.g., Adelman, Antonucci, Crohan, & Coleman, 1989; Fiske & Chiriboga, 1991) suggest that modern parents cope fairly well with their children's transitions towards adulthood. On the other hand, when parents fail to coax young adults to leave the parental home, then tensions can occur (Aquilino, 1996; Ryff & Seltzer, 1996). Mitchell (2004, p. 438) advocates that future research 'needs to examine the role that parents perceive themselves to play in their children's home-leaving decisions'.

As an extension of Mitchell's request, attention needs to be drawn to the ways parents cope with this important transition in their own lives and its impact on their family roles. Previous investigations have tended to take the perspective of how this transition affects adult children (e.g., Bucx & van Wel, 2008; Roberts & Bengtson, 1993; Thornton, Orbuch, & Axinn, 1995), but the present study attempts to focus on the parental viewpoint, as a significant 'turning point' in their life course. At the time when their children reach 'emerging adulthood', parents have reached 'emerging middle age' (Hendry & Kloep, 2007), with about half of their life still ahead of them. The way they cope with their children's leaving home, young people's prolonged dependency or striving to reach adult status, will have crucial repercussions for the parents' immediate personal psychosocial adjustments and for their future relationships with their adult children and their families.

In order to gain some insights into this family transition and transformation from this perspective, we investigate the period of emerging adulthood through the eyes and reported experiences of parents, as linked social actors in this crucial episode of family life (Elder, 1998). More specifically, this exploratory study sets out to consider the following research questions:

(1) How do parents perceive the experiences of the period of emerging adulthood in the family?
(2) What are their reported reactions to their children's growing up and striving for independence; or, alternatively, their reluctance to take on adult responsibilities?
(3) What do they say about coping with this prolonged period of parental responsibilities, and about parental role redundancy as young people prepare to gain adult status?

Methods

An exploratory interview study was carried out with a purposive sample of British mid-life parents between the age of 34 and 62 (mean age $M = 47.30$, $SD = 6.50$), whose 63 children were between the ages of 18 and 25 years (mean age $M = 20.59$, $SD = 2.04$).

Sample

An opportunity sample was created by having a number of trained fieldworkers approach parents who had at least one adult child in the age range 18–25 years in order to select a group of parents with the age characteristics appropriate to the study's aims, their children coming from a range of occupational backgrounds, such as university students, full-time employed, those in temporary unskilled jobs, and unemployed young people. Parents could roughly be categorized as belonging to working and lower and upper middle class. In more detail, the sample consisted of 59 middle-aged parents ($N = 29$ mother/daughter dyads; $N = 26$ mother/son dyads; $N = 5$ father/daughter dyads; and $N = 2$ father/son dyads). Of the young people, 26 attended university, 7 went to school or college, 22 were in full-time employment, 2 worked in temporary jobs, and 5 were unemployed. Five had already a child of their own, 2 were pregnant, 28 still lived at home, and 34 lived elsewhere away from home.

Procedure

Participants were informed that participation was voluntary and anonymous, that the interviews and any other data would be treated confidentially, and that they had the right to withdraw from the study at any stage. By choice, the interviews took place either in the participants' home or at university, were conducted by trained fieldworkers and were audiotaped. They lasted between 40 and 60 min.

A semi-structured individual interview was conducted with each parent. The 'open' interview was intended to allow parents to provide an unprompted description of family relationships in emerging adulthood. It began by asking them about their child's maturity level (Would you consider your son/daughter to be an adult or an adolescent?). Thereafter, and only if necessary to ensure the progress of the interview the following prompts were employed, based on major topics of family life before and during this transition (e.g., Talk about differences between how s/he is now and a few years ago, describe your relationship to him/her now and a few years ago, how you were as a parent when your child was around 12 years old, what you still have to provide for her/him [money, advice, household chores, shopping etc.], what things is s/he now doing for you, particular likes/dislikes about his/her lifestyle just now, and how s/he will be within the next few years). Later, tapes were transcribed verbatim, including non-verbal sounds such as laughter.

Analysis

The transcripts of the interviews were read several times by the first author, in order to become familiar with the narratives. Then, the first five transcripts

176 *Parental views of emerging adults*

were subjected to a detailed micro-analysis. This involved a line-by-line coding of each interview, following the procedure recommended by Charmaz (1995). Thus, responses on various topics of family life were grouped under broad headings in order to elicit general themes which clustered these parental comments. The other interviews were then read and reread several times, and analysed, looking for recurrent themes derived from the first interviews, together with any new themes that might have emerged from the ongoing analysis. The emergent themes, from all the interviews, were grouped and categorized, to provide a variety of superordinate themes, which were inter-related to each other and jointly associated and grouped with particular subthemes (see Figure 12.1). These themes were then cross-validated in a separate analysis conducted by the second author utilizing an identical procedure. Both authors' analyses were compared, and, where necessary, minor adjustments to the labels of themes were made after discussion. A high agreement between the two separate analyses was found.

A number of superordinate themes such as 'responses to emerging adulthood', 'perceptions of maturational change', 'hopes and fears for the future', 'pride and guilt' were extracted from this first-step analysis, but since the major focus of this paper was on the superordinate theme of 'responses to emerging adulthood', which appeared as a significant theme in all interviews, the other superordinate themes are only referred to, if relevant, in relation to this selected major theme in the remainder of the paper (see Figure 12.1).

Further, as we were interested in different parental reactions to the period of emerging adulthood, as a second-step, a person-centred analysis was employed. All interviews were read again to extract an individual picture of each participant's narrative. Interviews were then clustered according to the different themes they contained (like a qualitative 'cluster analysis'). Four broad clusters emerged (Figure 12.1), and again, this procedure was cross-validated by both authors.

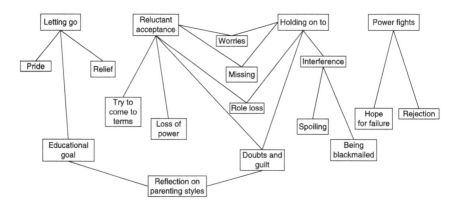

Figure 12.1 Tree-diagram of themes illustrating different parental strategies.

Results

From the first variable centred analysis extracting themes, the superordinate theme clearly present in all the interviews was of parents' perceptions of the issue of 'letting go'. A range of subthemes emerged, showing the different ways parents described their experiences of witnessing their offspring's increasing independence and maturity, and their own reactions to these. The feelings they described ranged from pride and relief, through concerns of not being needed anymore to rejection (see Figure 12.1), suggesting a continuum of perceived parental responses from acceptance of this family transition, albeit somewhat reluctantly in some cases; through concerns of role loss; to conflict, and even to gloating about young people's failed attempts to become independent by one or two parents. In the second, person-centred analysis, parents with similar styles of 'letting go' were clustered together. Broadly four 'clusters' were evident, though there was some overlap between the groups:

- One cluster indicated fairly happy acceptance of their children's developing autonomy ($N = 14$, see Table 12.1),
- Another demonstrated some regret and ambivalence, but also indicated an understanding of their children's need for independence ($N = 19$, see Table 12.2),
- A third, apparently less accepting cluster, appeared to use, consciously or unconsciously, strategies to delay their children's growing up ($N = 23$, see Table 12.3), and
- A fourth cluster illustrated conflict, where adult children's independence was a power struggle that resulted in rejection or triumph ($N = 6$, see Table 12.4).

Table 12.1 'Happy to let go' identification number, age of offspring, gender of interviewed parent, and life-style characteristics of the offspring in this group

Gender	ID No.	Age	Parent	Life-style
Daughters	02	23	Mother	Lives at home, college
	05	20	Mother	Lives away, works
	06	22	Mother	Lives away, works
	09	20	Mother	Lives at home, works
	13	20	Mother	Lives at home, university student
	17	22	Mother	Lives away, university student
	21	20	Mother	Lives away, university student
	22	19	Mother	Lives at home, works
	25	22	Mother	Lives away, unemployed, one child
	29	20	Father	Lives away, university student, one child
	32	22	Father	Lives away, university student
Sons	52	20	Mother	Lives at home, works
	56	18	Mother	Lives away, works
	59	20	Father	Lives away, works

178 *Parental views of emerging adults*

Table 12.2 'Reluctant to let go' identification number, age of offspring, gender of interviewed parent, and life-style characteristics of the offspring in this group

Gender	ID No.	Age	Parent	Life-style
Daughters	03	19	Mother	Lives away, works
	04	25	Mother	Lives away, university student
	07	18	Mother	Lives at home, works
	10	25	Mother	Lives away, university student
	12	21	Mother	Lives away, university student
	24	23	Mother	Lives away, university student abroad
	26	20	Mother	Lives away, works
	28	18	Mother	Lives away, university student
	28	21	Mother	Lives away, university student
	30	21	Mother	Lives away, university student
	31	19	Father	Lives at home, works
	33	25	Father	Lives at home (again), university student, works
Sons	04	22	Mother	Lives away, occasional jobs
	46	21	Mother	Lives away, university student, works
	48	20	Mother	Lives at home, works
	49	18	Mother	Lives at home, university student
	50	23	Mother	Lives away, university student, works
	53	21	Mother	Lives at home, university student
	55	23	Mother	Lives at home, works

Figure 12.1 shows these four groupings together with the subordinate themes on which the groupings were based. It can be seen from Figure 12.1 that some subordinate themes were associated with more than one cluster, mainly between the second (i.e., parents showing reluctant acceptance) and the third (i.e., those 'hanging on' to their children). In the following sections, these groupings are discussed in more detail, with relevant quotations to illustrate the parents' varying perceptions. (Subordinate themes from Figure 12.1 are marked in italics where they appear in the text).

Happy to let go

As can be seen in Table 12.1, 14 parents indicated that they were happy with their adult children becoming independent. Of these, only 3 parents stated that it would be a *relief* to see their children growing up and leaving:

> 'I'd love to see him in his own place (within 5 years), please God, (loud laugh) he can't be living with me at that age! But they do, don't they? They do! But the thought of it . . . Oh no, I can't imagine – I want my life back, you know. We'll always be there as parents but by then he's got to go'.
>
> (52, mother about son 20)

Parental views of emerging adults 179

Table 12.3 'Holding on' identification number, age of offspring, gender of interviewed parent, and life-style characteristics of the offspring in this group

Gender	ID No.	Age	Parent	Life-style
Daughters	01	19	Mother	Lives at home, university student
	11	18	Mother	Lives at home, works
	13	22	Mother	Lives at home, university student
	14	23	Mother	Lives away, one child, pregnant, unemployed
	15	24	Mother	Lives away, works
	16	18	Mother	Lives at home, school, works
	18	21	Mother	Lives at home, college
	19	18	Mother	Lives at home, school
	23	20	Mother	Lives away, university student
Sons	36	23	Mother	Lives away, university student
	37	18	Mother	Lives at home, unemployed
	38	20	Mother	Lives away, works
	39	21	Mother	Lives away, works
	40	20	Mother	Lives away, university student
	41	20	Mother	Lives at home (again), works
	42	23	Mother	Lives away, works
	43	20	Mother	Lives away, university student
	44	22	Mother	Lives away, university student
	45	18	Mother	Lives at home, college
	47	18	Mother	Lives at home, works
	51	18	Mother	Lives at home, college
	57	18	Mother	Lives at home, works
	57	22	Mother	Lives away, university student

Table 12.4 'Power fights' identification number, age of offspring, gender of interviewed parent, and life-style characteristics of the offspring in this group

Gender	ID No.	Age	Parent	Life-style
Daughters	08	18	Mother	Lives at home, school, pregnant
	27	21	Mother	Lives away with female partner, works
Sons	34	18	Mother	Lives at home, unemployed
	35	19	Mother	Lives at home, occasional jobs
	54	22	Mother	Lives at home (again), unemployed
	58	22	Father	Lives away, university student, one child

All the other parents who were happy with their children's increasing independence also showed a deep *satisfaction* with their life choices, and a *pride* in their achievements as if they were their own.

> 'She allows – and I've always said this to her – me and her mother to live her dream as well. And we do appreciate that. Both of us, although wanted to go

to university, neither of us were able to for financial reasons. She has been able to, she's going for her dream and we want to go with her'.

(32, father about daughter 22)

'To be honest I'm really proud of her, she even got a new job in a posh office in town ... she keeps her flat tidy which was a total shocker to me; I'd expected to be a laundry and maid service to her but fair play, she's done all her own washing and cleaning'.

(5, mother about daughter, 20)

Parents in this group were most likely to define their children as 'adults', using a number of traditional indicators of adulthood, such as having a good job, living away from home, having a child, or living with a partner. However, they also used a range of internal 'markers', such as the young people being able to make their own decisions, being able to handle money, showing concern for others, and taking on responsibilities, as signs of maturity. This often coincided with a description of their parenting style as 'authoritative', i.e., there had been rules and expectations for their children, but also support, and it had been their aim from the first to educate them for independence. However, it is difficult to interpret whether these parents saw their parenting style as effective because of their satisfaction with the outcome – or whether they saw the outcome as successful in order to justify their parenting style.

Reluctant to let go

On the other hand, nearly a third of the parents were somewhat reluctant to accept their child's increasing autonomy (see Figure 12.1 and Table 12.2). They talked about the difficulties of *losing their role* as parents and of having to come to terms with the fact that they were *not needed* anymore.

'Um, I don't always like the idea that they are grown-up but yeah I do see them as two adults. I'm aware that they want to be left to their own devices, don't want me dropping around every other day asking if they've eaten a proper meal or asking them where they've been and what they've been doing, and who they've been seeing. I'm very conscious of that. I think the main thing that I've noticed is that of their differing attitude towards me, in that I'm not needed all the time anymore [long pause]'.

(4, mother about son 22 and daughter 25)

Some parents regretted that they had *less power* to intervene in their children's life choices and behaviours, that they could not 'ground them any more', and that they had too *little information* about what their adult children were doing in their lives. It seemed they would like to retain their parental role longer, and they appeared quite surprised if their children could actually organize their own lives effectively. This was occasionally combined with feelings of doubt and *guilt* about whether they had been good parents – whether they had been too strict or too indulgent.

They *worried* about their children's welfare and also *missed* them, if they had moved out, and were aware of the loss of intimacy as a natural result of spending less time together (e.g., Aquilino, 1997).

> 'Um (pauses) sad sometimes (laughs) um, that she's not um, that she's not a child anymore, but I think I've got over that now. At the beginning it's worse and I did have lots of times where I just sat here (pause) you know, she not here and I missed her, but I think it's important to have other things going on'.
> (12, mother about daughter 21)

> 'I don't like that she lives away, I miss her and worry about her, not knowing what she is doing all the time but I know I um . . . have to accept that she has grown up now and needs to be independent, I can't help still wanting to protect her, what mother doesn't? (pause) I know she is a woman now and I should leave her get on with it, but 21 still seems young, but I know I have to let her get on with it'.
> (30, mother about daughter 21)

These parents were somewhat reluctant to allocate full adult status to their children, sometimes accepting that all the signs of maturity were there, but admitting that they would wish otherwise:

> 'Also because my son is the baby and I know it sounds a bit clichéd and a bit of a stereotype but I still regard him, although he's now 22, I still regard the youngest one as the baby (laughs) even though he's sometimes more mature than all of us put together at times!'.
> (4, mother about son, 22)

> 'I suppose he is (an adult). But he'll never be an adult in my eyes, compared to how others see him. Anybody over 20 (is an adult) but not my children . . . I don't really see my youngest as an adult because he is my child but then someone else's child the same age I would think as an adult'.
> (55, mother about son 23)

However, all the parents in this group accepted the inevitability of having to allow their children freedom of action and independence. There is supporting evidence from their narratives that they did try to come to terms with their new roles, working hard to keep interference to a minimum and admitting that to behave otherwise would be irrational. This characteristic of attempted role change made them different from the third group.

Holding on

As Table 12.3 shows, more than half of the parents belonged to this group, which was similar to the last grouping (illustrated in Figure 12.1), as they also talked

182 *Parental views of emerging adults*

about *role loss*, and *missing* their children, but they revealed the use of quite different strategies to come to terms with this situation: consciously or unconsciously they steered their behaviour towards delaying their children's independence and continued to *interfere* in their lives. The most frequent strategy was the use of rewards: providing services and continuing to spoil them in order to keep them at home longer or at to encourage them to visit often:

> 'He is still my little boy, a mummy's boy if you like. I still see him as being young and 'cos he lives at home still, he depends on me quite a lot. I still do a lot for him, I do his clothes, washing, tidy his room, make his tea most evenings and even still do packed lunch for him to take to work everyday. He earns his own money as he works full time as a plumber . . . But whether he decides to move out is another thing 'cos he probably thinks he has got it quite cushy as it is. But I do know he will move out in the very near future and I will miss him, but I know what he is like, he'll probably be back round here wanting his food cooked for him'.
>
> (47, mother about son 18)

> 'Well, although he's 23 and he lives away, he still comes home almost every weekend and he likes me to do the washing for him (smiling to herself about comments made) the ironing, I cook and make different things for him to take back with him. I also buy him food. No, he is good, he is at the end of the phone if I need him for anything, he knows I'm a worrier so he always phones me in the week to see how me and his father are, so you know that means a lot to me'.
>
> (36, mother about son 23)

The last quote demonstrates the continuing emotional dependence of this mother on her son, needing him as much or even more than she believes he needs her. Another mother was blatantly aware, that she should not make her son so dependent on her, but she did not really plan to change this:

> 'He's still my baby, boy really, I think I should get him to help out more, I probably shouldn't do everything for him, like when he was younger, umm . . . he needs to grow up and I probably shouldn't treat him like I did when he was a child' (laughs).
>
> (38, mother about son 20)

However, this strategy of *bribery* and spoiling backfired sometimes, particularly when money was involved. Many parents complained that their offspring had problems in learning how to handle money, relying on their parents to bail them out. Some parents felt exploited and blackmailed, when children only contacted them to borrow money. However, they tended to give into their children's requests, in spite of negative feelings:

'I feel so hurt. Because of we were so close. She had everything. She could want for anything. So I think ... it's my fault. She wanted money, she had money. She wanted new clothes, she had it all time, I think I spoiled her. When she started going out, I was giving her money to stop her shouting at me. She would shout a lot at me. Although none of my children still live with me, I still support her that way. Eh, me as a mother,I think we should always be there for them, but I do feel that ... a week or fortnight and then she comes for money: 'Mum can you ...' and then, you know, she says 'lend' but I've never had any money back'.

(14, mother about daughter 23)

Some parents felt pressurized in other contexts, too. One mother of an 18-year-old son told us that she felt that she had to give into all his demands, because otherwise he would drop-out of college and blame her for it. Another admitted that she did not dare to ask her 18-year-old daughter to participate in household tasks, because then 'she would kick up a fuss', which the mother dreaded. Other parents were bitterly disappointed about the thanklessness of their children 'to whom we gave everything', though some did see a link between their permissive parenting style and their adult children's behaviour towards them now:

'I wasn't strict, he had a time to come home, but he didn't take much notice. I would shout, but it didn't really make much difference, I didn't shout enough, definitively not enough. I didn't really discipline him as such, I was laid back, shouting doesn't work anyway ... I always gave in. We didn't have any household rules to be honest. I still look after him, do his washing, ironing, cooking, cleaning, picking up after him ... he's still my baby boy really'.

(37, mother about son 18)

'I should have been a bit more strict on her when she was little, but I never really wanted any help around the house, I wanted her to enjoy her childhood not having to do things I could easily do myself'.

(5, mother about daughter 20)

'Well, he is my only child, my blue-eyed beauty – he was such a beautiful baby all you would want to do is pamper him. I had visions of university when he was younger, I encouraged reading and never saw myself as strict, I wanted him to spread his little wings and fly – which he has done (pauses). Maybe at times I wasn't strict enough (laughs) that boy got away with murder (laughs) at least he grew up with enough common sense to stay out of prison'.

(42, mother about son 23)

These highly emotional quotes reveal poignantly how little parents had prepared for or come to terms with their children growing up. Within the sample, seven parents referred to their sons and three to their daughters as 'babies' and 'little boy/girl'. However, young people were reportedly not too happy with their parents' interference, and tried to prevent them becoming involved. Even with awareness, parents seemed unable to stop 'babying' and forcing their attentions on their grown-up children:

> 'He doesn't ask for this but I just feel that he is my baby and I feel as though I am still providing for him. Obviously he likes his independence now and doesn't like being my little baby anymore, as he does get quite angry when I do this'.
>
> (44, mother about son 22)

One example of a son's perceived immaturity and the mother's attempted resolution, illustrated how parents confused support with interference:

> 'Like with his flat for example, he has been living there for nearly two years now, and I have told him and told him and told him that it would be lovely, if he just did a bit of decorating here and there; eventually I went round and did it for him'.
>
> (39, mother about son 21)

The same mother already had clear plans of how she would intervene in her son's marriage – even though he did not even have a girlfriend yet. Thus, she described her son as immature, which gave her the perfect excuse for a continuing involvement in his life.

Power fights

The most obvious forms of continuing *power struggles*, found in the narratives of the few parents ($N = 6$) who completely disagreed with their children's life-style choices, was expressed, for example, in the non-compassionate, even triumphant, descriptions of a son's failure to achieve independence:

> 'He moved out to spend time with his girlfriend, now he doesn't know what he wants to do, so he's come back home. He's back home with his tail between his legs! Well his mother has to come to the rescue doesn't she ha-ha. He's lucky we've got room for him otherwise he'd be out on the street ha-ha. He tries to be clever, he's learning now though that he doesn't know it all! He's found out the hard way . . . he wants us now he's got nowhere else to go ha-ha, whereas before I'm sure he wanted to get away from us as soon as he could. It didn't last long! He was talking about going to university and doing music, that would be good if he did, but I'll believe it when I see it! Ha-ha!'
>
> (54, mother about son 22)

Similarly, a mother of a pregnant daughter could hardly disguise her hopes that her daughter would run into difficulties as a consequence of not following parental advice:

> 'M does not see that I have more life experience and more insight into possible consequences of clumsy choices she makes. I am shocked how resilient M is in regards to challenges she meets. Also she does keep her home clean. I suppose she has coped with her pregnancy quite well, although her father and I have offered her a lot of support. Maybe she needs to realise the consequences of her actions for awhile. I will certainly not be baby-sitting and M is well aware of this. I think that now is the time for her to face her responsibilities (smiles and nods)'.
>
> (8, mother about daughter 18)

Another example of how disagreement with a child's life-style choices could colour parental perceptions of maturity was vividly exemplified by a mother whose daughter lived independently:

> 'Because of how she lives her life, because I'm disappointed in her. Because of her sexuality, definitely! How would you describe it, is she gay, is she bisexual, what is she? And to be honest this is why I say she's not responsible. Because she doesn't want to hurt me, but what all the lies and false promises do is hurt me, to me all this just proves how immature she is because she won't take responsibilities for her actions, she'd rather lie'.
>
> (27, mother about daughter 21)

In the last few quotes, it also became evident that failure to follow parental advice was seen as a sign of immaturity – whereas in other quotes parents cited continuous reliance on parental advice as equally immature. This contradiction suggests that making the 'right' choices (i.e., agreement with the parental point of view), but without having to be told to do so, was seen as a 'real marker' of maturity in the eyes of some parents.

The four groups compared

As Tables 12.1–12.4 show, young men are slightly overrepresented in the groups 'Reluctant to let go' and 'Hold on', while there are more women in the 'Happy to let go' group. However, the difference does not reach statistical significance (χ^2 (3, N = 62) = 7.13, p = .07). Equally, the difference in mean age between the groups, with the 'Reluctant to let go' group being slightly older than the others ('happy to let go' M = 20.57, SD = 1.40; 'reluctant to let go' M = 21.11, SD = 2.28; 'hold on' M = 20.17, SD = 2.01; and 'power fight' M = 20.00, SD = 1.90) is not significant ($F(3, 58) = 0.931, p = .431$). Further, there are more young people still staying at home in the 'Hold on' group, but that might be equally a cause as a consequence of their parents' attitude.

Discussion

The majority of parents appeared to have certain difficulties in allowing their adult children to seek and gain mature independence. Some parents tried with reluctance to accept their offspring's striving for autonomy, whilst others employed various strategies, whether consciously or unconsciously, to delay 'letting go'. Whether or not parents perceived their sons and daughters as mature adults had a great deal to do with the parent's willingness to 'let go'. This willingness was influenced by whether or not parents approved of their offspring's choice of lifestyle: with approval, parents could enjoy their children's achievements, keep interference to a minimum, and concede adult status to them. Any striving for independence, which did not coincide with parental views, however, was often met with hostility and seen as a sign of immaturity. In many cases, the willingness to 'let go' appeared to have little to do with young people's own behaviour, but to reflect a parental need to maintain their parental role as long as possible. These parents tended to describe their children as not fully mature, thus justifying their continuing involvement. It seemed particularly difficult for parents to separate from a child of the opposite gender, though such a conclusion should be seen as tentative, given the small number of fathers in our exploratory sample. There are many 'emerging adulthoods', as Arnett and Tanner (2010) suggest, but there are equally many different ways for parents to deal with them, and future research should show what processes and mechanisms play a role in forming the varying responses of parents to this and other family transitions.

However, the present study is of an exploratory, qualitative nature and its aim was to produce a greater understanding of the parents' perspective during the important family transition of emerging adulthood. Thus, it remains unclear as to whether we are presenting a uniquely White Anglo-Saxon British story, or whether it holds true for other Western societies, and whether this finding is further influenced by structural factors such as social class, gender, and ethnicity (e.g., Bynner, 2005). Within this study, not all possible parental perspectives could be presented. In particular, there were few fathers in the sample, and it did not contain any parents who are in some way or another dependent on their children because of a disability, nor were there any parents of children with special needs. Parents were only interviewed on a single occasion, and their narratives might well have been influenced by their emotional frame of mind on that day. Given these particular limitations, a number of key issues emerging from this study are discussed, namely, macro shifts and micro effects, some implications for 'emerging adults', and some implications for parents.

Macro shifts and micro effects

The finding that so many parents had difficulties in 'letting go' contradicts earlier research (Adelman *et al.*, 1989; Aquilino, 1996; Fiske & Chiriboga, 1991; Ryff & Seltzer, 1996) that showed that parents were quite happy for their children to leave the parental home to live their own lives. Twenty years ago, when these studies were conducted, the social norm was that young people should leave home in their early twenties. If a young adult continued to live at home, parents were disappointed and believed that they had failed to adequately socialize their offspring for adulthood (Clemens & Axelson, 1985; Schnaiberg & Goldenberg, 1989). Nowadays parents seem to report a different attitude.

Societal changes have not only affected young people, but also changed family interactions and the role of parents. Women are now urged to embark on independent careers. Care tasks have been taken over to a great extent by the welfare state (e.g., care for children and the elderly), and household chores have been simplified by commercial products (e.g., ready cooked meals, sophisticated appliances, throw-away nappies). All this has had a profound effect on family life. Children are no longer an economic investment for old-age. Rather, they are an economic liability, which is reflected in the decreasing birth rates all over Europe (Douglass, 2005). If parents decide to have children, it is mainly for emotional reasons (Jensen, 1994). In effect, this is partly a consequence of young couples being faced with the choice between acquiring expensive consumer goods and having a child (Kalle, Lambrechts, & Cuyvers, 2000). Not surprisingly, parents who take the latter option may have a different view of independence in emerging adulthood and have different feelings about adult children leaving home. Mitchell (2006) used the metaphor of the 'pendulum swing' of family transformations over historical times, and our findings suggest that parents' perceptions of the 'empty nest' might be about to change again, at least among some parents.

Some implications for 'emerging adults'

Given the reluctance of a number of parents to lead their children towards independence, this might have repercussions for transitions into adulthood. Over-indulging young people actually seems to negatively influence their development of many adult skills. For example, Seiffge-Krenke (2006) has shown that over-protective parenting leads to over-dependence and reduced autonomy in early adulthood. Thus, it seems that parental reluctance to let their children achieve maturity may play some role in creating Arnett's (2004) 'emerging adults' who are reluctant to take on adult responsibilities. The ambivalence of parents seems to be matched by the ambivalence of emerging adults themselves. This interpretation has recently received some justification by the results of a quantitative study with a sample of emerging adults who were in the middle of the home-leaving process, showing that mothers' and fathers' separation anxiety played a crucial role in young people's separation-individuation process: parents who showed high anxiety about the distancing of their emerging adults used dependency-oriented psychological control, which in turn predicted higher levels of pathological separation in emerging adults (personal communication with Kins & Beyers, May, 2009).

Thus, emotionally satisfying as a prolonged mutual dependency of parents and their adult children might be (Scabini, Marta, & Lanz, 2005), it has its problematic side. Emerging adults who live independently tend to report better relationships with their parents than those who still live in the parental home (Buhl, 2007; Flanagan, Schulenberg, & Fuligni, 1993) and are more likely to develop mature adult-to-adult relationships. Dependency engenders an increased risk for maladjustment (Beyers & Goossens, 2003). Young people who consider themselves as emerging adults are more depressed (Nelson & McNamara Barry, 2005) than those who see themselves as adults and are less likely to achieve independent and self determined citizenship.

> 'On the one hand, the identity moratorium allows people to experiment with various identities and future selves, but on the other hand it leaves them open to various forms of identity manipulation; the very thing mass marketers are looking for. Moreover, the identity moratorium has helped create a virtually powerless group, with no one to speak positively and forcefully for it. The 'time-out' from adulthood also means a time-out from political and economic participation in mainstream society'.
>
> (Côté, 2000, p. 173f)

More research, and particularly longitudinal studies that run from the adolescent years into adulthood, is needed to tease out the effects of different parental styles on young people's well-being, adjustment to adulthood, and ongoing relationships with their parents, before, during, and after the transitions to adulthood.

Some implications for parents

If parental perceptions are accurate and dependency does last for an extended period, this might create a difficult situation for parents, sandwiched between caring for their adult children and their own ageing parents. With delayed entry into parenthood and longer child dependency, some parents could face ongoing parental responsibilities until their mid-sixties. This would have implications for their own life course, and might complicate their coping with further life transitions such as menopause, retirement, and ageing.

In the past, research on parent–child relationships has almost exclusively concentrated on long-term effects on the children and has not taken into consideration how parents themselves are affected. It becomes clear from this study that children's transitions to adulthood as part of one family transformation are equally behavioural and role transitions for the parents. Further, in the interactive context of family life, the dynamics of development mean that both parents and children affect and influence parenting styles and child behaviour, and interdependent forces such as emotions, perceptions, and behaviours consolidate and crystallize over time (Granic, 2000). The emerging relational patterns might not always create an outcome which is optimal and desirable for all participants in the long run, and may have possible effects for society. As Buhl (2008) argues, individuation is co-constructed in the family, and if achieved successfully, is a predictor of a satisfying lifelong relationship between parents and children. Thus, we strongly advocate that transitions to adulthood need to be researched and analysed from a more systemic and ecological perspective – within the cultural and psychosocial dynamics of the whole family and linked lives (Elder, 1998), with attention given to the transitional patterns of parents and other family members as well as to the young person on the brink of adulthood.

References

Adelman, P. K., Antonucci, T. C., Crohan, S. E., & Coleman, L. M. (1989). Empty nest, cohort, and employment in the well-being of midlife women. *Sex Roles, 20*, 173–188.

Aquilino, W. S. (1996). The returning adult child and parental experiences at midlife. In C. Ryff & M. Seltzer (Eds.), *The parental experience in midlife* (pp. 423–458). Chicago, IL: University of Chicago Press.

Aquilino, W. S. (1997). From adolescent to young adult: A prospective study of parent–child relations during the transition to adulthood. *Journal of Marriage and the Family, 59*, 670–686.

Aquilino, W. S. (2005). Impact of family structure on parental attitudes toward the economic support of adult children over the transition to adulthood. *Journal of Family Issues, 26*, 143–167.

Arnett, J. J. (2004). *Emerging adulthood: The winding road from late teens through the twenties.* Oxford: Oxford University Press.

Arnett, J. J. (2006). Emerging adulthood in Europe: A response to Bynner. *Journal of Youth Studies, 9*, 111–123.

Arnett, J. J., & Tanner, J. (2010). Lifestyles in emerging adulthood: Why we need a new stage. In J. J. Arnett, M. Kloep, L. B. Hendry, & J. Tanner (Eds.), *Divergent perspectives on emerging adulthood: Stage or process?* New York: Oxford University Press.

Beyers, W., & Goossens, L. (2003). Psychological separation and adjustment to university: Moderating effects of gender, age and perceived parenting style. *Journal of Adolescent Research, 18*, 363–382.

Bronfenbrenner, U., & Morris, P. A. (1998). The ecology of the developmental process. In D. Damon & R. M. Lerner (Eds.), *Handbook of child psychology* (5th ed., Vol. 1, pp. 993–1028). New York: Wiley.

Bucx, F., & van Wel, F. (2008). Parental bond and life course transitions from adolescence to young adulthood. *Family Therapy, 35*(2), 109–127.

Buhl, H. M. (2007). Well-being and the child–parent relationship at the transition from university to working life. *Journal of Adolescent Research, 22*, 550–571.

Buhl, H. M. (2008). Significance of individuation in adult parent–child relationships. *Journal of Family Issues, 29*, 262–281.

Bynner, J. (2005). Re-thinking the youth phase of the life course: The case for emerging adulthood? *Journal of Youth Studies, 8*, 367–384.

Carr, D. (2004). 'My daughter has a career; I just raised babies': The psychological consequences of women's inter-generational social comparisons. *Social Psychology Quarterly, 67*, 132–154.

Carr, D. (2005). The psychological consequences of midlife men's social comparisons with their young adult sons. *Journal of Marriage and Family, 67*, 240–250.

Charmaz, K. (1995). Grounded theory. In J. Smith, R. Harre, & L. Van Langenhove (Eds.), *Re-thinking methods in psychology* (pp. 27–49). London: Sage.

Clemens, A. W., & Axelson, L. J. (1985). The not so empty nest: The return of the fledgling adult. *Family Relations, 34*, 259–264.

Coleman, J. C., & Brooks, F. (2009). *Key data on adolescence*. Brighton: Trust for the Study of Adolescence.

Côté, J. E. (2000). *Arrested adulthood: The changing nature of identity-maturity in the late-modern world*. New York: New York University Press.

Dennerstein, L., Dudley, E., & Guthrie, J. (2002). Empty nest or revolving door? A prospective study of women's quality of life in midlife during the phase of children leaving and re-entering the home. *Psychological Medicine, 32*, 545–550.

Douglass, C. B. (Ed.), (2005). *Barren states: The population 'implosion' in Europe*. New York: Berg.

Elder, G. H., Jr. (1998). The life course as developmental theory. *Child Development, 69*, 1–12.

Eurostat (2006). *Eurostat New Cronos*. European commission population statistics. Luxembourg: Office European Communities.

Fingerman, K. L. (1996). Sources of tension in the aging mother and daughter relationship. *Psychology and Aging, 11*, 591–606.

Fiske, M., & Chiriboga, D. A. (1991). *Change and continuity in adult life*. San Francisco, CA: Jossey-Bass.

Flanagan, C., Schulenberg, J., & Fuligni, A. (1993). Residential setting and parent–adolescent relationships during the college years. *Journal of Youth and Adolescence, 22*, 171–189.

Gitelson, I. B., & McDermott, D. (2006). Parents and their young adult children: Transitions to adulthood. *Child Welfare, 85*(5), 853–866.

Granic, I. (2000). The self-organization of parent–child relations: Beyond bi-directional models. In M. D. Lewis & I. Granic (Eds.), *Emotion, development and self-organization: Dynamic systems approaches to emotional development* (pp. 267–297). New York: Cambridge University Press.

Hendry, L. B., & Kloep, M. (2002). *Lifespan development: Challenges, resources and risks*. London: Thompson.

Hendry, L. B., & Kloep, M. (2007). Conceptualizing emerging adulthood: Inspecting the emperor's new clothes? *Child Development Perspectives, 1*, 74–79.

Hendry, L. B., Shucksmith, J. S., Love, J., & Glendinning, A. (1993). *Young people's leisure and lifestyles*. London: Routledge.

Jensen, A. M. (1994). Feminization of childhood. In J. Qvortrup, M. Bardy, G. B. Sgritta, & H. Wintersberger (Eds.), *Childhood matters: Social theory, practice and politics* (pp. 59–75). Aldershot: Ashgate.

John, B., & Alwyn, T. (2005). *Promoting safe and sensible attitudes to alcohol in children and their families: From lollipops to alcopops*. Report to the Alcohol Education Research Council, London.

Kalle, P., Lambrechts, E., & Cuyvers, P. (2000). *Partner interaction. Partner interaction, demography and equal opportunities as future labour supply factors*. European Commission SOC 98 101387-05E01. Netherlands Family Council.

Kins, E., Beyers, W., Soenens, B., & Vansteenkiste, M. (2009). Patterns of home-leaving and subjective well-being in emerging adulthood: The role of motivational processes and parental autonomy support. *Developmental Psychology, 45*, 1416–1429.

Kloep, M. (1999). Love is all you need? Focusing on adolescents' life concerns from an ecological point of view. *Journal of Adolescence, 22*, 49–63.

Lachman, M. E. (2001). *Handbook of midlife development*. New York: Wiley.

Lachman, M. E., & James, J. B. (1997). *Multiple paths to midlife development*. Chicago, IL: University of Chicago Press.

Matthews, T. J., & Hamilton, B. E. (2006). *Delayed childbearing: More women are having their first later in life*. NCHS Data Brief. Centers for Disease Control and Prevention. Retrieved from http://www.cde.gov/nch/data/databriefs

Mitchell, B. A. (2004). Making the move: Cultural and parental influences on Canadian young adults' home-leaving decisions. *Journal of Comparative Family Studies;, 35*, 425–441.

Mitchell, B. A. (2006). Changing courses: The pendulum of family transitions in comparative perspective. *Journal of Comparative Family Studies, 37*, 325–343.

Nelson, L. J., & McNamara Barry, C. (2005). Distinguishing features of emerging adulthood: The role of self-classification as an adult. *Journal of Adolescence Research, 20*, 242–249.

Pudrovska, T. (2006). Psychological implications of motherhood and fatherhood in midlife: Evidence from sibling models. *Journal of Marriage and Family, 70*, 168–181.

Roberts, R. E. L., & Bengtson, V. L. (1993). Relationships with parents, self esteem, and psychological well-being in young adulthood. *Social Psychology Quarterly, 56*, 263–277.

Ryan, R. M., Deci, E. L., Grolnick, W. S., & La Guardia, J. G. (2006). The significance of autonomy and autonomy support in psychological development and psychopathology. In D. Cicchetti & D. J. Cohen (Eds.), *Developmental psychopathology: Vol. 1. Theory and method* (2nd ed., pp. 795–849). New Jersey, NJ: Wiley.

Ryff, C., & Seltzer, M. (1996). The unchartered years of midlife parenting. In C. Ryff & M. Seltzer (Eds.), *The parental experience in midlife* (pp. 3–28). Chicago, IL: University of Chicago Press.

Scabini, E., Marta, E., & Lanz, M. (2005). *The transition to adulthood and family relations: An intergenerational perspective*. Hove: Psychology Press.

Schnaiberg, A., & Goldenberg, S. (1989). From empty nest to crowded nest: The dynamics of incompletely-launched young adults. *Social Problems, 36*, 251–269.

Seiffge-Krenke, I. (2006). Leaving home or still in the nest? Parent–child relationships and psychological health as predictors of different leaving home patterns. *Developmental Psychology, 42*, 864–876.

Settersten, R. A., Furstenberg, F. F., & Rumbaut, R. G. (2005). *On the frontier of adulthood: Theory, research and public policy*. Chicago, IL: University of Chicago Press.

Shucksmith, J., Hendry, L. B., & Glendinning, A. (1995). Models of parenting: Implications for adolescent well-being within different types of family context. *Journal of Adolescence, 18*, 253–270.

Soenens, B., Vansteenkiste, M., Luyckx, K., & Goossens, L. (2006). Parenting and adolescent problem behavior. An integrated model with adolescent self-disclosure and perceived parental knowledge as intervening variables. *Developmental Psychology, 42*, 305–318.

Statistics Canada (2008). *Summary tables*. Retrieved from http://www40.statcan.ca/l01/cst01/

Thornton, A., Orbuch, T. G., & Axinn, W. L. (1995). Parent–child relationships during the transition to adulthood. *Journal of Family Issues, 16*, 538–564.

White, N. R. (2002). 'Not under my roof!' Young people's experience of home. *Youth and Society, 34*, 214–231.

Willis, S. L., & Reid, J. D. (1999). *Life in the middle: Psychological and social development in middle age*. San Diego, CA: Academic Press.

Wittmann, S., Buhl, H. M., & Noack, P. (2000). Arbeitsbericht aus dem Forschungsprojekt '*Erwachsene und ihre Eltern,' 1999 bis 2000* [Research report from the research project 'Adults and Their Parents,']. Jena: Friedrich-Schiller-University Jena.

13 Pathways to retirement

In this study we wanted to trace possibly different 'pathways' into retirement and how these transitions were perceived by the individuals concerned. The article attempted to show the various interactive elements that combine to create transitions into retirement in ways that make the process pleasant or difficult. The article takes a series of empirical findings about transitions into retirement to discuss social and community roles for senior citizens together with a range of professional roles for counsellors and psychologists and other services working with older people. Significantly, the core of the article's argument is that transitions of old age share similar basic elements to those in coping with earlier life-course transitions.

Earlier, my research focus had been describing and offering some interpretations of adolescent lifestyles. In doing so, I became somewhat frustrated by the limitations of research methods available – often cross-sectional designs, which do not allow causal explanations to be made and do not effectively capture transitional processes of change. Furthermore, societal influences on the individual developmental pathways were often 'missing' from accounts of findings.

With regard to methods which do attempt to get 'under the surface' of change and transitions in development, I have felt that many quantitative methods were often too restricted to reflect dynamic change or reveal the variety of individual behaviours. Hence, in my research I tried increasingly to apply qualitative methods (often in combination with quantitative approaches) in attempts to uncover both major trends and individual variations. (One can even use qualitative methods – though not in all cases – to test hypotheses as in quantitative analysis (see e.g. Hendry & Kloep, 2010).

Thus, as my career continued, I became aware that my publications, based mainly on empirical findings, had led me to present a number of theoretical frameworks: Some were wholly original, and others were adaptations of others' ideas but applied differently. Nevertheless, theoretical models are not without their critics; and being the kind of academic that I am, the first theoretical framework I criticized was one of my own creations! At the time of writing a book about adolescent development (see Hendry, L B (1983) Growing Up and Going Out, Elsevier Science), I used John Coleman's (1974) focal theory to show how adolescent leisure transitions were differentiated by gender, age, social class and relational factors, amongst others. It was, in essence, a descriptive model, though useful in exhibiting the emergent multi-variable pathways. I also adapted Coleman's focal model in devising an explanatory theoretical mapping of adolescents' coping with unemployment (see Hendry, 1987).

RETIREMENT

A new beginning?

Marion Kloep and Leo B. Hendry

With the societal changes and shifts of the last few decades, the elderly population of the UK now matches the numbers of teenagers (Coleman & Schofield, 2005). Does this change in the composition of British society mean that we now have 'emerging old age' as a new life phase?

One of the problems in trying to answer this question is the difficulty in defining old age. Given the de-standardised life course in our society, where few jobs are for life, relationships and marriage are less permanent, age of retirement is flexible, more active lifestyles exist and there is greater longevity, it is not easy to state when old age actually begins or what describes the hallmarks of emerging seniority.

Transitions across the life course encompass a range of maturational tasks, and these are no easier for older adults to negotiate than for adolescents (see Coleman & Hendry, 1999). What causes the more dramatic change in one's self-identity: the development of pubic hair during puberty or one's hair turning silver within the process of ageing? Old age transitions encompass many shifts in physical appearance, the 'empty nest' syndrome when adult children leave home, the menopause, moving into retirement, economic changes, the loss of parents, and so on.

One of the uncertainties in understanding how old age is experienced compared to other life shifts is that all of us, social scientists and lay people alike, have passed through adolescence, but most of us have not yet been aware of more than a glimpse or two of our pending entry into old age. Traditionally, retirement was seen as the last normative shift – the marker of entry into old age – but now, thanks to governmental decree, the age of retirement can vary from middle age onward depending on individual circumstances. Nevertheless, the transition into being retired is still significant both for the individual and for their status in the eyes of other members of that society.

However, little professional help is available to assist people to plan for this major transition in their life. Existing retirement planning consists of little more than financial advice, and does not cover preparation for the social, emotional and health changes of later life. This article explores the multifaceted shifts that accompany retirement for different individuals, and suggests that psychologists – both within and beyond the workplace – could play a key role in assisting people to gain greater life satisfaction out of this life phase.

The meaning of retirement

A large number of studies have been conducted over the last few decades, identifying health, gender, economy, educational level, marital status and the quality of social networks as the main factors influencing both decisions about when to retire and the degree of adjustments to retirement (see Barnes *et al.*, 2002; Kim & Moen, 2001, 2002), in addition to 'push–pull' factors at the workplace and in other life spheres (Hanisch, 1994). However, what this research shows are complex, interacting, and mainly social factors that do not always explain individual decisions and adaptations particularly well, and do not take into account the accumulative influences of lifespan experiences.

A case study of two women by August and Quintero (2001) illustrates nicely how individual careers are constantly shaped throughout the whole of the life course: Different cumulative experiences, career options and individual resources led to different retirement choices, ultimately causing one woman to opt for security and retirement, and the other to face new challenges and plan a different late life career. In our own Norwegian qualitative research of transitions into retirement (Kloep & Hendry, 2006) we identified three groups, but with many individual psychosocial variations within them (see box).

Clearly, retired people are a varied, heterogeneous group, who do not experience this life shift all in the same way. Retirement counselling should take this into account. For example, it seems to us that our 'distressed' group might have benefited from much earlier life interventions, focused on their current, injurious life events rather than on retirement issues. The second group, whose life resources were mostly associated with occupations, would require help in developing social and leisure skills for the time when they might be forced to leave employment. On the other hand, some members of our 'well-adjusted' group, might have been persuaded to remain working for longer, at least part-time, if greater flexibility had been allowed to enable them to pursue their other interests. In other words, they would have been more suited to the services of an organisational psychologist rather than those of a counsellor or life coach.

EXPERIENCES OF RETIREMENT – THREE GROUPS?

High distress: This was a very small group, who showed signs of high distress. These were individuals who reported a range of debilitating experiences, such as major health problems, loss of partner, lack of skills or hobbies, and family tragedies. They had not liked their work, but neither did they adjust well to the experiences of being retired. Their problems did not stem from the retirement transition per se, but were the result of accumulated negative life-course experiences and events impinging on their development.

You see, I just find I have this problem of going into a room of people I don't know and getting started. I can't do it ... I've just got this enormous inferiority complex. Everybody else seems so much cleverer than I am. ... I don't particularly want to go and work in a charity shop. I did try that sort of by mistake on one occasion. I got lured into it, but I didn't fancy that – you know, if I could do something behind the scenes. I haven't done anything in a sort of civil, if that's the right word, capacity, organisation or anything like that. That is the feeling I have, that everybody else seems so ridiculously efficient and knowing what they're doing, and who to talk to, and all this kind of jazz, ... but I just sort of feel it's all a bit late in the day now for anything like that ... I'm about fifty years behind the times! You see, I'm going to be behind the times. I'm obsolescent, if not obsolete, I've decided.

(Female, 76)

Work as a lifestyle: Gaining high administrative or academic posts in their careers, the majority of the interests and social networks of this group were linked to their professional positions, and they were reluctant to yield these and accept the role and status of a retired person. If forced to do so, they had considerable adjustment problems and suffered quite badly from their perceived loss of social status.

When you retire from your job, then you feel now you've joined the group of retired people, whom you always regarded as people who are a bit senile and who need help to get up from a chair and that kind of thing ... And of course, that you do not signify anything any longer is the essential thing. I have been in such a position for my entire career – I had a leading position ... I don't even have a dog to command now! So now it's the wife that commands me, because she is still working, but that is ok ... But it is very clearly quite a big transition from being in work to making hoovering the house one's biggest task in life!

(Male, 67)

Life beyond work: This was the largest group. They had enjoyed their jobs, but had retired willingly, and often earlier than required, in order to have time to enjoy other activities, hobbies and commitments. They usually adapted well to retirement after an initial adjustment phase, and led busy, well-structured and active lives. Nevertheless, there were strong indications that they had developed a range of interests, hobbies and skills that facilitated their transition much earlier in the life course, not during the process of retirement. Once again, this demonstrates the need for advanced preparations to successfully achieve anticipated future life shifts.

... well, I left work when I was 63 ... that will soon be nine years since I left, so that way I got a lot out of life. This, that I could let go of thinking of the work situation all the time, meant that I could develop myself, have hobbies. Two times a week I am an instructor of a work-out

> *group, and there, there too, we are on such fabulous terms . . . because we developed through work and leisure, we gained a great deal of new friends (apart from childhood friends) with whom we have contact . . . we are a gang, we, and we love to meet in the streets and take the last bus home!*
>
> (Male, 71)

Community participation

The group who were best adjusted to a retired lifestyle showed high involvement in community organisations and activities. Social participation seems to be not only a sign of good adjustment, it also adds to life quality after retirement. It enhances cognitive functioning and functional ability (e.g. Avlund *et al.*, 2004; Lee, 2000; Singh-Manoux *et al.*, 2003) and perceived life quality (Bowling *et al.*, 2004), and it reduces morbidity (Hyyppa & Maki, 2003). Apart from being good for the individual, older citizens' social participation is a valuable asset to the community. Many retirees continue in paid employment part-time; some provide educational networks locally or nationally; some keep communities alive by organising events, participating in local political decision-making, looking after grandchildren and providing DIY help to their grown-up families, friends and neighbours. If communities fail to capitalise on engaging the resources that older citizens invest in local events and activities, they risk losing them. An increasing number of active older people use their energies on trips and travelling around the world instead (Feldman & Oberlink, 2003; Staats & Pierfelice, 2003).

In other words, social participation by older citizens has important functions both for the individual and for society. In our latest study, seeking to find out what older people do in retirement, their motivations, and what facilitates or hinders their social engagement, we trained a number of volunteers from the University of the Third Age in South Wales as co-researchers, to interview age peers in their own communities about the daily life of a pensioner (Kloep & Hendry, 2007).

A picture of highly active senior citizens emerged, engaged in a wide range of activities, from wind surfing, to studying for degrees, to participation in the running of community organisations such as charities, councils or churches. Some were so busy with a variety of pursuits that they could hardly find time to be interviewed!

While the number of activities, and the time invested in these, decreases somewhat with increasing age, a separate analysis by Jenkins (2006) showed that the majority of older citizens are extremely active, engaging on average in 11 different activities, and spending nearly 20 hours a week in community organisations. Some rural communities were kept alive by the involvement of senior citizens initiating events not only for each other but for the whole community: running clubs, organisations and church events, arranging charity car boot sales, lotteries and other events, entertaining at local fairs, and assisting in local government. All these contributions demonstrate how older citizens can provide valuable resources for local communities and society generally.

The reasons for their individual involvement varied, but one important point that many made was that participation was not necessarily taken up after retirement – they had always been engaged in these or similar activities. This was particularly true for being active in clubs, organisations and charities, and for hobbies like gardening, golf and water sports. Some mentioned that they were particularly delighted to find more time for these activities after retirement, while others felt somewhat pressurised to take over responsibilities 'because no one else was willing to do it'.

Apart from enjoying the activities in themselves, many emphasised the social values of participating. Shared activities of all kinds offered opportunities to meet and make new friends. For some, these community engagements provided the only venues they had to meet others, and offered a social lifeline after bereavement.

On the other hand, a few participants could not be bothered with involvement in activities beyond their family. Reasons for this were twofold: some had had an exhausting life, busy with organising meetings and events, and now, in retirement, preferred to do things on their own. By contrast, others lacked socialising experiences and were too shy to join a group or to learn a new skill.

Many would like to be more involved, but were prevented by individual or social circumstances. Having to care for a relative, lacking economic means, declining health and loss of mobility were the most quoted individual reasons for this. Directly connected to non-participation were social factors: limited information and few possibilities for respite care: lack of transport and travel problems in visiting adult children, who had moved away because of rising house prices or the lack of educational and vocational opportunities locally: and few opportunities to influence relevant local government policies on these, and other, issues.

New directions for research and practice

In general, people have concerns about the next life phase they are about to enter. For example, in an ongoing interview study (Hendry & Kloep, 2007) of transitions from late adolescence to adulthood, several teenagers expressed the view that adulthood brings responsibilities and with these the end of 'fun' as they know it. Similarly, many adults perceive old age as a time when personal resources deteriorate and the future is bleak. However, from the narratives of many older people, old age can be fun if one has an array of psychosocial resources to draw on. From their perspective, this is a period of the lifespan filled with positive enjoyment and productive social engagement.

So, with various transitional pathways into old age, starting for some in their fifties, and for others in their eighties, do we have to expand Erikson's (1968) eight stage theory by adding another developmental stage between adulthood and old age, something like 'emerging old age'? We think not. We would argue that understanding the processes and mechanisms of any lifespan transition is more insightful than merely inventing new stages that do not explain development, but are simply descriptive – and only for some individuals in certain cultures in certain historical periods. For the researcher, the onset of old age is the result of a complex interaction of physical, physiological, psychosocial, ecologic and cultural factors, that cannot be investigated by simply assuming the linear and causal relationships of a few variables. Thus, we need more holistic research approaches that do not treat individual differences merely as 'error variance', but rather develop a range of innovative strategies that get under the skin of becoming and being retired and of other lifespan transitions.

It seems to be true that with increasing age people are pressed towards being less active. This is not necessarily self-chosen: it can be caused by limitations in their physical abilities, social expectations or legal regulations that reduce possibilities of activity in later life. However, it can also be the result of a proactive decision to preserve self-agency. Thus, neither disengagement nor sustained involvement are inevitable outcomes of ageing: they are the result of a dynamic lifelong process of accumulating and losing resources, which is different for every individual (Hendry & Kloep, 2002). Looked at in this way, dealing with the transitions of old age is not especially different from coping with the transitions of earlier life.

Such an ecological life span approach also has repercussions for counsellors, occupational and health psychologists. For the practitioner, research from a lifespan perspective might guide new approaches to our psychological services. People of all ages need to learn and relearn the skills involved in lifespan transitions, such as reflecting upon their individual needs, setting goals and making decisions that are appropriate to, and optimal for, their development within the life course. As this article has illustrated, many of the skills demonstrated by those who had adjusted successfully to retirement have had their genesis much earlier in the lifespan.

In the case of the transition to retirement itself, there may be a growing need for counselling and advisory services that go well beyond providing financial guidance. Such services, together with greater flexibility in workplace arrangements, could help people to explore different sectors of their lives and their life course. The focus might be on how to develop new friendships; actively taking care of one's health, selecting an appropriate place to live, re-adjusting marital life, and perhaps most importantly, how to make optimal use of time – at work, within the family, at leisure, within community organisations, and in learning new activities and hobbies.

References

August, R.A. & Quintero, V.C., (2001). The role of opportunity structures in older women workers' careers. *Journal of Employment Counselling, 38,* 62–81.

Avland, K., Lund, R., Holstein, B.E. & Due, P. (2004). The impact of structural and functional characteristics of social relations as determinants of functional decline. *Journals of Gerontology, 59B,* 44–56.

Barnes, H., Parry, J. & Lakey, J. (2002). *Forging a new future. The experiences and expectations of people leaving paid work.* London: Policy Press in association with the Joseph Rowntree Foundation.

Bowling, A., Gabriel, Z. Banister, D. & Sutton, S. (2004). *Adding quality to quantity: Older people's views on their quality of life and its enhancement.* ESRC Growing Older Programme Sheffield.

Coleman, J.C. & Hendry, L.B. (1999). *The nature of adolescence* (3rd edn). London: Routledge.

Coleman, J.C. & Schofield, J. (2005). *Key data on adolescence* (5th edn). Brighton: Trust for the Study of Adolescence.

Erikson, E. (1968). *Identity, youth and crisis*. New York: Norton.

Feldman, P.H. & Oberlink, M.R. (2003). The AdvantAge Initiative: Developing community indicators to promote the health and well-being of older people. *Family and Community Health, 26,* 268–274.

Hanisch, K.A. (1994). Reasons people retire and their relations to attitudinal and behavioural correlates in retirement. *Journal of Vocational Behavior, 45,* 1–16.

Hendry, L.E., & Kloep, M. (2002). *Life-span development: Resources, challenges and risks*. London: Thomson Learning.

Hendry, L.B. & Kloep, M. (2007). *Emerging adulthood or eternal youth?* Paper presented at the 3rd conference on Ernerging Adulthood. February, Tucson, Anzona.

Hyyppa, M. & Maki, J. (2003). Social participation and health in a community rich in stock of social capital. *Health Education Research, 18,* 770–784.

Jenkins, J. (2006). *Senior Citizens, Third Agers, Silver Surfers – But do they wear purple?* Unpublished MSc thesis, University of Surrey and Pre-Retirement Association.

Kim, J.E. & Moen, P. (2001). Moving into retirement: Preparations and transitions in late midlife. In M.E. Lachman (Ed.) *Handbook of midlife development* (pp. 487–527) Wiley; New York.

Kim, J.E. & Moen, P. (2002). Retirement transitions, gender, and psychological well-being: A life course ecological model. *Journals of Gerontology, 57B,* 212–222.

Kloep, M. & Hendry, L.B. (2006). Entry or Exit! Transitions into retirement. *Journal of Occupational and Organizational Psychology, 79,* 569–593.

Kloep, M. & Hendry, L.B. (2007). *Being over 60 in Wales*. Unpublished Report, University of Glamorgan. Available from the authors on request.

Lee, Y. (2000). The predictive value of self assessed general, physical, and mental health on functional decline and mortality in older adults. *Journal of Epidemiology and Community Health, 54,* 123–129.

Singh-Manoux, A., Richards, M. & Marmot, M. (2003). Leisure activities and cognitive functioning in middle age: Evidence from the Whitehall II study. *Journal of Epidemiology and Community Health, 57,* 907–921.

Staats, S. & Pierfelice, L. (2003). Travel: A long range goal of retired women. *Journal of Psychology, 137,* 483–494.

Appendix

The quotations below are not from the original article but from the research itself:

> So he died six years ago now and it was traumatic when he had the stroke, because he couldn't speak, not only could he hardly move, he couldn't speak either ... and I think that had a tremendous effect on my outlook on life, you know, 'cos I sort of thought: this is not going to be the end of the world kind of thing, so I sort of stopped, well not really stopped wanting to do things, but

you do sort of take control of yourself and face the situation as it is, and not necessarily as you would like it to be . . . and we were both very, very happy in P . . . shire.

(female, 76)

Well, I finished that research project one and a half years before I reached 70. And then I worked with this project here, so that I could continue until I was 70. But it was far from ready, so I have been working here all the time, all the time up till now . . . I still have an office . . . I love to be here, because I also do something that has nothing to do with the Institute, but with my subject discipline. An investigation on water resources. This I do on a totally voluntary basis.

(male, 75)

Our U3A is unusual, it has a jazz band. I run the jazz band, I started the jazz band, I learnt the banjo to play in the jazz band and once a week on a Friday morning we practise, we play New Orleans jazz, there are six people in the band and we play at local fetes, lots of charity things, but also evening concerts, indoor, outdoor events, jazz festivals, theatres, all the usual things, where a jazz band would play. I was a founder member of our U3A and I was, I would say the first Vice Chairman and member of the founding committee. I now belong to several other groups, the Natural History group, the local history group, I go to armchair travel, mobility for men, the picture group, the photography group and occasionally other groups and I usually go along to the monthly business meeting. Well, some things in the village. I'm Secretary of the local parish church and the Treasurer of the village hall committee. I belong to the National Trust group and the Historical Society and the West Wales National Trust and I attend quite a few of those meetings, trips etc.

(male, 75)

14 Reflecting on theories

One nice thing about being an academic writer is that it is possible to change one's previous ideas, even theories or models, and no-one seems to mind terribly! With time for reflection, the strengths and weaknesses of the original focal model applied to leisure transitions became evident, and it was necessary to re-assess the initial theoretical framework and to test if the basic elements of the model were affected by contextual and societal change. So, this extract demonstrated, by using data from a three-nation study, that additional, associated factors are a good test of a particular model's robustness. The effects of cultural change and of geographic context made a significant impression on the empirical results, thereby showing that the original 'theory' was, in essence, merely a description and that changing social conditions had caused the various patterns of transition to alter significantly.

LEISURE TRANSITIONS – A RURAL PERSPECTIVE[1]

Leo B. Hendry, Marion Kloep, Geir A. Espnes, Jan E. Ingebrigtsen, Anthony Glendinning and Sheila Wood

The paper examines leisure focal theory from a cross-cultural perspective by utilizing adolescent samples from rural Norway, Scotland and Sweden. Both quantitative and qualitative methods were used to explore the robustness of the model across countries. Results revealed effects of both culture and rurality on the patterns of adolescents' leisure transitions, and these were discussed in relation to the original theoretical framework.

Introduction

The social and economic forces that have been destabilizing employment, gender, and age roles have not left leisure unscathed. Leisure is affected by the same new technologies and globalization that have been transforming working life (Roberts, 1997). These wider changes are linked to trends in young people's leisure: A greater age-span is involved in present-day youth scenes, gender and social class differences are more diffuse, and tastes and styles have fragmented. However – as

Roberts pointed out – these are only trends, and the main systematic differences in leisure pursuits are still somewhat associated with the same old structural predictors. In this paper we set out to explore the possible influences of cultural differences and socio-geographical settings on adolescents' leisure transitions.

Hendry (1983) theorized that the leisure patterns of both young women and young men move through three stages in early-, mid- and later-adolescence, namely: 'organized leisure', 'casual leisure' and 'commercial leisure', with males making the transitions from one phase to the next slightly later than females. It was further hypothesized that these leisure transitions tended to coincide with transitions in relational issues across adolescence as Coleman (1974) had outlined earlier. Organized leisure includes sports participation and adult-led activities, and tends to decline from the early adolescent years. Casual leisure includes 'hanging around' with friends, and this tends to be less common after mid-adolescence. Commercial leisure becomes the predominant form in later-adolescence, and includes cinema attendance as well as visiting discos, pubs and clubs: on average, 75% of 16–24-year-olds in Britain, for example, visit pubs four times a week (Willis, 1990). With a representative sample of approximately 8,000 Scottish adolescents, Hendry et al. (1993, 1997), found these same general trends in leisure transitions. The results confirmed the theoretical model proposed by Hendry in 1983, and suggested that casual and informal leisure activities outside the home, such as 'hanging about with friends' in the local neighbourhood, are at a peak in middle adolescence and fall away rapidly thereafter, whilst commercial leisure venues, such as cinemas, discos, clubs and pubs, steadily increase in importance across the adolescent years to reach a peak in later adolescence. Gender differences were evident in these leisure transitions, with a decline in the use of the local neighbourhood seen as more marked amongst young women, and an increase in pub attendance more marked amongst young men. The results also suggested that young people's leisure involvement was linked to social class background (where social class differences related to casual leisure pursuits rather than commercial involvement). There was nevertheless some overlap in the uses of leisure by adolescents from the different social classes: These days, young peoples' leisure tastes do *not* fall within neat gender, social class or geographic boundaries (Roberts and Parsell, 1994). There is great variety within all groups related to the wider processes of individualization (Maffesoli, 1994), and various offerings of the consumer industries from which to select. However, the key finding from Hendry's research was that trends in *leisure transitions* were broadly similar for all social groupings.

In the last two decades there have been changes in the leisure patterns of young women, yet gender has remained a strong predictor of participation in 'active' pursuits (e.g., Glyptis, 1989; Wold and Hendry, 1998). In particular, leisure opportunities are sometimes restricted through conventions governing the use of 'space' (Coakley and White, 1992). By contrast, there are fewer conventions that restrict the activities of young males. Hendry et al. (1993) have reported that many leisure settings are male preserves and that this lack of access to leisure 'space' for girls means that they often retreat into home-based activities. More recent changes in young women's leisure behaviour, however, are related to their progress in education and the labour market, and gaining control over their own fertility (Roberts, 1995). Young women are as likely as young men to use indoor sports facilities (Department for Education, 1995). They also visit other public spaces – without male escorts – such as city centres, wine bars and all aspects of the club scene. Nowadays in Western societies it may often be young men who lead narrower leisure lives, doing little except drink, watch and talk about sport and sex while young women develop broader leisure interests, relationships and skills (see Roberts *et al.*, 1990; Roberts, 1996). Yet Coakley and White (1992) argued that young men regard sporting activity as congruent with a dominant masculine role and gain kudos from engaging in competitive activities. On the other hand, many young women are less likely to connect sports activity with the process of becoming a woman and may avoid participating in leisure activities that may be perceived as threatening to their femininity. Focusing on sports participation, Hendry *et al.* (1993) found that among 13–20-year-olds, around three-quarters of males but less than half of the females participated in sports on a weekly basis. Coakley and White (1992, p. 32) suggested that: 'the decision to participate in sport was integrally tied to the way young people viewed themselves and their connection in the social world'. Throughout adolescence, young people's involvement in sporting activities declines, with young women 'dropping out' at an earlier stage than men (Hendry *et al.*, 1993).

What has been said so far is mainly applicable to the UK, and based on urban findings. However, Roberts and Fagan (1999) found that traditional gender and class divisions persist in the leisure patterns of young people even in former communist countries, namely Armenia, Georgia and Ukraine. The influence of Western youth cultures causes a division by the consumer styles they adopt. A new socio-economic hierarchy based primarily upon the amounts of money that people can spend, is emerging.

Hence, if the socio-economic order of various societies is important to leisure, what similarities and differences appear when we consider youth from a *cross-cultural* perspective? Do different cultures create different patterns of leisure transitions across the adolescent years? Are gender differences similar across cultures? The present paper sets out to consider these questions by examining the leisure transitions within adolescent samples in Norway, Scotland and Sweden. In order to compare cultural influences as rigorously as possible, the samples were selected from comparable rural areas in the three countries involved in the study.

Methodology

Given the key points outlined in the introduction, the paper sets out to examine rural youth cross-culturally in a variety of socio-geographic situations using both qualitative and quantitative research approaches.

The questionnaire survey had its genesis in pilot focus group interviews with young people in the first half of 1996, along with issues raised from previous studies concerning, amongst other topics, leisure transitions. The main purpose of

204 *Reflecting on theories*

the survey was to develop a general picture based on young people in specified age–groups (12, 14 and 16-year-olds) in a wide diversity of rural locations and settings in Norway, Northern Scotland and Sweden. We defined 'rural locations', using Randall's (1992) definition of rural districts, as small communities that were located at least 40 kilometres from large urban conurbations. Variability with regard to socio-demographic profiles, such as fishing, farming or tourism-based communities, geographic location, such as inland, coastal or island areas and settlement size was taken into consideration in selecting the catchment areas.

The survey was designed to provide a context and backdrop to the 'young person centred' in-depth qualitative interview studies and essays that were conducted with a much more restricted sample of rural youth from the same locations. Table 14.1 shows the distribution of the sample over age groups and countries, yielding a total *n* of 4,100 young people (49% male and 51% female). The questionnaire was distributed during normal school hours in the classrooms in autumn 1996, and answered under the supervision of a researcher.

In Scotland five focus group interview study locations were chosen where selection was guided by responses to the baseline questionnaire–survey that had been conducted the previous autumn. The interview sites were representative of the original questionnaire survey. It was decided to interview two different age groups of young people across this diversity of site locations. Thus, a group of girls and a corresponding group of boys from Year 4 of each of five secondary schools (15/16-year-olds) and Year 6 groups along with some who had left school (17/18-year-olds) were interviewed in the second half of 1997. All of these young people had completed the survey questionnaire in the previous year. One individual in each age group and of each gender was chosen by a teacher or a community education worker in each location after discussions about the type of characteristics to be represented in the sample (i.e., coming from a local family or being an incomer, and whether the young person lived in a rural town, village or the surrounding countryside). The selected volunteers were asked to choose three or four friends to be interviewed as a focus group. In total a sample of 20 15/16-year-old girls and 18 15/16-year-old boys were interviewed, along with

Table 14.1 Distribution over age groups and countries

			Age group			Total
			12 yrs	14 yrs	16 yrs	
Country	Norway	Count	274	343	287	904
		% of Total	6.7%	8.4%	7.0%	22.0%
	Scotland	Count	754	800	938	2492
		% of Total	18.4%	19.5%	22.9%	60.8%
	Sweden	Count	219	263	222	704
		% of Total	5.3%	6.4%	5.4%	17.2%
Total		Count	1247	1406	1447	4100
		% of Total	30.4%	34.3%	35.3%	100.0%

19 17/18-year-old girls and 16 17/18-year-old boys, across the five interview study sites.

In Sweden, an essay competition was undertaken in co-operation with a local newspaper. Young people between 13 and 17 years were asked to describe in their own words: 'What is it like to be young in Jämtland: describe your life now, how it is and how you want it to become'. They were informed that their essays would be used in a research project. Participants were entered in a prize draw. 134 girls and 106 boys sent in essays varying in length between one and 12 pages. In Norway, some of the adolescents wrote short essays on their thoughts about organized activities and about living in their community. These are not relevant to the findings presented in this paper.

In deriving answers to the question of how the focal model might change in different, but similar, cultural settings, a Principal Component Analysis with Varimax rotation was carried out on the 32 leisure-time items from the 1996 questionnaire survey, resulting in six factors:

1 Friendship-based activities (e.g., visit friends, spend time with friends, 'hang around' with friends).
2 Sports (e.g., membership of a sports-club, play sports recreationally).
3 Organized leisure activities (e.g., membership of a youth group, a charity group, a hobby class, a choir).
4 Activities with parents (e.g., sit and talk with parents, go out together, watch TV together).
5 Commercial activities (e.g., go to a cinema, look around the shops, go to a pub, night-club).
6 Relaxing leisure (e.g., hang around the house doing nothing, read, listen to music).

Factor-scores were computed for each of the factors. On these, a number of ANOVAs were performed to examine the effects of gender, age group and country.

Findings and discussion

If we look at the results overall it is possible to note a number of leisure transitions occurring across the adolescent years of our international samples exactly as Hendry (1983) predicted. Sports (see Figures 14.1 and 14.2) and organized clubs and activities both reveal decreasing amounts of participation between early adolescence (i.e., 12/13 years), through mid-adolescence (i.e., 14/15 years), to later-adolescence (i.e., 16/17 years). Both these types of leisure activity are adult-led and mainly organized by adults. Such transitions can be explained in terms of young people's desire to increase their self-agency and autonomy of choice in their leisure pursuits as they move away from childhood towards adulthood. Nowadays many people have more money, some also have more time at their disposal, and they are surrounded by a plethora of consumer industries. Thus

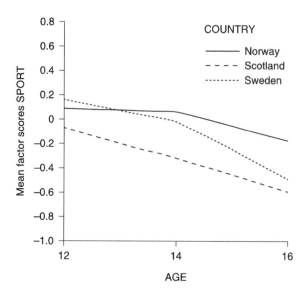

Figure 14.1 Girls' involvement in sports.

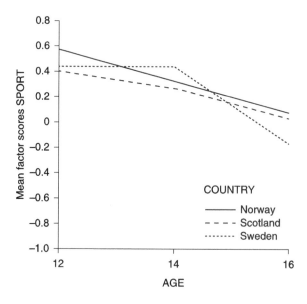

Figure 14.2 Boys' involvement in sports.

it is claimed that it is possible for individuals to create identities according to what, when and how they consume (e.g., Featherstone, 1991; Maffesoli, 1994). With regard to commercial leisure (see Figures 14.3 and 14.4), involvement augments with age and young women participate in the commercial leisure sphere more than

Reflecting on theories 207

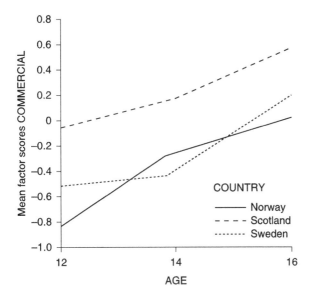

Figure 14.3 Girls' involvement in commercial activities.

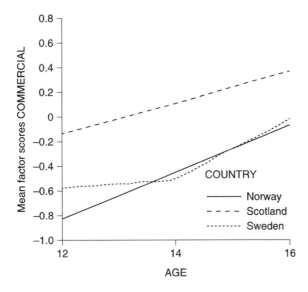

Figure 14.4 Boys' involvement in commercial activities.

young men. Again, this is in line with the transitions in the leisure focal theory model. This gender difference is explicable by young women's earlier physical and social maturity, and by the fact that adolescent young women often have older boy-friends who are themselves at a later transitional stage and 'draw' their female

208 *Reflecting on theories*

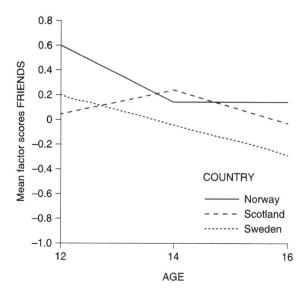

Figure 14.5 Girls' involvement in casual leisure with friends.

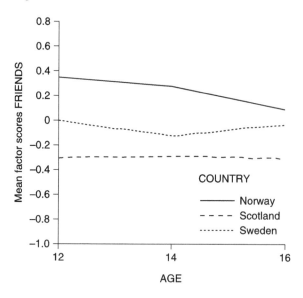

Figure 14.6 Boys' involvement in casual leisure with friends.

partners with them, so-to-speak in advance of male age-peers. However, when we consider participation in casual leisure activities with friends (see Figures 14.5 and 14.6), our general findings are *not* consistent with the focal model. For these activities, there is a decrease over the adolescent years. In contrast, the model claimed a peaking in mid-adolescence, where peer-oriented leisure was seen as a context for the rehearsal of various social skills away from the (prying?) eyes of adults, before trying them out within the commercial arena: A way of testing one's acceptance in the leisure world of adults. (Here we should note that Kloep, 1999, found similar results of lessening peer involvement in a sample of Swedish youths, while Flammer *et al.*, 1999, found contradictory results with an urban Norwegian sample.) Turning now to the cross-national perspective, it can be seen that cultural differences – and/or societal changes – alter the universality of Hendry's (1983) original model. In peer-oriented leisure the overall gender differences we have discussed above are especially powerful. Scottish young women in particular are more involved with peers in leisure time than young men (see Figures 14.5 and 14.6).

Involvement with friends shows a *curvilinear* pattern for Scots women, reaching a peak in mid-adolescence in accordance with the model. In contrast, this type of leisure *decreases* with age for young Norwegian and Swedish women. However, the finding for Swedish men represents a mirror image of the results for Scottish young women. Overall, Norwegian young people seem to be more involved in casual leisure activities with friends than the other two nationalities, a result also found by Flammer *et al.* (1999) in their cross-national study (ANOVAs reveal significant effects for gender and country, and a significant effect for age group for young women, but not for young men; as well as an age group × country effect for young women).

Within commercial leisure pursuits, where young women are consistently more involved than their male counterparts, Scottish women participate significantly more often than Swedes or Norwegians (ANOVAs revealed significant effects for age-groups, gender and country, see Figures 14.3 and 14.4). Since these are rural samples, it can be proposed that one explanation for the cross-cultural differences is that the distance between rural and urban areas is greater in the Scandinavian countries than in Scotland, and in addition many of the smallest rural settlements in northern Scotland have pubs, bars, or small tourist hotels. Further, the minimum legal age for holding a driving licence and drinking alcohol in bars or pubs differs between Scotland and Scandinavia (in Scotland a car driving licence can be obtained at 17 years and drinking is allowed at 18 years of age. In Scandinavia the situation is somewhat different. In Norway a driving licence can be obtained at 18 years, and drinking wine and beer in a restaurant is allowed from 18 years of age, but spirits cannot be drunk legally till 20 years of age. In Sweden both driving and drinking are legal from 18 years of age, though buying alcohol from the state-run liquor shops is only allowed at 20 years).

Overall, as we can see from Figures 14.1 and 14.2, young men are more involved in sports than young women in all three countries, though Scotsmen are least involved of the three male groups. The decline by age is linear in all three countries. 'Dropping out' from sports differs for young women by country, with Scottish women giving up sport earliest of the three groups and those in the other two countries ceasing to participate by mid- to later- adolescence (ANOVAs reveal significant effects for gender, age-group and country for all groups, but no interaction effects). However, we can note one interesting exception: participation in aerobics or dance classes *augments* as the only sports activity for young women with increasing age in all three countries (effects for age-group, but not for country are significant). This is in line with suggestions that it is the competitive male orientation of most sports activities that make young women give up sports earlier than their male peers (e.g., Coakley and White, 1992; Hendry et al. 1993).

In contradistinction to sports, young women participate more in organized leisure than young men in the three countries. The Scots are more associated with organized activities than the others, and younger adolescents are more involved than older youths are. Thus, there are gender differences in organized leisure participation for all three countries and for all age groups (ANOVAs reveal significant effects for gender and country, and for age-group among young women). The 'drop out' pattern shows country differences: in Scotland and Sweden the drift from adult-led clubs and organized activities is apparent from early-adolescence and then reaches 'steady state', whereas in Norway there is an *increase* in participation from early- to mid-adolescence for both young men and young women, then a decline from mid- to later-teens.

It seems likely that these organized groups and clubs provide a social context for rural adolescents in the absence of other more 'appropriate' venues better suited to their developmental stage. For instance, Hendry and Raymond (1986) found that unemployed urban teenagers used local leisure facilities such as youth clubs as social settings for meeting friends rather than 'down town' discos and pubs because of a lack of money, but at the same time disliked these 'childish' contexts as not relevant to their legitimate social needs and wishes. The authors suggested that such limitations on young peoples' leisure opportunities could have effects on their social skills and development. In a similar vein, it is possible that rural teenagers are 'forced' to maintain membership of local youth clubs because of limited alternatives of choice, lack of transport, distance to travel and so on, as the following quotes suggest:

> Well, there's a youth club that we still go to. It's a bit far for me to go to, but ... Well, it's just for secondary school pupils really. It's joined with two other villages. It's actually held in X and everyone comes to it mostly unless there's something on.
>
> (17/18-year-old girl, Scotland)

> There is a youth club there, but there are usually only five people around. To be there is like being at home, constantly supervised by parents.
>
> (16-year-old girl, Sweden)

Additionally, for both genders there were more complaints about lack of access to meeting places from the older age groups (ANOVAs reveal significant effects for gender, country and age groups). In relation to lack of transport, however, young men's complaints levelled off around 15–16 years – perhaps because they were by this stage in a position to own a motorbike or have access to a family vehicle.

What seems evident from the qualitative interviews and 'projective' essays used in our study is that young men and women have different views about rural leisure. These varying attitudes create different ways of behaving in the same contexts. Examining their perceptions of 'rurality', for instance, young women tended to complain earlier and more than young men about various aspects of rural life.

Too few places to meet

One alternative setting for young people to meet in the absence of formal meeting places in rural areas is to 'hang around', but rural adolescents are not particularly satisfied with this: 61% of the girls and 46% of the boys considered it to be a serious problem that there are too few places for young people to meet in rural areas. Or, as a Swedish girl says:

> We have to continue to walk up and down the road. This society is not made for us between 14 and 18, sad but true. One looks into the youth club, circles the village, and if one is lucky, one is picked up by a car. Bloody shit is all I can say. If you want to have fun, you have to drink till you drop. But that's not good neither.
>
> (15-year-old girl, Sweden)

Nothing to do for young people

Having nothing to do turned out to be *the* major complaint for both young men and women in the questionnaire data as well as in the qualitative data: The mean score on a 5-point scale of agreement to the statement that 'There is nothing to do here for young people like me'; (ranging from 1 = 'totally agree' to 5 = 'totally disagree') was 2.0 for girls and 2.3 for boys):

> I think about all these weekends that have been spent doing absolutely nothing. The only thing that can save me from fading away totally is sports ... What is there to do? The weekends all have the same pattern. Go down to the youth club, talk some shit, go up and down the main road. Is it that what life is about? I understand exactly why more and more get drunk during weekends.
>
> (15-year-old girl, Sweden)

> There's nothing to do in it, nothing at all. It's just a few shops and that's it. Dead ... it's like a ghost town, and you're miles away from everything and you've to travel, get a car into town or something before you can actually do something. But there's not anything to do in the [nearest local] town either.
>
> (15-year-old boy, Scotland)

Interestingly, relating complaints about the lack of things to do with the reported frequencies with which young people actually engaged in different types of leisure activities yielded only small correlations (e.g., commercial leisure $r = -0.21$ organized leisure activities $r = -0.02$, sports $r = +0.14$, peer-oriented leisure $r = +0.03$, relaxing leisure $r = -0.06$ and parent related activities $r = +0.19$). This implies that it is not so much the *quantity* of leisure time activities, but the perceived *quality* that leads to the conviction that there is 'nothing to do', as is nicely illustrated in the following quotes:

> In the summer holidays a whole group of us will go camping and fishing. Last year we walked 15 miles just to get to this fun fishing spot. We camped and walked back the next day. I've got a rowing boat, you know, so you can go fishing and that. We do that as well. We go off on mountain bikes. There's a lot of good places around here you can go. In the summer it's cool. You can go swimming and you just jump off the cliffs.
>
> (15/16-year-old boy, Scotland)

> I play in an orchestra on Mondays, tennis on Tuesdays, on Wednesdays and Thursdays the youth club is open, in winter I go skiing and skating and drive a snow-scooter, in summer I go swimming, cycling and play soccer . . . but there is nothing to do here, particularly on weekends. We are often together with some older guys whom we meet in the village and hang around with them, being generally bored. Because bored is exactly what you are nowadays.
>
> (14-year-old girl, Sweden)

No shops

One aspect of rural living that concerned young women was the difficulty of accessing shops and fashionable goods. Living in the country does not mean that young people are uninvolved in the global, commercial world of make-up and fashion. As several young women commented:

> Or if you need new clothes, you'll never make it to the town. There is a bus, but that costs that much that you have money left for only a three-pack of socks.
>
> (15-year-old girl, Sweden)

> And it's so far to go for everybody. Like it's 18 miles to get to one place and then 18 miles to get to another. It's just terrible. They're all bored out of their brains and it's all old people. It's old shops. It's all grannies and that.
>
> (12-year-old girl, Scotland)

Too little freedom to be the way one wants

In the process of growing towards adulthood, young people wish to develop a separate identity and individualism. Given the constraints of living in a small community the norms of the adult society and the influences of peer pressure both create certain restrictions on the growing self-identity of these adolescents, and this was evident in the statements of many. Here we illustrate this perception by the quote of one young woman:

> You can't do anything different or think differently or absolutely not dress differently. If you do, you have to be prepared to sometimes not be treated with respect, or to hear some shit-talk.
>
> (15-year-old girl, Sweden)

Too much gossip and no privacy

Linked to the issue of autonomy was the adolescents' experience of being the centre of village comment and gossip. This seemed to be a particular concern for young women, perhaps especially in relation to visiting the doctor to discuss contraception, for example, or more generally in connection with social encounters and meetings in public or engaging in 'adult' activities like smoking:

> But it's just if they see you, if anybody sees you do anything that maybe you shouldn't be doing, then obviously it's going to get back to your parents and even if it's maybe not something that you shouldn't be doing, just something you don't necessarily think your parents need to know and private things and it's going to get back to your parents because everybody knows everybody.
>
> (15-year-old girl, Scotland)

> I wouldn't go to my doctor about anything 'cos he's close to my family. I know it's all meant to be confidential but I couldn't sit there and talk to him. But if I go to the doctor, I go on a Wednesday when there's a doctor that comes [to another local rural practice] and usually it's a locum which comes, so I can talk to him or her. It's usually a him.
>
> (17-year-old girl, Scotland)

Lack of transport

Country life inevitably means that visits to the nearest town require private transport or a very efficient public service. Few countries provide such amenities, and teenagers are particularly disadvantaged unless or until they can access transport to suit their personal requirements. The following quote reflects the views of many teenagers in the study:

> But then living out in the country it's hard to do everything. You can't just nip to town in an evening. You've got to have it organized a week in advance.
>
> (17/18-year-old girl, Scotland)

214 *Reflecting on theories*

Difficulties in finding a job in the future

Given the importance of employment to the successful transitions of adolescents in present day society (e.g. Roberts, 1995), it is not hard to understand that a high percentage of young people wish to leave their rural area and move to towns and cities in order to pursue higher education and careers. This is particularly true for academically-oriented and socially motivated young women in all three countries. However, as stated in one of the following quotations, there is a yearning in *some* for a return to their rural idyll when they have children of their own, if only they could find a job:

> What I hate are these rural yokels who are completely intolerant against new things or changes. Their meaning of life is to go to dances and drink . . . leave school, move in with their sweetheart of the moment and produce children. Then they are hooked. I refuse to adjust to this. I want an education. Then I leave. Far away from here.
>
> (15-year-old girl, Sweden)

> I wonder if I will still be fishing up here in 20 years, or what I want to do. Most of all, I would like to go hill-walking with my children in summer, if I'll have any. But maybe I have to take a job in Stockholm or something.
>
> (13-year-old girl, Sweden)

> I don't want to live here in the future. There are no nice jobs and only a few people. I want to live in a big city or go abroad. Because I don't believe there is any future here.
>
> (15-year-old girl, Scotland)

Conclusions

While the leisure focal model (Hendry, 1983) has been useful for understanding the leisure transitions of (mainly British) urban youth, it seems clear on the basis of our study that rural and cultural imperatives heavily influence patterns of adolescent leisure transitions cross-culturally in the late 1990s. The possible effects of rapidly changing societies may further impinge on this picture. Uncertainty is a consequence of the sheer pace of economic and social change. Lifestyle formation is still happening to some degree within social class, ethnic and gender boundaries, and leisure still plays an important role in young people's life – basically as a source of fun, diversion, companionship and relaxation.

But some essential changes in leisure transitions cannot be denied: involvement in casual leisure in mid-adolescence described in the original focal model (Hendry, 1983), for instance, may have been a feature of the cultural and economic ecology of the times, where the street corner and friends' homes were peer venues for social engagement. It is possible to speculate that such settings have been replaced more and more by cafes, pizzerias and fast-food restaurants as social meeting places, even within many so-called rural areas in the new millennium. Additionally, many young people may today be more affluent and desire access to the various commercial contexts of 'globalized' Western societies. In the light of media advertising, such adolescent desires do not cease at the boundaries of suburbia but continue into the rural hinterland. Hence entry to commercial leisure has accelerated down the adolescent age-scale. Age has become a less useful social predictor. Youth as a life stage has become more varied in length, and more individualized. As a feature of these earlier leisure transitions, and as a manifestation of earlier social maturity, Kloep (1999), for example, has shown in her rural Swedish study that romantic love relationships feature early as an adolescent concern, whereas 'conflicts with parents' was seen by young people as a relatively unimportant relational issue.

All these findings point towards evidence of an earlier maturation – or at least social sophistication – of youth. Future research needs to consider more carefully and specifically the effects of commercialism on rural youth's social and leisure development (though see e.g., Gofton, 1990; Maffesoli, 1996; Parker *et al.*, 1998; Hendry *et al.*, 1998, who have commented generally about consumerism and youth). Additionally, in relation to young peoples' perceptions of the lack of things to do in rural settings, we need to consider more seriously, how they might be enabled within school, youth work and organized leisure settings to develop greater self-reliance and skills of self-efficacy in their leisure pursuits.

Further, the gender differences, which emerged, raise important questions regarding leisure provision that is relevant for young women in the rural context of the three countries. More appropriate leisure provisions might be a start in preventing further 'female de-population' of the countryside. Moreover the complexity of our findings across cultures indicates in general the need for a different approach towards understanding adolescence and adolescent leisure. We have to move on from the idea that there is a simple and generalized (theoretical) story to tell about adolescence: there are many individual pathways within leisure transitions resulting from different characteristics, social interactions and ever-changing cultural systems. We have to end our fixation with aggregated findings and single factor explanations and start to examine processes and mechanisms as Rutter (1996) and Kloep and Hendry (1999) amongst others have proposed. It is by disaggregating findings, culturally and across societies, that facts of real importance can be found. This is a somewhat similar claim to Bronfenbrenner's (1979) 'ecological' theory, which considered psychosocial development as the result of a series of ongoing interactions and adaptations between individuals and sets of variously overlapping social systems. These systems range from the micro-level to the societal macro-level within different cultures. We need to take account of all these 'interactions' in order to move from rather *'static' theoretical models* to gaining a clearer understanding of the *processes* of leisure transitions within and across cultures.

Notes

The Scottish part of this research project was funded by the Health Department, Scottish Office, Edinburgh. The views expressed in this paper are entirely those of the authors.

References

Bronfenbrenner, U. (1979) *The Ecology of Human Development: Experiments by Nature and Design*, Harvard University Press, Cambridge, MA.

Coakley, J. and White, A. (1992) Making decisions: gender and sport participation among British adolescents. *Sociology of Sport Journal* **9**, 20–35.

Coleman, J. C. (1974) *Relationships in adolescence*, Routledge and Kegan Paul, London.

Department for Education (1995) Young People's Participation in the Youth Service. *Statistical Bulletin* 1/95, London.

Featherstone, M (1991) *Postmodernism: Theory, Culture and Postmodernism*, Sage, London.

Flammer, A., Alsaker, F. D. and Noack, P. (1999) Time use by adolescents in an international perspective. I: The case of leisure activities, in *The adolescent experience. European and American adolescents in the 1990s* (edited by F. D. Alsaker and A. Flammer), Lawrence Erlbaum, Mahwah, NJ.

Glyptis, S (1989) *Leisure and Unemployment*, Open University Press, Milton Keynes.

Gofton, L. (1990) On the town: drink and the 'new lawlessness'. *Youth and Policy* **29**, 33–39.

Hendry, L. B. (1983) *Growing Up and Going Out*, Pergamon, London.

Hendry, L. B. and Raymond, M. (1986) Psychosocial aspects of youth unemployment: an interpretative theoretical model. *Journal of Adolescence* **9**, 355–366.

Hendry, L. B.,. Shucksmith, J. and Glendinning, A. (1997) Adolescent focal theories: age trends in developmental transitions, *Journal of Adolescence* **19**, 307–320.

Hendry, L. B., Glendinning, A., Reid, M. and Wood, S. (1998) *Lifestyles, Health and Health Concerns of Rural Youth: 1996–1998*. Report to Department of Health, Scottish Office, Edinburgh.

Hendry, L. B., Shucksmith, J., Love, J. G. and Glendinning, A. (1993) *Young People's Leisure and Lifestyles*, Routledge, London.

Kloep, M. (1999) Love is all you need? Focusing on adolescents' life concerns from an ecological point of view. *Journal of Adolescence* **22**, 49–63.

Kloep, M. and Hendry, L. B. (1999) Challenges, risks and coping in adolescence, in *Exploring Developmental Psychology* (edited by D. Messer and S. Millar), Arnold, London.

Maffesoli, M. (1996) *The Time of the Tribes*, Sage, London.

Parker, H., Aldridge, J. and Measham, F. (1998) *Illegal Leisure*, Routledge, London.

Randall, J. (1992) *Scottish Rural Life*, Department of Environment, Scottish Office, New St. Andrew's House, Edinburgh.

Roberts, K. (1995) *Youth and employment in modern Britain*, Oxford University Press, Oxford.

Roberts, K. (1996) Young people, schools, sport and government policies. *Sport, Education and Society* **1**, 47–57.

Roberts, K. (1997) Same activities, different meanings: British youth cultures in the 1990s. *Leisure Studies* **16**, 1–15.

Roberts, K. and Fagan, C. (1999) Young people and their leisure in former communist countries: four theses examined. *Leisure Studies* **18**, 1–17.

Roberts, K. and Parsell, G. (1994) Youth cultures in Britain: the middle class take-over. *Leisure Studies* **13**, 33–48.

Roberts, K., Campbell, C. and Furlong, A. (1990) Class and gender divisions among young adults at leisure, in *Youth in Transition* (edited by C. Wallace and M. Cross), Falmer Press, London, pp. 129–145.

Rutter, M. (1996) Psychological adversity: risk, resilience and recovery, in *Conflict and Development in Adolescence* (edited by L. Verhofstadt-Deneve, I. Kienhorst and C. Braet), DSWO Press, Leiden, pp. 21–34.

Willis, P. (1990) *Common Culture*, Open University Press, Milton Keynes.

Wold, B. and Hendry, L. B. (1998) Social and environmental factors associated with physical activities in youth, in *Young People and Physical Activity* (edited by S. Biddle and J. Sallis), Health Education Authority, London.

15 The lifespan challenge model re-visited

Finally, reflecting, like Uhtred of Bebbanburg, I want to re-assess the Lifespan Challenge Model in order to examine how my ideas on lifespan development may have changed and altered from the creation of the original framework. So, in this extract there is an attempt to bring my thinking up-to-date by including, and interpreting, concepts such as 'transitions' and 'transformations' and by offering a fanciful scenario of change. This leads to ideas about development as systemic change, where self-organization means that interactions among various elements in the system orchestrate a spontaneous emergence of order within that system. It is why, in development, there are often long periods where, for an observer, seemingly nothing happens, and why there are shifts when the system temporarily loses its ability to maintain order, and instability occurs before order is re-established at a different level.

A SYSTEMIC APPROACH TO THE TRANSITIONS TO ADULTHOOD

Marion Kloep and Leo B. Hendry

Introduction: transitions

In this chapter we present a theoretical perspective, which is distinctly different from the stage theory described by Tanner and Arnett in Chapter 2 [of the original publication]. Instead of arguing for a new life stage to be inserted into the life course, we will propose abandoning the concept of stages altogether, and, instead, will focus on the processes and mechanisms of developmental change.

It would seem at first sight to be fairly straightforward to consider the transitions from adolescence to adulthood. However, if we take a second look, the notion of transitions is somewhat complicated to understand. For example, what exactly is a "transition"? Dictionaries may describe it as "the process of moving from one place to another," which is an acceptable definition, if we are discussing a car traveling from A to B or someone crossing a border from one country to

The lifespan challenge model re-visited 219

another. If we speak about human development, however, it becomes more difficult to imagine what "movement" we are discussing, or, for that matter, what starting point we envisage and what the end goal may be.

Perhaps it is easier to grasp the ideas we are trying to convey by considering an example. Imagine a river flowing along. We can see eddies, currents, and calm backwaters, how the river divides as it encounters a rock, how different streamlets emerge round the rock then, perhaps, reunite, how the river diverts itself around fallen trees and other debris, how these "intruders" can even cause the river to change its course altogether, and how tributaries influence the strength of the river's flow. So, the river is in a constant state of movement. Now picture a little water sprite popping up onto the surface of the water (and let's call that "birth"). It floats along, moving with the flow of the river, often being driven from one streamlet to another, swerving round rocks and obstacles, sometimes swimming against a diagonal current that takes it toward one bank then steering on an opposite pathway, often pushed back by the power of the current. Our sprite is often in contact with others on the river. Sustenance is available to this mythical creature from the river and its inhabitants. In turn, our water sprite excretes and drops fishbones into the stream thereby causing the chemical composition of the river to change. Over time our little sprite sinks under the surface and disappears from our view (let's call this "death") but continues to be part of the river by supplying nutrients as its body slowly disintegrates and is absorbed back into the riverbed. Thus, the sprite is part of the river, and the river is part of the sprite: both are part of the one system!

Without expanding this fanciful description of the life and death of one water sprite, we can use this analogy to explain "transitions" and "transformations." Like our water sprite, when human beings are born into a society, that is itself in constant change, they develop and change by the interaction of their own motive forces with the shifts and changes of the cultural environment in which they live. Hence, for a variety of reasons some of us are continually changing developmentally whereas others remain in the backwaters for lengthy periods. Some experience both shifts and calm periods because there will be "turning points" and obstacles to be surmounted throughout their life, and changes and shifts may affect only some aspects of the individual (what psychologists call "domain-specific" development). This also means that at times some aspects of our life course can cause us to regress in certain areas of development. Evans (2007) describes human progress through the life course as follows:

> When people move in social landscapes, how they perceive the horizons depends on where they stand. The horizons change strongly as they move, sometimes opening up, sometimes closing down. Where they go depends on the pathways they see, choose, stumble across, or clear for themselves, the terrain and elements they encounter.

What we are arguing is that it is useless to describe human transitions as "stages" because in our "movement" through the life course we are advancing, regressing, developing in some domains and not others; in a sense ever-becoming but never arriving! Thus, conceptualizing stages provides only a simplistic description of broad life-phases and does not allow us to grasp the complexities of different transitions, processes, and underlying, operational mechanisms. This has been stated some decades ago. In the 1970s, Riegel (1975) stressed that the primary goal of a developmental analysis is the study of change, not stasis! Yet only in the past few years have these ideas been incorporated into undergraduate textbooks (e.g., Thornton, 2008) and thereby found their way into mainstream psychology. We believe with Thelen and Baltes "that there are general principles of development: mechanisms and processes that hold true whatever the content domain" (Thelen & Baltes, 2003, p. 378), and that it is these processes and mechanisms we should analyze, instead of creating (normative) labels based on chronological age and mistake them for an explanation. In the following sections of this chapter this is the task we address by saying something about transitions to adulthood, describing systems theory as a framework for understanding the complex nature of these transitions, explaining various societal shifts, and introducing a simplified model of resources and challenges as one way of describing and analyzing human development.

Transitions from adolescence and adulthood

So, from our river analogy, adolescence is not a starting "point." Rather, it is itself a transition, with no clearly defined start or finish. A similar problem exists with the definition of adulthood. It is not possible to indicate the moment it starts, and with the vast and rapid changes occurring in our societies, which we discussed in the introductory chapter [original publication], it has become increasingly obsolete to use traditional "markers" of adulthood—such as leaving home, completing your education, finding a job, and starting a family of your own—to determine whether an individual has reached adulthood.

From a traditional psychological point of view, transitions mean changes in the body, in behavior, cognition, emotions, and skills that make individuals in one age group different from individuals in another age group. These changes can be on a larger or smaller scale, such as the transition to adulthood or the transition from Piaget's primary circular reactions to secondary circular reactions. Developmental psychologists have often chosen to describe these "transitions" as a succession of stages and substages, but nevertheless have always run into problems when trying to find definite starting points and end points of these stages. One reason for these problems is that development is often domain specific. For instance, we might agree that an individual can develop a mature adult physique, while at the same time not possessing the instrumental skills needed for living independently in a particular society. Furthermore, since behavior is multiply determined and assembled from the interactions of multiple subsystems, an "end goal," a "completed stage" is never achieved, because characteristics of both individuals and their contexts vary and change, and a "good fit" on one occasion may not be good on another (Ford & Lerner, 1992; Spencer et al., 2006). An individual's skills for independent living might be excellent under good economic conditions, but not remotely sufficient to cope with an economic crisis.

Sociologists look at the different sociocultural demands that individuals have to meet, and define a transition as a change in identities, roles, and statuses that are within the awareness of the individual and members of their in-group, their subcultures, and the culture of society. However, not all groups in society treat young people in the same way; there are different criteria by which teachers, parents, girl friends, advertising companies, employers, or the military determine the "adultness" of a person. The right to vote, marry, purchase alcohol, visit a nightclub, or be voted into a parliament are not all granted at the same age in a society, and most of these "adult" rights vary between countries. With this, sociologists run into a problem similar to psychologists in trying to define the end of adolescence and the start to adulthood. Historically in some cultures, there were "rites of passage" to mark the transition to adulthood, but modern societies have mainly discarded these (though there are still some religious traditions, such as First Communion, Confirmation, and Bar Mitzvah, that remain as reminders of a time when rituals and ceremonies were of more transitional significance).

Thus, it is difficult to describe the changes that occur between adolescence and adulthood as "a transition from point A to B," because we cannot really define where "A" ends and "B" starts, since this differs between cultures and cohorts, between individuals, and even within individuals. What actually happens is a series of many minitransitions, some of which are reversible, some domain specific, and some more general: none of these occurs between two defined points.

So, adolescence and adulthood are not dichotomous. How the individual is seen depends, among other things, on the point of view of the observer, the task at hand, the personal circumstances of the individual, and the demands and support of the macrosystem. Rosenberger (2007) argued like this:

> What emerging adulthood is, what adulthood is, and how the two relate are moving targets in a constantly changing world. Emerging adulthood is a concept that allows us to think through rapidly changing, globalized lifestyles in richer countries in a new way. However, what may be a global phenomenon of emerging adulthood will take different forms and meanings in relation to economic, political, and historical differences. ... we should be open to elongated and ambiguous periods of emerging adulthood, that might even extend indefinitely, depending on the definition of adulthood and how quickly and in what way the definition changes in relation to cultural and historical logic.
>
> (Rosenberger, 2007, p. 95)

What we are really discussing are not transitions to adulthood, but a series of on-going transformations that occur, from the period labeled "adolescence" by stage theorists, through periods called "early adulthood," "midlife," and "old age," all the while experiencing changes and processes that enable us at any point in the life course to be defined concurrently as "a being," "a has-been," and "a becoming."

How do children eventually transform into adults? As we have argued above, we cannot answer that question by simply describing an array of stages they go through. Neither can we answer the question by looking at specific tasks they have to solve en route, as Havighurst (1972) proposed, because these tasks vary widely between individuals in different contexts and at different historical times. Nor can we decide when they have actually reached adulthood, because the definition of what characterizes "an adult" will vary in different societies at different times. "Assuming adult responsibilities" once historically meant that a man could be a hunter, endure pain, and survive in wild nature. Later, it meant being able to provide for a family. Now, in our modern society, it means being individually capable and responsible for our own life. However, even this might be changing. It would be a mistake to define "adult skills" as those our generation possesses, and then to measure the status of young people against this. Our grandmothers would have regarded the skill of preparing a family meal as absolutely basic for a fully adult woman. Today, with deep-frozen, ready-meals, this is a discretionary adult skill. On the other hand, with technology invading every part of our daily lives, the ability to handle electronic devices becomes more and more crucial for daily living—and young people may appear to be better equipped for this than present-day adults. So although some young people may not have acquired the skills that were traditionally seen as "markers of adulthood" (such as being economically independent), they do appear to possess certain survival skills in which the adult population of today may be less competent.

For all these reasons, we regard it as analytically fruitless to classify human beings as "children," "adolescents," or "adults" except for simple descriptive clarity, because the boundaries between these stages are vague, overlapping, and to a large extent arbitrary. To understand human development and change, we propose instead to analyze the processes and mechanisms that underlie developmental change in general. What is it that makes us change, and how does change occur—on the microlevel of the here and now, and on an ontogenetic level across the life span? Here we take and adapt a dynamic systems framework in analyzing these processes and mechanisms of human change.

A systemic perspective

What makes a systemic perspective different from traditional views of development is that it abandons the idea of simple, unidirectional and linear processes of cause and effect in explaining change. Instead, it sees nature as an open system that both consists of, and belongs to, a number of other open systems; and as human beings, we are part of this natural configuration. Hence, just like our water sprite in its river, the individual and the environment are not two entities separate from each other, but together form an open system (a point of view already offered by Vygotsky in 1930).

An open system does not have boundaries; it is embedded in larger systems and is in constant exchange with them. For example, from a systemic point of view, we would dismiss the question of whether it is "nature or nurture" that influences human development as a wrongly posed question. We do not regard "nature" and "nurture" as separate components: they are, as indeed is the developing individual himself or herself, part of the same system. Nor would it be correct to say that nature and nurture "interact"; that would be similar to describing your health as an interaction between heart and body. Individuals cannot interact with an environment of which they are integral elements (Thelen & Smith, 2006). Since this may be seen as an unorthodox way of thinking, we will clarify this idea by way of an illustration.

Consider, for example, that you are approaching a tray of apples in a fruit shop. Are they a part of you, or are they a part of your immediate and current environment? (The answer may not be as easy as you might at first consider.) If you are thinking of these apples, they are already "in your mind." When you see the apples lying in front of you, perceiving them, they have an impact on your perceptual system (and most likely on your digestive hormones). Now, you touch the apples, then choose one and buy it. Is the apple more certainly a part of you now than it was before? Or will it be when first you smell it, bite it, taste it, chew it, digest it? Then, how long will it be part of you? For as long as it remains within your digestive system or will it still be when pieces of it have left your body and are remitted (together with your body fluids) back to nature and transformed into other substances? What we want to demonstrate with this simple, yet complex, example is that there is no definitive answer as to when exactly the apple is part of you or when you are part of the apple.

In contrast to closed systems, which have no input from outside, so that their elements can maintain a stable relationship with each other (like water in a hermetically sealed bottle at constant temperature), open systems exchange matter and energy with other systems. Thus, they are never stable, but always in a dynamic flow. Hence even an apparently inactive adolescent lingering on the sofa is going through changes—hormones circulate in his or her body influencing mood, sounds are heard, thoughts are reflected on, the digestive system works, cells are renewed, beer and popcorn might enter the system, perspiration occurs, a nagging parent needs to be fended off . . . and all this is just a small part of his or her overall, continuous development.

Each system consists of many heterogeneous elements—such as molecules in body tissues, cells in a body, the body's physiological composition and anatomical make-up, individuals in a dyad or in society and in historical time. Each of these elements has certain degrees of freedom, which means it has different possibilities to "behave." Neurons may fire or not, action potentials can be transmitted or inhibited at synapses, eyes may be open or closed, an arm can be flexed or straightened, and moved in all directions, objects can be big or small, heavy or light, within reach or beyond reach and so on. Imagine what a complicated action it is to see an object, then reach out and grip it! This needs the organization and coordination of all these elements and is possible only if the degrees of freedom of each of the elements are considerably limited. Otherwise human movements would be chaotic, haphazard, and unpredictable. Compared to the full possible range of arm movements, there are only a few restricted types of movement that will lead to a seemingly simple skill such as successfully gripping an object. How much more difficult is it to master tasks that involve many more elements and different systems, such as learning the "adult skills" of planning ahead, managing time, and assuming responsibilities?

This process of "self-organization" in open systems means that the interactions of their elements lead to the spontaneous emergence of order within the system, because elements inhibit each others' degrees of freedom. The resulting patterns themselves are not static, but can undergo further changes in space and time. If the elements of the system interact repeatedly to reach a particular goal, they coordinate spontaneously and form a novel system. More or less erratic hand movements are, over time, organized into a goal directed grip, and young people through puberty will eventually learn to cope with their newly elongated limbs and changed body proportions and move gracefully again without needing to be taught. The ability to self-organize is essential for successful adaptation to changing circumstances (Guastello, 2002).

Apart from being complex and consisting of highly heterogeneous elements, open systems have another quality: they exist far from a so-called "equilibrium." A system is said to be at "equilibrium" when the energy and momentum of the system are uniformly distributed and there is no flow from one region to the other, as, for example, when salt is completely dissolved in water (Thelen & Smith, 1998). This "equilibrium" can be thought of as an "attractor" state, a stable place at which the system tends to settle or get stuck, and where least energy is used. However, though living systems "strive" to find homeostasis, they never achieve or stay in complete equilibrium, because they interact all the time with surrounding elements, which disturb the order and force the system to reorganize. Therefore, if a system receives sufficient input, it will move away from its attractor state and new ordered structures may spontaneously appear that were not formerly apparent: development has occurred.

This is why in human development there are often long periods in which seemingly nothing happens. Parents have been driven to despair by endlessly nagging their teenage children to get up in the morning in time for school: staying in bed is obviously a very stable attractor state in the teenage years. For most people, however, sleeping patterns change along the way to adulthood: the system is reorganized and finds a quite different attractor state. It is called developing a work-commitment!

Developmental changes are difficult to predict, because open systems are nonlinear systems. What does that mean? A linear relationship is, for example, number and weight: two spoons of sugar weigh exactly double one spoon of sugar. But an adolescent, who has passed two of the so-called "markers of adulthood" (e.g., has a job and a girlfriend) is not twice as adult than another adolescent who has achieved only one of these "markers"; and two nagging parents are not necessarily twice as effective in getting their teenager out of bed as one.

These are examples of nonlinear relationships: elements do not change proportionally with the variables that define them—the values of all the defining variables do not simply sum up or multiply. Because of this non-linearity, minimal change in one of the elements of a system can lead to abrupt shifts in the state of the system, much in the same way as the famous last drop that makes the glass overflow or the straw that is supposed to break the camel's back!

During these shifts, the system temporarily loses its ability to maintain its order and thereby loses dynamic stability, but can, after going through a period of "confusion," gain it again on a different level. A perfectly well-adapted teenager might start to act seemingly erratically, changing his or her behavior from day to day (or even from minute to minute) in a range from truculent aggression to complete cooperation (e.g., Coleman & Hendry, 1999), and then, within a short time, "suddenly" settling down to behave in a consistent and amicable way.

However, over time the more order that has accumulated through self-organization of the system, the more input is usually needed to shift its direction. Once a system has created an order of patterns through self-organization, a precedent for the direction of further change is created—and certain other pathways are more or less excluded. Lewis (2000) calls this phenomenon "cascading constraints," because it constrains possibilities for the system's future pathways: once stem cells have been arranged to form a hand, they can no longer transform into another body part, and once a young person has decided on a particular career, has taken out a large mortgage to buy a house, or has become pregnant, the range of further lifestyle options is somewhat restricted. Like the degrees of freedom of each single element, the number of possible attractor states is eventually reduced by the increasing order and complexity of the interactions of the dynamic system. Though behavior emerges in the moment, the effects of each behavioral decision accumulate over longer time scales, as each change sets the stage for future changes, so that past behavior still has an influence on present behavior (Spencer et al., 2006). This is not only true for single individuals, who forge their particular and varied paths through life each time they make a decision. Because our lives are linked to others, traces of contemporary and former generations' life choices are woven into the system in which our own behavior emerges. Current historical events shape, to some extent, the conditions under which a young person enters adulthood, but so too do decisions that have been taken by the parents and grandparents long before the individual was born. Their choices about where to live, what kind of family to form, and what employment to seek still affect descendant generations (Elder, 1997).

Thus, we can see here other examples of self-organization and shift from macrolevels to microlevels of a society. The economic base of a society, its traditional values system, the distribution of hegemonic power and social status within it, and individual characteristics all interact and lead to the self-organization of relatively stable roles for different members in that society, for example, gender roles or the norms and expectations directed toward different age groups. Bynner (2005) uses the concept of individual pathways to explain how they link one "status passage" to the next:

> Such biographical pathways are longitudinal in the sense that each step along them is conditioned by the steps taken previously, by the personal, financial,

social and cultural resources to which the growing individual has access, and by the social and institutional contexts through which the individual moves.

(Bynner, 2005, p. 379)

The social system itself is never completely stable; there are always exceptions and rebels, the status quo will always be questioned, so that the system is continuously in a state of flux and changing in concert with the elements within it. Leaving this attractor state would lead to instability and crisis, which is unsettling for individuals, whose resistance to change and nostalgic yearnings about "keeping to the old ways" add to the system remaining in a particular attractor state for a lengthy time period, in spite of dynamic currents to create disequilibrium. It needs a powerful force (such as an industrial, technological, or political revolution) to get a society out of balance and eventually change toward a new attractor state.

In summary, from a systemic perspective human development is seen as the interplay of various elements in an open system, which self-organizes and is relatively stable from time-to-time, but ever so often is brought into imbalance and has to reorganize itself on a different, more complex level.

Resources and challenges

So in what ways can dynamic system theory help us to understand human transformations from child to adult (and beyond)? We will utilize our simplified theoretical framework of developmental change (Hendry & Kloep, 2002) to illustrate this.

At the outset, we want to take a closer look at the resources for development that are available to human beings. All healthy children are born with a certain range and level of fairly similar resources that help them to develop into adult human beings (no one has yet been reported as having developed into a frog Prince!) and to cope with life's challenges. Importantly, these resources will change and alter over the life course. Furthermore, all babies get bigger, all have a predisposition to learn to walk and speak a language, to see, to hear and to smell, to learn new things, and to feel varying emotions. Consequently, Indian and Russian, British and Maori neonates, and those in rich and poor families, behave in much the same way.

Accepting these similarities, we are also very different from each other from the day we are born, and even as fetuses in the womb. Many of our resources are innate, such as certain reflexes. Others are learned, since learning starts in the first seconds of life and will go on until death. Still others are structurally determined, such as nationality or social class. Just as certain potential resources exist for every individual from the very first moments of life in the womb, so too does the inequality in their distribution among individuals. Furthermore, some resources are more "personal" to the individual (such as intelligence) and some are more societal. Indeed they can potentially include all the groups from family, school, clubs, peers, to the local community itself that may have a function of intermediary between the individual and society (e.g., Shucksmith & Hendry, 1998; Small & Supple, 2001), and which create different opportunities, such as whether education is available and affordable, the employment situation, climate, laws, health system, and cultural traditions. Hence, they encompass conditions of the individual's micro-, meso-, and macrosystems (Bronfenbrenner, 1979) and they are all potential resources.

The idea of a "resource system" to describe an individual's potential to cope with various challenges has also appeared in sociological literature. Côté (1996) uses the concept of "identity capital" (which consists of sociological assets, such as educational level, and psychological resources, such as critical thinking abilities) to describe the resources an individual possesses to deal with the demands of modern living and development throughout the life course. The number and kind of resources can vary at any moment in time and over the lifespan. New resources are added, others disappear, some characteristics become resources, and some lose their resourceful quality.

None of the variables within these different categories should be seen in isolation from the others, rather they should be regarded as highly interactive. Biological and sociostructural variables, for example, interact with acquired skills, and together form the basis of self-efficacy, which in turn enhances the learning of new skills. Consider for a moment a female child who is, because of her gender (i.e., structural resource), not allowed to play boisterously with her peers. She may not develop the skills of self-defense (i.e., skills resource), and thus be at higher risk of becoming an assault victim, which in turn, might have an impact on her self-efficacy and health resources. Low self-efficacy can lead to shyness, fewer social contacts, and thus to fewer social resources, and so on.

To take a positive example, a child born with a musical talent might find an adult who is willing to further this gift. Having a mentor and a skill that is admired by peers and potential romantic partners is a good prerequisite to stay out of "trouble" by not having to impress peers with more risky, perhaps delinquent behaviors. All this can strengthen self-esteem and lead to further social contacts and new associated skills.

Now this view of individual resources would not be a systemic one if we regarded the resource system as static and closed. Of course, this is not the case. First, as already mentioned, potential resources interact with each other so that they can enhance and/or inhibit each other. For example, physical attractiveness can be a resource in many social contexts and enhance self-esteem. However, it can also inhibit the learning of social skills—the individual relying solely on good looks to be accepted by peers. Or being a talented soccer player can enhance your health and fitness and gain peer approval, yet it can also lead to sports injuries and fiercely competitive attitudes to others—and in some young people, being an active sports participant during adolescence even predicts heavy alcohol use in young adulthood (Peck, Vida, & Eccles, 2008).

Second, the resource system participates in other open systems. So whereas in some situations being a creative, critical thinker could bring you a King's sponsorship, in other circumstances it could lead you to the hangman's noose! Or to take a more contemporary example, being a creative and critical thinker could win you a doctoral scholarship, in other contexts it could bring you the boss's disapproval and dismissal. Social embeddedness in a community and strong links with your family can be a powerful resource in meeting various challenges, but it can turn into a disadvantage when it prevents a young person from moving away to pursue a university education or a career (Henderson et al., 2007). A plethora of material resources can buy better food, healthier housing, and better health care, as we can observe in the richer countries of the world. It also enhances the probability for obesity, alcohol and drug dependency, and inactivity, as the same statistics show (World Health Organization, 2008). Thus, potential resources can become disadvantageous while potential disadvantages can become beneficial, depending on the interaction with other elements in the participating systems.

Third, some resources that are beneficial in the short term can become potentially harmful or even highly risky in the longer term. The increasing availability of unskilled, temporary part-time work in Western societies does give young people work experience and a wage. However, if they continue to rely on the same or similar jobs for some years into the future it may constrain their opportunities to gain complete freedom from their parents, because these wages are too low and too unpredictable to allow for independent living (Martín, 2002). Or even more dramatically, drugs prescribed to offset depression may in the long term lead to drug dependency.

Hence, we cannot define what a resource actually is—or what might become one—without considering it in interaction with the challenges the individual will meet. Likewise, we would not know whether to put salt or sugar into a dish without knowing what kind of food the dish contained! For this reason, it is advantageous for individuals to build up a whole range of different skills in various domains, as it is impossible to predict what kinds of challenges they are going to face across the life span, and which of these skills might become a valuable resource one day.

This is particularly relevant because challenges are defined by resources, and vice versa. Only by knowing an individual's resources can we decide whether a particular task is a challenge, and only by knowing a particular task can we decide if an individual has the resources to deal with it. What we are trying to say here is that it is impossible to view resources without looking at challenges at the same time: the two are inexorably linked, in fact they are part of the same open system, and what we are really analyzing is not resources on the one hand and challenges on the other, but the relationship between the two.

To illustrate this further, no potential resource is a resource in isolation. For example, is it a challenge for young people to manage their own apartment? It can well be, if they never had to do any housekeeping before. But it is no more than a routine task for those who have previously participated in household tasks in their parental home. Similarly, having a lot of money can most certainly be a resource, if the challenge is of a nature that can be solved with money (for example, hiring a cleaner, if the individual lacks cleaning skills). However, money can also be completely irrelevant in other situations (e.g., when sitting for an examination) or even a disadvantage (e.g., looking at an array of expensive Belgian chocolates while trying to maintain a healthy diet). Actually, money can be changed from a potential resource into a challenge, if there is a lack of economic planning skills (as is often observed in lotto millionaires, for whom sudden riches can be more than they can handle).

Similarly, whenever young people's risk behaviors and lifestyle choices are regressed on a series of potential predictors in psychological research, "education" emerges as a strong protective factor (Jessor, 2008). This kind of research, however, springs not only from a relatively static cause-and-effect view of the world, it is also biased with a normative definition of what constitutes a "healthy outcome," thereby ignoring all the microprocesses that become invisible in a regression model and/or lost in the error variance. It might be true that a higher level of education is correlated with less risky behavior, but it is also true that in many peer cultures today, academic ability and an aptitude for studying are regarded as "uncool" and make the "nerd" vulnerable to bullying and social exclusion. That might effectively stop her or him from participating in drinking sprees—but is it really a healthy outcome? Furthermore, what is it that seems to be "protective" about education? Is it the academic skills achieved, is it the teachers' supervision that keeps young people off the street, is it the better work prospects that come along with better grades, or is it enhanced self-esteem? Again, we need to know the processes and mechanisms that function to protect some young people from engaging in certain risk behaviors. Simply forcing thousands of disengaged, alienated teenagers to attend two more years of compulsory schooling, as is currently being debated in the UK, seems unlikely to solve anything. Education might be a resource for many young people in many contexts, but being a good statistical predictor does not necessarily make it a panacea. It is the obvious limitations of this kind of research that have led dynamic system theorists to urge abandoning variable centered studies in favor of person-centered research (Valsiner, 1997).

Thus, although the task determines what a resource is, the number and kind of potential resources within an individual's resource system determine whether the particular task the individual meets turns out to be a routine chore, a challenge, or a risk. Elder (1986, 1987), for example, has shown that during the Great Depression in the United States, being called up for military service had a differential impact on young men depending on when in their life course it happened. It had positive effects on younger men, who had just left high school, because it saved them from unemployment and gave them the opportunity to learn entrepreneurial skills, which were important for their future careers. Nevertheless, the same military service had negative effects on older men, because it disrupted their careers and their families.

In other cases, stressors that disrupt the continuity of your life can act as "catalysts for change" (Fiske & Chiriboga, 1991). Therefore, a certain amount of stress can be regarded positively from a developmental point of view, because it can lead to the acquisition of new skills (Aldwin, 1992). Hence, a task can be a clearly positive experience, or it may contain negative elements that, nevertheless, lead to growth. For example, having a physical handicap has, for some people, been the antecedent to enormous personal growth, whereas something as apparently desirable as getting a promotion can be disastrous for a person who lacks the managerial skills to cope with new responsibilities. Gottlieb, Still, and Newby-Clark (2007), in analyzing the impact of life events on development in emerging adulthood, concluded that whereas development could be limited only by negative experiences, growth could be stimulated by all kinds of life events, ranging from those perceived as very undesirable to those perceived as very desirable.

As a systemic framework, the resources-challenge model is a useful, simplified tool for analyzing the changing life courses of individuals in changing societies by taking into account the ways different individuals encounter different experiential challenges by utilizing a varying set of resources in meeting these and by explaining how challenges, resources, and risks are all dynamically linked across the life course. It can also provide insights into how some individuals develop and others "stagnate" either by choice of lifestyle or through lack of relevant challenges and resources.

Development and change

Each time an individual meets a challenge, the system of challenges and resources becomes unbalanced, as the individual is forced to adapt his or her resources to meet this particular challenge. This adaptation can be short-lived if the resources easily match the challenge, as in dealing with routine tasks. On the other hand, it can be a long, anxiety-provoking process when the challenge is significant (or when there are several challenges encountered at the same time; see Coleman & Hendry, 1999) and matching resources are not easily available. If the individual is eventually able to solve the task, his or her resources are transformed and increased, and it will be easier to cope with similar challenges in the future. In other words, the individual has changed, and development has occurred.

What this means is that there need to be challenges for development to occur—or to use the terminology of dynamic systems theory, the system needs an input to become unbalanced and to reorganize on a more complex level. The idea of a "conflict" that triggers change is actually not new within developmental psychology; we can find it, for example, in the notion of equilibration in Piaget's theory, in the necessity of crises in Erikson's stage theory, and in Riegel's (1979) dialectical psychology.

If we leave the theoretical terminology for a moment and turn to some real life examples, we can easily see how young students, starting for the first time at a university, see themselves confronted with a whole range of new challenges. To leave home, find new friends, adjust to a different way of teaching and learning, manage their own economy, and spend their evenings unfettered by parents are all new experiences that tax their resource systems and bring them out of equilibrium. There will be a time of confusion, during which all elements of the system—existing resources and existing challenges (which vary with the history of the individual) as well as emerging challenges and emerging resources (which vary with the new environment, such as support systems of the university, subject-specific demands, peer group climate, housing conditions, etc.) to interact and reorganize themselves into a new system with a new attractor point: a competent student is evolving from the confused freshman. However, when the time comes, this system will be shaken up again, and the student will have to reorganize into an employee!

Meeting a challenge that "disturbs" the system can be both exciting and anxiety provoking. Every organism has processes by which it defends itself against, overcomes, or adapts to such perturbations (Ford & Lerner, 1992), and each response to such a disruption means simultaneously losing an existing secure position (i.e., development as risk) and an increase in possibilities (i.e., development as progress). This creates feelings of both hope and insecurity in the individual (Dreher, 2007), and explains why it is sometimes more comfortable to try to avoid further challenges and to choose "the way of least resistance" (in systemic terms: to keep to the old attractor state). Subjectively this is a comfortable state, but it does not offer a great deal of potential development. Hendry and Kloep (2002) have chosen to call this situation "contented stagnation." An example of this can be a young person who objectively has the resources (e.g., money, skills, available housing) to leave the parental home, but finds it much cheaper and more comfortable to stay and have his meals cooked, his room cleaned, and his laundry washed. This is a reasonable adaptation to the existing circumstances, but it does not offer him the chance to learn the skills of independent living.

Conversely, when an individual does not have the resources to seek out further challenges, this also prevents development because the individual just maintains the status quo and is not able to change. Hendry and Kloep (2002) have called this "unhappy stagnation" because it is imposed, not chosen. An example could be a young girl who had poor grades in school and is unable to find work locally, yet wants to have her own apartment. However, she ends up without education or employment and unable to leave her parental home as she hoped.

To summarize, human change comes about by a systemic interaction of different resources and challenges, and not simply by the passing of time. Every new challenge causes the system to change. This can consist of a reorganizing of the system and a major transformation or of avoiding challenges and keeping the system more or less near to equilibrium. Only the first of these options leads to what we would term "development."

Shifts

The processes and mechanisms of change are the same for all humans independent of culture, cohort, and age; yet what makes them so different across these parameters are life experiences. On the one hand, all normal babies develop into adults, and eventually they grow old and die. On the other hand, some of them will become parents and some will not; some of them will be outstanding in intellectual pursuits and others will hardly learn to read or write. Some will spend most of their adult lives in prison, others will live in mansions, and still others will live in a tin hut in the forest or in an urban slum.

In addition, each young person will have unique experiences from the very first day of birth. A second child in a family is actually not living in the same environment as its older sibling, even if it might appear so superficially. First, an older brother or sister exists. Second, the parents are some years older, more experienced, and, possibly, in a different phase of their life; friends and relatives do not react in the same way to the arrival of each new child; there are different peers to interact with in the nursery school, and so on. In other words, everyday life is different in many small aspects, which collectively and interactively lead to a different life course. The different challenges individuals meet across their life span play a significant role in human diversity in development.

If we look at teenagers across the world, we see that what happens to their bodies during puberty is similar no matter where and when they live. Their hormonal system starts to change, which causes them to develop their primary and secondary sex characteristics, and they eventually reach a state of adult maturity. There is some variability as to when exactly they have their menarche or first nocturnal emission, but it will, with great certainty, happen within the second decade of their life, given that they are healthy and well nourished. Thus, it is important to note that even for a biological shift such as puberty we have to take context variables into account.

In other words, there are certain changes in life that will happen to all humans relatively independently of the influences of their physical and cultural environment. These changes are "maturational shifts" caused mainly by normal biological mechanisms, such as puberty, the menopause, and ageing. Even if there are certain variations in the onset and duration of these maturational changes between individuals within the same culture, and between groups in different cultures, the processes involved, and the biological outcomes, are similar for all human beings. These shifts are expected and experienced by everyone. They are nevertheless a challenge, because the individual will have to cope with and adjust to them psychosocially. However, the ability to prepare for them and the presence of older role models make them relatively easy to face. It is maturational shifts that account for the similarity in human development throughout the world, and which led some earlier psychologists to believe that all development follows a given, genetically determined pattern.

Human beings within one cultural setting are closely similar. Hence, the people in individualistic societies of rich Western nations differ significantly from the collective cultures of the developing countries. However, even within the same culture, there are sub-cultural differences (i.e., men compared to women, working classes compared to middle and upper classes, different religious groups, youth subcultures, and regional variations). For example, in the United States, differences have been observed as to when and why young people from varying cultural backgrounds leave home. Catholics leave home later than all other groups, whereas fundamentalist Protestants leave home at a fairly early age for marriage, and liberal Protestants do so to go to college (Goldscheider & Goldscheider, 1994).

As we have previously commented, cultures change over time: ancient Britain was different from modern Britain, and being a teenager in the 1970s posed different challenges than those facing an adolescent today. Thus, although all members of all cultures share the same maturational shifts, one significant set of influences that causes differences between cultures is the developmental transitions

The lifespan challenge model re-visited 233

we call "normative-social shifts," and to a certain degree those we call "quasi-normative shifts."

Normative shifts are changes in our life that are prescribed by law for all members of certain well-defined groups. Within a country, these could be, for example, starting school, achieving adult legal status, and retiring from paid employment. These shifts occur in the lives of almost all members of a particular culture at given times in their life. Thus, they are predictable, expected, and shared with peers. Age-graded procedures like these are to be found in every society, though their enforcement varies considerably by culture.

Quasi-normative shifts are experiences which are not prescribed to the same degree, but common and socially expected to occur within a certain age range in a given culture. Examples for these shifts are leaving the parental home, age at first marriage, getting a first job, parenthood, and other cultural symbols like age-related clothes fashions, hair style and musical interests. Both normative and quasi-normative shifts account for similarities between members within certain cultural groups, and for differences between cultural groups; and these normative and quasi-normative shifts are not static within a culture or subculture. Since cultures themselves are open systems, expectations vary concurrently with changes in the cultural system. Hence, expectations about childhood, adolescence, and young adulthood continuously change over the course of history, between societies and within societies.

Moreover, there is a range of non-normative shifts awaiting individuals across their life course. Non-normative shifts are changes that do not occur for everyone, but only for some, perhaps for very few individuals. The number of possible non-normative shifts that can occur across the life course is almost infinite, though examples could include a serious accident or injury, but also moving to a foreign country or a radical career change. These shifts can be developmental "turning points" (or "turning processes"), and they can have enduring consequences by affecting subsequent events through a process of cumulative advantages or disadvantages ("cascading constraints," in the language of dynamic system theory). However, we should keep in mind that many of these "transitions" do, in reality, consist of multiphasic processes of relatively long duration. They frequently comprise a succession of several "points of choice," and not single, short-lived events (Elder, 1998). Thus, these shifts present the individual with a host of challenges, and each of these can be dealt with more or less successfully.

To sum up, we argue that it is these individual processes of change, acting in concert with all other elements of the wider system, that explain human development rather than the simple passing of time. We develop by meeting and coping with a myriad of challenges from day to day—and not by moving through age-bound stages.

Summary: a new way of analyzing transitions to adulthood

In this chapter we have discussed the difficulties inherent in defining the notions of "adolescence," "adulthood," and, as a consequence, "transitions," and argued that trying to describe human development by these vague, ill-defined concepts does not add to our understanding of what causes human change across the lifespan. Therefore, by way of an analogy about a river and a river sprite, we proposed an alternative systemic view, that seeks to analyze the processes and mechanisms that underlie human transformations, by considering the resources and challenges involved in development across the life span. We regard the individual as an open system, embedded in a diversity of microsystems and macrosystems, which in turn influence the kind and number of challenges met. Hence, the mechanisms involved in meeting normative and quasi-normative shifts do not vary between cultures and historic cohorts, whereas cultural conditions and their associated challenges do. For this reason, the individual pathways from childhood to adulthood vary enormously. For some children, there are non-normative shifts that cause them to grow up very quickly, whereas for others, different non-normative shifts have prolonged their period of "transition" to more than a decade. Some are forced by societal conditions to shorten or prolong this period, whereas others have some choice in the pace of their transition, depending on their resources. In subsequent chapters [of the original publication] we will utilize this theoretical perspective and way of thinking to interpret the varying pathways of transformation that exist for young people in culturally different societies throughout the world.

References

Aldwin, C. M. (1992). Aging, coping, and efficacy: Theoretical framework for examining coping in lifespan developmental context. In M. L. Wykle & J. Kowal (Eds.), *Stress and health among the elderly* (pp. 96–113). New York: Springer.

Bronfenbrenner, U. (1979). *The ecology of human development: Experiments by nature and design*. Cambridge, MA: Harvard University Press.

Bynner, J. (2005). Rethinking the youth phase of the life course: The case for emerging adulthood? *Journal of Youth Studies, 8*, 367–384.

Coleman, J. C., & Hendry, L. B. (1990, 1999). *The nature of adolescence* (3rd ed.). London: Routledge.

Côté, J. E. (1996). Sociological perspectives on identity formation: The culture-identity link and cultural capital. *Journal of Adolescence, 19*, 417–428.

Dreher, E. (2007). Optimierung von Selbstwirksamkeit. In A. Bucher, E. Lauermann, & K. Walcher (Eds.), *Ich kann. Du kannst. Wir können. Selbstwirksamkeit und Zutrauen* (pp. 33–58). Wien: Lanz.

Elder, G. H. Jr. (1997). The life course and human development. In W. Damon & R. M. Lerner (Eds.), *Handbook of child psychology* (4th ed., Vol. 1, pp. 939–991). New York: Wiley.

Elder, G. H. Jr. (1998). The life course as developmental theory. *Child Development, 69 (1)*, 1–12.

Evans, K. (2007). Concepts of bounded agency in education, work and the personal lives of young adults. Invited Symposium Paper, 3rd Conference on Emerging Adulthood. Tucson, Arizona, February 15–16.

Fiske, M., & Chiriboga, D. A. (1991). *Change and continuity in adult life*. San Francisco: Jossey Bass.

Ford, D. H., & Lerner, R. M. (1992). *Developmental systems theory: An integrative approach.* New York: Sage.
Goldscheider, F., & Goldscheider, C. (1994). Leaving and returning home in 20th century America. *Population Bulletin, 48(4),* 2–35.
Gottlieb, B. H., Still, E., & Newby-Clark, I. R. (2007). Types and precipitants of growth and decline in emerging adulthood. *Journal of Adolescent Research, 22(2),* 132–155.
Havighurst, R. J. (1972). *Developmental tasks and education* (3rd ed.). New York: McKay.
Henderson, S., Holland, J., McGrellis, S., Sharpe, S., & Thomson, R. (2007). *Inventing adulthoods: A biographical approach to youth transitions.* London: Sage.
Hendry, L. B., & Kloep, M. (2002). *Lifespan development: Resources, challenges and risks.* London: Thomson Learning.
Jessor, R., Turbin, M. S., & Costa, F. M. (2010). Protective and risk factors in healthy eating and regular exercise among adolescents in China and United States: Accounting for developmental change. *Journal of Research on Adolescence.* In press.
Lewis, M. D. (2000). The promise of dynamic systems approaches for an integrated account of human development. *Child Development, 71,* 36–43.
Martín, M. (2002). La prolongación de la etapa juvenil de la vida y sus efectos en la socialización. *Revista de Estudios de Juventud, 56,* 103–118.
Peck, S. C., Vida, M., & Eccles, J. S. (2008). Adolescent pathways to adulthood drinking: Sport activity involvement is not necessarily risky or protective. *Addiction, 103,* 69–83.
Riegel, K. F. (1975). Toward a dialectical theory of development. *Human Development, 18,* 50–64.
Riegel, K. F. (1979). *Foundations of dialectical psychology.* New York: Academic Press.
Rosenberger, N. (2007). Rethinking emerging adulthood in Japan: Perspectives from long-term single women. *Child Development Perspectives, 1,* 92–95.
Shucksmith, J., & Hendry, L. B. (1998). *Health issues and adolescents: Growing up, speaking out.* London & New York: Routledge.
Small, S., & Supple, A. (2001). Communities as system: Is a community more than the sum of its parts? In A. Booth & A. C. Crouter (Eds.), *Does it take a village? Community effects on children, adolescents and families* (pp. 161–174). Mahwah, NJ: Erlbaum.
Spencer, J. P., Clearfield, M., Corbetta, D., Ulrich, B., Buchanan, P., & Schöner, G. (2006). Moving toward a grand theory of development: In Memory of Esther Thelen. *Child Development, 77(6),* 1521–1538.
Thelen, E., & Baltes, E. A. (2003). Connectionism and dynamic systems: Are they really different? *Developmental Science, 6,* 378–391.
Thelen, E., & Smith, L. B. (1998). *A dynamic systems approach to the development of cognition and action* (3rd ed.). Cambridge, MA: MIT Press.
Thelen, E., & Smith, L. B. (2006). Dynamic systems theories. In W. Damon & R. M. Lerner (Eds.), *Handbook of child psychology* (6th ed., Vol. 1, pp. 258–312). New York: Wiley.
Thornton, A. (1988). Cohabitation and marriage in the 1980s. *Demography, 25,* 497–508.
Valsiner, J. (1997). *Culture and the development of children's action: A theory of human development* (2nd ed.). New York: Wiley.
World Health Organisation. (2008). WHO Statistical Information System (WHOSIS), available online at http://www.who.int/whosis/en/ (last accessed June 2008).

Concluding remarks

Looking back on life, as Uhtred is doing for Bernard Cornwell, and as Erikson would expect me to do within his theoretical framework: What would I hope was different? What disappointments? What successes? What about the future?

Firstly, there have been a few disappointments – but no disasters. Generally, it concerns me that we are slow to engage in inter-disciplinary research more often, especially since systemic analysis is emerging as an extremely insightful way of interpreting findings. There is still little collaboration and still insular 'empires' within the various social science disciplines. When once I asked a very eminent sociologist why we do not more often share our insights about development, I was told that then there would be less conformity to disciplinary-accepted knowledge and few, if any, single-discipline international associations or societies (as exist today with Psychology and Sociology amongst others). Would that be so disastrous?

Next, I would have liked to engage with policy-making and professional practices more consistently and to have made a greater impact on them. I have been lucky insofar as newspapers and the media have provided some reportage of my findings. But, on the other hand, I have written mainly for my academic peers and published scholarly articles and texts. So, to my mind, there are, in general terms, 'gaps' among what is readily available for academic audiences, what is often 'distilled' as useful for policy-makers and practitioners, and what is offered to the general public via the media. Then, there is a need for 'real' dialogue between adults and teenagers to be conducted on a rational basis and not as imposition from adult-prejudice: Give young people a *genuine* 'voice'.

Turning now to what I consider to have been successful ventures, I would like to emphasise my own transitions towards a lifespan perspective and dynamic systems theory have been crucial: From the various contexts that contribute to the young person's development – school, family, leisure – to other interactive, developmental forces such as relationships with peers and mentors, to contexts and geographic settings, then, to mid-life and old age. I also believe that my proffered theoretical frameworks have benefited by being developed from empirical findings, creating a strong baseline of evidence for formulating my interpretive ideas.

It seems to me that in some ways the ideas inherent in Dynamic Systems Theory have been around for as long as I can recall, yet not really implemented empirically or theoretically. So, there have been few inter-disciplinary projects over the years, which might have begun to tease out the various, interactive, multi-directional elements involved in human change. Even now, research is slow to demonstrate the values of gaining a systemic view of development. Thus, I am encouraged when I discover supporting evidence for my stance from such disparate perspectives as vocational development and neuroscience. Vondracek, Ford and Porteli (2014), in discussing occupational socialization, state that individual functioning and development result from patterns of multi-directional, multi-causal processes among the dynamic attributes of individuals and their contexts. They consider developmental processes are similar, in the sense that people are somewhat alike, but individual differences in purposes and contexts, for which people construct patterns of functioning, produce significant behavioural variations. Equally powerfully, fifteen German scientists under the leadership of Professors Felix Tretter and Boris Kotchoubey have published their reflections on neuroscience in which they criticize today's neurological research (*Psychology Heute*, 4, 2014). They write that neurologists over-estimate the explanatory power of their research, arguing that a multi-disciplinary, systemic-scientific approach is needed, for which an intense and institutionalized collaboration of several disciplines is necessary: medicine, psychiatry, neurology, clinical psychology, systems-biology, anthropology and philosophy, together with ecology, to develop a theory of bio-systems.

So, my reading of recent academic trends leads me to believe that the sciences are on the cusp of a very powerful 'paradigm shift' where many traditional ways of researching and theorising may be swept away, to be replaced by systemic and interdisciplinary approaches, and the challenges this will make to methodologies, research focus, interpretations, and theorising about human change will be fascinating to observe. Yet, paradoxically, linked to the problem of revealing 'variability', is the need to discover universal explanations, not culture-bound or simply confined to particular sub-groups: a task for these ecological theorists of the future.

Possible future directions for the social sciences have to some extent been parallelled by the growth of my own theoretical ideas and academic thinking since my first venture into academic publishing. In a recent book for budding psychologists (Hendry and Kloep, 2012) a number of ideas from Dynamic Systems Theory are presented to illustrate important processes and mechanisms in lifespan development, and currently, I am writing a book with ex-colleagues, which takes a systemic approach to highlight developmental pathways from adolescence to early adulthood (see Kloep *et al.*, forthcoming, 2015).

However, the issue of new theories, paradigm shifts, and methodologies I leave largely to the next generation of researchers and theorists – As my semi-fictitious hero, Uhtred of Bebbanburg, might write: "My life pages turn over and over, and then I'm finished. The book is closed!"

Yet I trust, like me, Uhtred is planning to leave some kind of inheritance to his son and to future generations (at least, that's what Bernard Cornwell has whispered in my ear!). My approach has been to encourage my post-graduate students to think systemically in their research and writings. I consider that I have succeeded somewhat in this venture and in running research methods courses on behalf of the European Association for Research on Adolescence for doctoral students in Europe, North, Central and Latin America I have left behind me on an international level, some exciting new talents.

Then, till fairly recently, I acted as Co-Editor, with Professors Marion Kloep and Inge Seiffe-Krenke, for a Psychology Press series, and two recommended books illustrate my inheritance scheme. For the first book (Taylor and Gozna, 2011), I encouraged Rachel Taylor to adopt a systemic framework, and she used Dynamic Systems Theory as a framework for arguing that 'deception' as a learned social skills 'package' is a necessary component in young people's development. In the second, we created a forum for Saskia Kunnen's ideas to develop (2012). In her work, a Dynamic Systems approach is taken to adolescent development. Strengths and weaknesses of different systemic styles and methodological approaches are considered.

So now, having briefly outlined my career, provided examples of my earlier and more recent writings and interpretations and offered a few ideas into the future, I can, like Uhtred, finally claim: "My book is truly closed".

References

Hendry, L.B. and Kloep, M. (2012) *Psychosocial Aspects of Adolescence and Adulthood: Transitions and Transformations* (London: Palgrave).

Kloep, M., Hendry, L.B., Taylor, R. and Stuart-Hamilton, I. (2015) Development from Adolescence to Early Adulthood: A Dynamic Systemic Approach to Transitions and Transformations, Hove: Psychology Press.

Kunnen, S., (2012) *A Dynamic Systems Approach to Adolescent Development* (Hove: Psychology Press).

Taylor, R. and Gozna, L. (2011) *Deception* (Hove: Psychology Press).

Vondracek, F.W., Ford, D.H. and Porfeli, E.J. (2014) A Living Systems Theory of Vocational Behavior and Development. Rotterdam: Sense Publishers.

Index

alcohol 103, 123, 129, 209, 221, 227–8

body image 84, 124

challenges 6, 7–9, 86, 90, 94, 96, 98, 99, 101, 103, 105, 106, 114–15, 122–35, 151, 153–4, 159, 163–5, 194, 220, 226–34
cluster analysis 10, 33, 36, 38–42, 44, 47, 48, 49, 84, 176
communication 89–107
community, centre 40, 51–60, 78, 141; education 61–2, 65, 138, 204; participation 52, 65, 196–7
conflict 12, 115, 125, 126, 164, 230; with parents/adults 73, 80–1, 84, 86, 123, 125, 145, 173, 177, 215; with peers 73, 76–7, 85, 156
coping 8, 90, 114, 115, 122–35, 137, 166, 171, 174, 188, 192–3, 198, 233
cross-cultural 89, 201–51
crowds 68–86, 101

delinquency 126, 130, 153,
developmental stage 112, 159–68, 197–8, 210, 218–22, 233
disaggregation 6, 10, 21, 215
drugs 74, 80, 89, 111, 126, 129–30, 228
dynamic systems 7, 33, 167–8, 222–6, 230, 233, 236–8; *see also* theory, dynamic systems

emerging adulthood 103, 154, 157, 159–68, 171–89, 221, 230,
environment 6, 8, 33, 63, 65, 111, 123, 124, 127, 151, 156, 222–3, 230, 231, 232

family 29, 30, 35, 37, 69, 99, 123, 125–7, 141, 147, 151, 163, 171, 172, 174, 186–7, 188–9, 222, 226, 228, 231
family relationship 7, 115, 123, 172, 173, 175

goodness of fit 6, 8, 105, 106, 137, 153

health 15, 25, 27, 28, 52, 165, 172, 193, 194, 197, 223, 227, 229; adolescent perceptions of 110–20; behaviour 7, 111, 115; influences on 111–14; mental 105; needs 110–11
hidden curriculum 12–19, 64, 131
homosexuality (incl. gay and lesbian) 113, 127, 185

identity 44, 52, 68, 69, 78, 80, 83, 85, 92, 94, 101, 105–6, 113, 127, 130, 134, 146, 154, 161, 163, 166, 167, 172, 188, 193, 206, 212, 221

leaving home 125, 172–4, 186–7, 193, 220, 231, 232
leisure 28, 32, 37, 39, 43, 51, 52, 58, 79, 86, 89–107, 111, 138–40, 142–3, 145, 151, 156–8, 201–12, 215; casual 91, 96–100, 142, 152, 202, 208; commercial 52, 55, 91, 100–1, 103, 146, 202, 206–7, 209; facilities 51, 63, 70, 77, 78, 210; organised 91, 95–6, 102, 152, 202, 210; rural 72, 79, 111, 201–15; *see also* sport
lifespan 7–9, 89, 105, 123, 157, 159–61, 164, 167, 194, 197, 198, 218, 227–8, 234

mentors 2–3, 9, 10, 12, 61, 69, 94, 119, 156, 227, 236
meta-skills 131–4,
middle-age 160, 166, 172, 173, 174, 193

Norway 2, 92, 104, 201–10

old age 192, 193, 197–8, 221, 236
over-protection 150–4, 165,

parents 24, 26, 28, 29, 31, 39, 42, 43, 64, 71, 80, 82, 84, 86, 90, 91, 93, 94, 96, 98, 102, 111, 112, 117, 122, 125, 128, 131, 145, 147, 152–3, 156, 157, 162, 165, 166, 167, 171–81, 193, 212, 213, 215, 223, 224, 228, 230, 231, 232
parental views 171–81
parenting styles 7, 125
pathways, educational 33–44; occupational 165, 172, 192–8; transitional 111, 159, 163, 164, 215, 225, 234, 237
peers 43, 58, 63, 91, 96, 102, 106, 114, 124, 152, 162, 208, 209, 227, 233; groups, types of 68–86; influence 35, 111, 112–13, 114–15, 128–9, 131, 213
personality 9–11, 21, 29, 35
physical education 12, 13–19, 21–32, 34–44, 131

resources 7–10, 90, 96, 98, 106, 122, 125, 126, 128, 153, 165, 166, 172, 194, 197, 220, 226–31, 234
retirement 160, 172, 188, 192–8
risks 7–10, 25, 30, 94, 105, 106, 114–15, 122, 123–35, 156, 165, 188, 227, 229, 230
risk-taking 74, 85, 98, 103, 104, 111, 122, 127–31, 153, 154, 166, 229
romance 126–7

school 12, 13–19, 21–32, 35–44, 54, 56, 58, 63, 68, 69, 70, 73–4, 78, 95, 113, 114, 137, 138, 145, 153; leaving 56, 58, 131, 137, 139, 141–2, 146
Scotland 15, 36, 61, 62, 63, 65, 71, 89, 92, 104, 201–15
sex roles 35, 114, 115
sexual, behaviour 89, 99, 126–7, 128, 129, 131, 132; relationships 94, 111–12

shifts, developmental 8, 105, 232; non-normative 123–5, 132, 134, 166, 233, 234; normative 123–5, 134, 161, 172, 193, 233
smoking 59, 74, 83, 84, 85, 104, 111, 112, 128, 129, 213
social-class 13, 27, 30, 35, 38, 39, 43, 44, 51, 52, 58, 59, 63, 105, 106, 111, 112, 115, 117, 126, 157, 163, 164, 165, 175, 186, 193, 201, 202, 203, 214, 226, 232
sport, and academic attainment 14, 34–45; and leisure 50–60, 64, 78, 95, 97, 100, 102, 129, 131, 144, 152, 157, 202, 203, 205, 206, 209–10, 227; in school 15–16, 18, 19, 21–32, 34–45
stress 91, 115, 122, 152, 154, 167, 194, 229
sub-cultures 44, 51–60, 69, 83, 105, 111, 112, 116, 129, 221, 232, 233
Sweden 91, 92, 104, 157, 167, 201–16

teachers *see* physical education teachers
theory, dynamic systems 7, 33, 167, 220, 226, 230, 233, 236, 237, 238; *see also* dynamic systems; ecological 33, 167, 171, 215; focal 91, 95, 105, 106, 115, 193, 201, 202, 207; life span 7–9, 105, 156, 167, 226–31
transitions, to adulthood 13, 68, 89, 90, 101, 104, 105, 117, 122, 127, 131, 132, 147, 150, 159, 160–8, 171, 174, 187–9, 218–34; leisure 91, 99, 201–15; occupational 123, 192–200

unemployment 97, 125, 172, 229; coping with 137–47, 193

values, school 13, 28, 30, 31, 34, 58; social 39, 51, 57, 68, 86, 111, 116, 125, 147, 152, 197, 225

weight 27, 31, 36, 124, 224

youth, centres 12, 25, 26, 30, 50–60, 78, 95–102, 142, 145, 152, 157, 210; workers 61–7, 92, 118, 140, 157